D0230087

Books should be returned on or before the
last date stamped below.

- FEB86 23   - 6 MAR 1987   26 MAR 1990

2 4 MAY 1986   - 8 MAY 1987   - 7 DEC 1990
- 4 JUN 1986   2 1 NOV 1987   1 7 DEC 1991
                1 7 FEB 1988
1 3 JUN 1986   - 2 OCT 1993
- 5 SEP 1986   2 8 SEP 1988
2 8 NOV 1986   - 5 NOV 1988

2 4 DEC 1986   2 5 NOV 1988   2 6 JUN 1995

= 7 JAN 1987   1 1 FEB 1989
                - 7 MAR 1989

                                1 8 FEB 1997
                                2 5 SEP 1997

NORTH EAST OF SCOTLAND LIBRARY SERVICE
14 Crown Terrace, Aberdeen

WITHDRAWN FROM LIBRARY

CROCHET sweaters

4.   746.43

N E S L S
644835

CROCHET SWEATERS

NORTH EAST SCOTLAND
LIBRARY SERVICE
WITHDRAWN
FROM LIBRARY

CROCHET SWEATERS

NORTH EAST SCOTLAND
LIBRARY SERVICE

WITHDRAWN
FROM LIBRARY

HAMLYN
London · New York · Sydney · Toronto

Published 1985 by
Hamlyn Publishing,
A division of the Hamlyn Publishing Group Ltd,
Bridge House, London Road,
Twickenham, Middlesex

©Marshall Cavendish Limited 1985

ISBN 0 600 50165 5

All rights reserved. No part of this publication
may be reproduced, stored in a retrieval
system, or transmitted, in any form or by any
means, electronic, mechanical, photocopying,
recording or otherwise, without the prior
permission of Hamlyn Publishing and the
copyright holder.

746.43
4.
644835

INTRODUCTION

If you're a crochet fan you'll find this book a great source of inspiration. In these pages are 46 beautiful, stylish crocheted garments for women, men and children, chosen to appeal to all tastes and ages. There are warm cardigans and jackets for out-of-doors, glamorous evening sweaters, cool cotton tops for summer, charming little sweaters for babies and warm, handsome pullovers for men – to name but a few. The wonderful range of crochet textures is well represented: bobbles, filet work, lace patterns, woven crochet, as well as the basic fabric stitches are all here. And if you've ever wanted to learn Tunisian (afghan) crochet or hairpin lace, here is your chance, for we've included several garments using these techniques, along with photographs and step-by-step instruction to make it easy.

Most of the other projects, too, include illustrated instructions for a special technique used in that project – for example, how to work a shell lace edging, how to work surface slip stitch and how to make a frogging loop.

Yarns needed for the projects are specified by generic type (e.g. double knitting yarn, 4 ply yarn, medium-weight mohair), rather than by brand name. We strongly recommend that you buy good-quality yarn for any crochet project – those made of natural fibres, such as wool and cotton, or natural-synthetic blends. There are some good all-synthetic yarns available, but many are of poor quality. The colours are less attractive and they are unpleasant to the touch. Often they do not wear well, loosing their resilience after a few washings. Today many pure wool yarns are even machine washable; and hand-washing is not really such a chore when the sweater is a treasured part of your wardrobe. So, avoid cheap yarns – they're a false economy.

When buying any yarn, check the wrapper or ask the shop assistant to make sure that it is appropriate for the garment. The right choice of yarn will help to ensure that the garment is fun to make and to wear.

Before you begin work on a project, remember to check your tension. This step is *absolutely essential* if you are to obtain a garment of the correct size. Even professional crocheters make a tension sample to make sure that they get the same number of stitches (and sometimes rows) to the centimetre as did the designer of the pattern. The sample should be at least 10cm square. If you get more or fewer stitches per centimetre than the stated tension, try a larger or smaller hook, respectively, until you get the right tension. The short time you spend at the outset getting the tension correct may save you hours of wasted time making something the wrong size.

CONTENTS

LACY BLOUSE

Made in white or a pastel colour, this blouse is perfect for a summer day. Made in black, with ribbon threaded through the rows, it becomes an elegant evening top.

Size
To fit 86-96cm bust
Length 48cm

Materials
Approx 1250m of a No. 5 crochet cotton
2.00mm crochet hook

Tension
20tr and first 17 rows of patt should measure 10cm using 2.00mm hook

To save time, take time to check tension.

Back and front (worked in one piece)
Beg at centre back, make 95ch.
1st row 1tr into 3rd ch from hook, 1tr into each ch to end.
Turn. 93tr.
2nd row 3ch, 1tr into each st to end.
Turn.
3rd row 1ch, 1dc into each st to end.
Turn.
4th row Working into front loops only, work a row of crab st (dc worked from left to right) back along the row. Do not turn.
5th row 1ch, working into back loops of row 3, work 1dc into each st to end. Do not turn.
6th row As row 4.
7th row As 5th row working into back loops of row 5. Do not turn.
8th row As row 4.
9th row As row 5, working into back loops of row 7. Turn.
10th row 3ch, 1tr into each st to end. Turn.
11th row 4ch, * miss next tr, 1tr into next tr, 1ch, rep from * to end of row, ending with 1tr into last st. Turn.
12 row 3ch, * 1tr into next 1ch sp, 1tr into next tr, rep from * to end of row. Turn.
13th row 3ch, 1tr into each of next 4tr, * miss 1tr, 1ch, 1tr into each of next 7tr, rep from * to end of row, ending with 1tr into each of last 6tr. Turn.
14th row 3ch, 1tr into each of next 4tr, *1ch, miss next tr, (yrh, insert hook into 1ch sp, draw through a loop) 5 times, yrh, draw through 10 loops, yrh, draw through rem 2 loops on hook (1 puff st), 1ch, miss next tr, 1tr into each of next 5tr, rep from * to end, ending with 1tr into each of last 4tr. Turn.
15th row 3ch, 1tr into each of first 3tr, *1tr into next 1ch sp, 1ch, 1tr into next 1ch sp, 1tr into each of next 5tr, rep from * to end of row, ending with 1tr into each of last 4tr. Turn.
16th row As 10th.

17th row As 11th.
18th row As 12th.
Work rows 3-12 twice.
39th row 4ch, * miss next tr, 1 puff st into next tr, 1ch, rep from * to end of row, ending with 1tr into last st. Turn. 45 puff sts.
40th row 3ch, * 1 puff st into next 1ch sp, 1ch, rep from * to end, ending with 1 puff st into last 1ch sp, 1tr into 3rd of 4ch. Turn.
41st row 3ch, * 1tr into top of puff st, 1tr into next 1ch sp, rep from * to end of row, ending with 1tr into top of turning ch. Turn.
42nd row As 11th.
43rd row As 12th.
44th row As 11th.
45th row As 12th.
Divide for armhole
46th row 3ch, 1tr into each of next 42tr, leave rem of tr unworked.
47th row Make 52ch, 1tr into 4th ch from hook, 1tr into each ch, then 1tr into each tr to end of row. Turn. 93tr.
Work rows 11 and 12 twice.
52nd row As 39th.
53rd row As 40th.
54th row As 41st.
55th row As 11th.
56th row As 12th.
Work rows 3-9.
64th row 3ch, 1tr into each of next 50 sts. Turn.
65th row Ss over next 2 sts, 4ch, miss next tr, 1tr into next tr, *1ch, miss next tr, 1tr into next tr, rep from * to end of row. Turn.
66th row 3ch, * 1tr into next 1ch sp, 1tr into next tr, rep from * 22 times. Turn. 47tr.
Decreasing 1 st at neck edge on every row until there are 41 sts, work rows 3-9. Turn.
74th row 3ch, 1tr into each tr to end of row. Turn. 41 sts.
75th row As 11th.
76th row As 12th.

SPECIAL TECHNIQUE
Corded rib

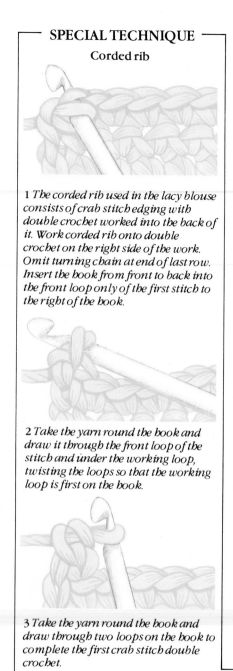

1 *The corded rib used in the lacy blouse consists of crab stitch edging with double crochet worked into the back of it. Work corded rib onto double crochet on the right side of the work. Omit turning chain at end of last row. Insert the hook from front to back into the front loop only of the first stitch to the right of the hook.*

2 *Take the yarn round the hook and draw it through the front loop of the stitch and under the working loop, twisting the loops so that the working loop is first on the hook.*

3 *Take the yarn round the hook and draw through two loops on the hook to complete the first crab stitch double crochet.*

4 *Insert the hook from front to back into the front loop only of the next stitch to the right of the hook, and work another crab stitch as before.*

5 *Continue to work into the front loop of each stitch in the same way. Make sure you twist the loops each time to achieve a corded effect.*

6 *To complete the first corded rib row, make one chain, then work a double crochet into the back loop of each stitch worked in the previous row, working behind the crab stitch row.*

77th row 3ch, 1tr into each of next 3tr, * miss 1tr, 1ch, 1tr into each of next 7tr, rep from * to end of row, ending with 1tr into each of last 4tr. Turn.

78th row 3ch, 1tr into each of next 2tr, * 1ch, miss next tr, 1 puff st into next 1ch sp, 1ch, miss next tr, 1tr into each of next 5tr, rep from * to end, ending with 1tr into each of last 3tr. Turn.

79th row 3ch, 1tr into each of next 2tr, * 1tr into next 1ch sp, 1ch, 1tr into next 1ch sp, 1tr into each of next 5tr, rep from * to end of row, ending with 1tr into each of last 3tr. Turn.

80th row As 10th. 41tr.

81st row As 11th.

82nd row As 12th.

Work rows 3-12 twice.

103rd row As 75th.

104th row As 76th.

105th row As 77th.

106th row As 10th.

107th row As 11th.

108th row As 12th.

109th row 1ch, 2dc into next tr, 1dc into each tr to end. 42 sts.

110th row Work crab st into front loops only.

111th row 1ch, working into back loops, work 2dc into next st, 1dc into each st to end. 43 sts.

112th row Work crab st into front loops only.

113th row 1ch, working into back loops, work 2dc into next st, 1dc into each st to end. 44 sts.

114th row Work crab st into front loops only.

115th row 1ch, working into back loops, work 2dc into next st, 1dc into each st to end. Turn. 45 sts.

116th row 3ch, work 1tr into each st to last 2 sts, 2tr into each of next 2tr.

Turn. 47tr.

117th row Ch 4. 1tr into next tr, * 1ch, miss next tr, 1tr into next tr, rep from * to end of row. Turn.

118th row 3ch, * 1tr into 1ch sp, 1tr into next tr, rep from * to last sp, 2tr into last sp, 1tr into 3rd of turning ch. Turn. 50tr.

119th row Make 44ch, 1dc into 2nd ch from hook, 1dc into each ch, then 1dc into each tr to end of row. 93dc. Work rows 4-12.

Now work rows 39-63.

Next row As 10th.

Next row As 11th.

Next row As 12th.

Now work rows 3-18, then rows 3-10.

Next row 3ch, 1tr into each tr to end. Fasten off.

Yoke
Make 52ch.

1st row 1tr into 3rd ch from hook, 1tr into each of next 22ch, 1ch, miss 1ch, 1 puff st into next ch, miss 1ch, 1tr into each of next 24tr. Turn.

2nd row 3ch, 1tr into tr at base of 3ch, 1 puff st into 1ch sp, 1ch, 1 puff st into next 1ch sp, 1tr into each of next 21tr, 2tr into each of next 2tr. Turn.

3rd row 3ch, 1tr into tr at base of 3ch, 1tr into each of next 5tr, 1ch, miss 1tr, 1tr into each of next 10tr, 1ch, miss 1tr, 1tr into each of next 7tr, 1ch, 1 puff st into next 1ch sp, 1ch, miss next puff st, 1tr into each of next 7tr, 1ch, miss 1tr, into each of next 10tr, 1ch, miss 1tr, 1tr into each of next 5tr, 2tr into last tr. Turn.

4th row 3ch, 1tr into tr at base of 3ch, 2tr into next tr, 1tr into each of next 5tr, 1ch, 1tr into each of next 10tr, 1ch, 1tr into each of next 7tr, 1tr into next

1ch sp, 1ch, miss next puff st, 1tr into next 1ch sp, 1tr into each of next 7tr, 1ch, 1tr into each of next 10tr, 1ch, 1tr into each of next 5tr, 2tr into each of last 2tr. Turn.

5th row 3ch, 1tr into each of next 8tr, 1ch, 1 puff st into next 1ch sp, 1ch, 1tr into each of next 9tr, 1ch, miss 1tr, 1 puff st into next sp, 1ch, miss next tr, 1tr into each of next 7tr, 1ch, 1tr into each of next 7tr, miss next tr, 1 puff st into next sp, miss 1tr, 1ch, 1tr into each of next 9tr, 1ch, 1 puff st into next 1ch sp, 1ch, 1tr into each of last 9tr. Turn.

6th row 3ch, 1tr into each of next 7tr, 1ch, miss 1tr, 1 puff st into next sp, 1ch, 1 puff st into next sp, 1ch, miss 1tr, 1tr into next 7tr, 1ch, miss 1tr, 1 puff st into next 1ch sp, 1ch, 1 puff st into next sp, 1ch, miss 1tr, 1tr into each of next 6tr, 1ch, 1tr into next 6tr, 1ch, miss 1tr, 1 puff st into next sp, 1ch, 1 puff st into next sp, 1ch, miss next tr, 1 puff st into next sp, 1ch, 1 puff st into next sp, 1ch, miss 1tr, 1tr into each of last 8tr. Turn.

7th row 3ch, 1tr into each of next 7tr, 1tr into 1ch sp, 1ch, 1 puff st into next sp, 1ch, 1tr into next sp, 1tr into each of next 7tr, 1tr into next sp, 1ch, 1 puff st into next sp, 1ch, 1tr into next sp, 1tr into each of next 6tr, 1ch, 1tr into each of next 6tr, 1tr into next sp, 1ch, 1 puff st into next sp, 1ch, 1tr into next sp, 1tr into each of next 7tr, 1tr into next sp, 1ch, 1 puff st into next sp, 1ch, 1tr into next sp, 1tr into each of last 8tr. Turn.

8th row 3ch, 1tr into each of next 8tr, 1tr into next sp, 1ch, 1tr into next sp, 1tr into each of next 9tr, 1tr into next sp, 1ch, 1tr into next sp, 1tr into each of next 7tr, 1ch, 1tr into each of next 7tr, 1tr into next sp, 1ch, 1tr into next sp, 1tr into each of next 9tr, 1tr into next sp, 1ch, 1tr into next sp, 1tr into each of last 9tr. Turn.

9th row 3ch, 1tr into each of next 9tr, 1ch, 1tr into each of next 11tr, 1ch, 1tr into each of next 8tr, 1ch, 1tr into each of next 8tr, 1ch, 1tr into each of next 11tr, 1ch, 1tr into each of next 10tr. Turn.

10th row 3ch, 1tr into each of next 8tr, 1ch, miss next tr, 1 puff st into next sp, 1ch, miss next tr, 1tr into each of next 9tr, 1ch, miss 1tr, 1 puff st into next sp,

1ch, miss next tr, 1tr into each of next 7tr, 1ch, 1tr into each of next 7tr, 1ch, miss next tr, 1 puff st into next sp, 1ch, miss next tr, 1tr into each of next 9tr, 1ch, miss next tr, 1 puff st into next sp, 1ch, miss 1tr, 1tr into each of last 9tr. Turn.

11th row 3ch, 1tr into each of next 7tr, 1tr, miss 1tr, 1 puff st into next sp, 1ch, 1 puff st into next sp, 1ch, miss 1tr, 1tr into next 7tr, 1ch, miss 1tr, 1 puff st into next 1ch sp, 1ch, 1 puff st into next sp, 1ch, miss 1tr, 1tr into each of next 5tr, 1 puff st into top of next tr, 1ch, 1 puff st into top of next tr, 1tr into each of next 5tr, 1ch, miss 1tr, 1 puff st into next sp, 1ch, 1 puff st into next sp, 1ch, miss next tr, 1tr into each of next 7tr, 1ch, miss next tr, 1 puff st into next sp, 1ch, 1 puff st into next sp, 1ch, miss 1tr, 1tr into each of last 8tr. Turn.

12th row 3ch, 1tr into each of next 7tr, 1tr into sp, 1ch, 1 puff st into next sp, 1ch, 1tr into next sp, 1tr into next 7tr, 1tr into next sp, 1ch, 1 puff st into next sp, 1ch, 1tr into next sp, (1ch, miss next st, 1tr into next st) 3 times, 1 puff st into next sp, 1tr into next st, (1ch, miss next st, 1tr into next st) 3 times, 1ch, 1 puff st into next sp, 1ch, 1tr into next sp, 1tr into next 7tr, 1tr into next sp, 1ch, 1 puff st into next sp, 1ch, 1tr into next sp, 1tr into each of last 8tr. Turn.

13th row 3ch, 1tr into each of next 8tr, 1tr into next sp, 1tr into next st, 1tr into next sp, 1tr into each of next 7tr, 1ch, miss next tr, 1tr into next tr, (1ch, 1tr into next st) 5 times, 1ch, miss puff st, 1tr into next st, (1ch, 1tr into next st) 5 times, 1ch, miss next tr, 1tr into each of next 7tr, 1tr into next sp, 1tr into next st, 1tr, into next sp, 1tr into each of last 9tr. Turn.

14th row 3ch, 1tr into each of next 16tr, 1ch, miss 1tr, 1tr into next tr, (1ch, 1tr into next tr) 13 times, 1ch, miss next tr, 1tr into each of last 17tr. Turn.

15th row 3ch, 1tr into each of next 14tr, 1ch, miss 1tr, 1tr into next tr, (1ch, 1tr into next tr) 15 times, 1ch, miss next tr, 1tr into each of last 15tr. Turn.

16th row 3ch, 1tr into each of next 12tr, 1ch, miss 1tr, 1tr into next tr,

(1ch, 1tr into next tr) 17 times, 1ch, miss next tr, 1tr into each of last 13tr. Turn.

Divide for neck

Next row 3ch, 1tr into each of next 12tr. Turn.

Work another 12 rows of tr on these 13 sts. Fasten off.

Rejoin yarn to other side of neck and work 13 rows of tr over the 13tr. Fasten off.

To make up

Join centre back and shoulder seams. Work a row of crab st round front neck edge of main bodice piece. Ss yoke in place.

Welt

Join yarn to the lower edge at one side and work approx 156tr round lower edge. Work 2 more rows in tr.

Next row 4ch, miss 1tr, * 1tr into each of next 10tr, 1ch, miss next tr, rep from *, ending with a ss into 3rd of 4ch.

Next row 3ch, 1 puff st into next sp, 1ch, miss next tr, * 1tr into each of

next 8tr, 1ch, 1 puff st into next sp, 1ch, miss next tr, rep from * to end, ending with a ss into top of 3ch.

Next row 4ch, * 1tr into next sp, 1tr into each of next 8tr, 1tr into next sp, 1ch, rep from * to end, ending with a ss into 3rd of 4ch.

Now work another 3 rows of tr working into every st.

Next row 4ch, 5tr into same place as 4ch, * miss 2tr, 6tr into next tr, rep from * to end, ending with a ss into top of 4ch. Fasten off.

Armhole edging

Join yarn at underarm, 4ch, 5dtr into same place as 4ch, miss 4tr along armhole edge, * work 4dtr into sp between next 2tr, miss next 4tr, rep from *, ending with a ss into top of 4ch. Fasten off.

Neck edging

Work a row of dc evenly round neck edge. Work shell edge as for armhole, missing 3dc between each shell. Fasten off.

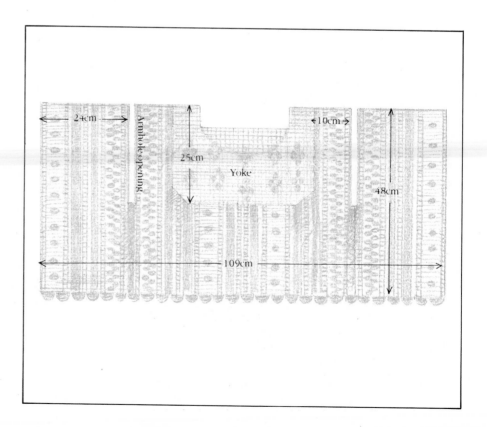

SOFT
SUMMER BLOUSE

A double row of shell edging finishes the neckline of this flattering blouse.

Size

To fit *81-86cm bust*
Length *50cm*
Sleeve seam *15cm*

Materials

Approx 1200m of a No. 5 crochet cotton
Nine 1cm buttons
2.50mm crochet hook
1 pair 3¼mm knitting needles

Tension

22tr and 11 rows to 10cm using 2.50mm
hook

To save time, take time to check tension.

Front

Make 92ch. 1tr into 4th ch from hook, 1tr into each ch to end. Turn.
Next row 3ch, 1tr into each tr to end. Turn. 90tr.
Rep last row 29 times more.
Shape armholes
Ss across first 5tr, 1htr into next tr, 1tr into each of next 78tr, 1htr into next tr. Turn.
Next row Miss first htr, ss into each of first 2tr, 1htr into next tr, 1tr into each of next 72tr, 1htr into next tr. Turn.
Next row Miss first htr, ss into next tr, 1htr into next tr, 1tr into each of next 68tr, 1htr into next tr. Turn.
Next row 3ch, 1tr into each tr to end. Turn. 68tr.
Rep this row 13 times more.
Shape neck
Next row 3ch, 1tr into each of next 22tr, 1htr into next tr. Turn.
Next row Ss into each of first 1htr and 1tr, 1htr into next tr, 1tr into each tr to end. Turn.
Next row 3ch, 1tr into each of next 18tr. Turn.
Work 3 more rows of tr on these 19 sts.

Fasten off.
Miss centre 20tr, then rejoin yarn to work 2nd side of neck, matching first side and reversing all shapings.

Back (worked in two pieces)
Make 45ch. 1tr into 4th ch from hook, 1tr into each ch to end. Turn.
Next row 3ch, 1tr into each tr to end. Turn. 43tr.
Rep this last row 29 times more.
Shape armholes
Ss across first 3tr, 1htr into next tr, 1tr into each tr to end. Turn.
Next row 3ch, 1tr into each of next 35tr, 1htr into next tr. Turn.
Next row Miss 1htr, ss into next tr, 1htr into next tr, 1tr into each tr to end. Turn.
Next row 3ch, 1tr into each tr to end. Turn. 34tr.
Rep this last row 19 times more.
Shape shoulders
Next row 3ch, 1 tr into each of next 18tr.
Fasten off.
Work 2nd back to match, reversing all shapings.

Sleeves
Make 61ch.
1tr into 4th ch from hook, 1tr into each ch to end. Turn.
Next row 3ch, 1tr into each tr to end. Turn. 59tr.
Work 9 more rows in tr.
Next row (inc row) 3ch, 1tr into each of next 2tr, * 2tr into next tr, 1tr into each of next 3tr, rep from * to end. Turn. 73tr.
Work 4 rows in tr.
Rep inc row working only 1tr after last inc. 91tr.
Work 3 rows in tr.
Shape sleeve top
Next row Ss over first 4tr, 1htr into next tr, 1tr into each of next 81tr, 1htr into next tr. Turn.
Next row Ss into htr, 1htr into next tr, 1tr into each of next 79tr, 1htr into next tr. Turn.
Next row Ss into htr, 1htr into next tr, 1tr into each of next 77tr, 1htr into next tr. Turn.
Cont dec as on last row working 2tr less on each row until 37tr rem.
Fasten off.

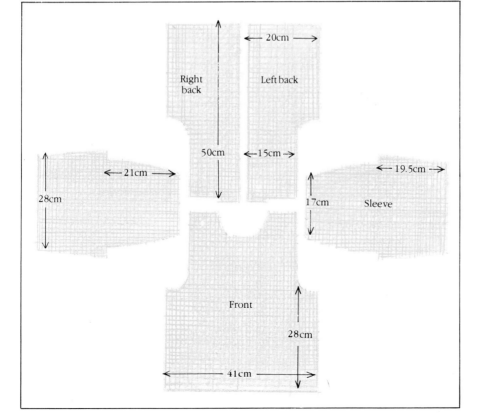

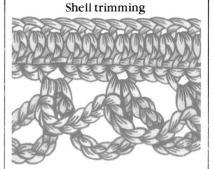

SPECIAL TECHNIQUE
Shell trimming

1 *Work the basic treble row as instructed in the pattern. Then work a series of short chain loops into the treble row, catching the chain into the treble with a double crochet at regular intervals. Work a second row of longer loops behind the first, catching them into the same places.*

2 *Work small shells into the first row of short loops and larger shells into the second row of longer loops. Make sure that the right side of the treble stitches faces the front on both rows of shells by breaking off yarn and starting shells at same side on each row.*

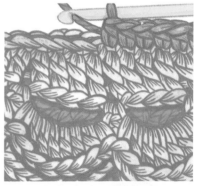

3 *Place the wrong side of the edging on the right side of the main fabric. Hold the two pieces together and use half treble to join in the two pieces, working each stitch through the two edges.*

Working buttonholes

Where small buttons are used on a crocheted garment, they are often fastened simply by inserting them between the fabric stitches. However, buttonholes can easily be worked in crochet —either horizontally or vertically, into the main fabric or into a separate band that is sewn on to it. If you are making separate button and buttonhole bands, make the button band first and mark the button positions with pins. Use these marks as guides when placing the buttonholes. Double crochet is usually used for the bands.

Horizontal buttonholes

1 Work in double crochet to position for first buttonhole. Make 2 chain to form top of medium-sized hole. The number of chain varies depending on size of hole required.

2 Miss next double crochet and work into the following stitch. The number of stitches missed is always the same as the number of chain.

3 On the next row, work in double crochet into the chain made in the previous row to complete the top of the buttonhole.

To make up

Join side seams. Using knitting needles, pick up and K133 sts along lower edge.
1st row K1, * P1, K1, rep from * to end.
2nd row P1, * K1, P1, rep from * to end. Work 7 more rows in rib. Cast off loosely in rib.

Buttonhole

Using crochet hook, work approx 112tr along centre back edge. Rep for buttonhole band (the sps between tr serve as buttonholes). Sew on buttons, spacing them evenly.

Sleeve edging

Join yarn at side edge, using crochet hook work 1sc into sp between first 2tr, * 1htr between next 2tr, (1tr between next 2tr) 3 times, 1htr between next 2tr, 1sc between next 2tr, rep from * to end. Fasten off. Join sleeve seam. Join shoulder seams. Set in sleeves gathering excess at top of sleeve.

Collar

Make 93ch. 1tr into 4th ch from hook, 1tr into each ch to end. 91tr.
Next row * 7ch, miss the next 5tr, ss into next tr, rep from * to end. Turn.
Next row Into each 7ch loop work 13tr.
Next row *10ch, ss into the same place as ss of 7ch loop, rep from * to end. Turn.
Next row Into each 10ch loop work 14tr. Fasten off.
Hold collar in place along neck edge, WS of collar to RS of neck, and work a row of htr through both thicknesses. Fasten off.

Vertical buttonholes

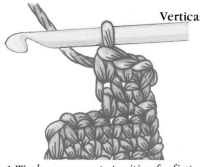

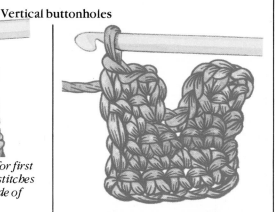

1 Work across row to position for first buttonhole. Here the band is 6 stitches wide, with 3 stitches on each side of buttonhole.
Turn and work 2 rows (or more, for a longer buttonhole) on these stitches, ending at the inner edge of work.

3 Work 2 rows on these stitches, ending at side edge so that second side of buttonhole is same height as first.

2 Slip stitch down side of buttonhole and into double crochet immediately below.
1ch to count as first double crochet, work to end of row, so that there are 3 stitches on second side.

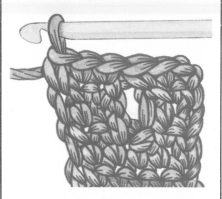

4 Work double crochet across both sides of buttonhole, joining the two sides in this way.

LATTICEWORK TOP

Mouth-watering ice cream colours are used for this cool cotton sweater decorated with horizontal and vertical stripes.

Sizes
To fit *82 [87:91] cm bust*
Length *57cm*
Sleeve seam *11cm*

Note *Instructions for larger sizes are in square brackets [ ]; where there is one set of figures it applies to all sizes.*

Materials
4-ply pure cotton:
Approx 150g in each of 2 colours (A and B)
25g in contrast colour (C)
5.50mm crochet hook
1 pair 4mm knitting needles

Tension
11 dtr and 5 rows to 11cm using 5.50mm hook

To save time, take time to check tension.

Note *When shaping, work edge sts at a slightly looser tension to keep work flat.*

Back
* * Using crochet hook and A, make 47 [49:51] ch *loosely*.
Base row 1dtr into 5th ch from hook, 1dtr into each ch to end.
Turn. 44 [46:48] sts.
Patt row 4ch, miss first dtr, 1dtr into each dtr, 1dtr into top of turning ch.
Turn.
Work 12 more rows in patt.
Shape armholes
1st row Ss into each of first 4dtr, 4ch, 1dtr into each dtr to last 3 sts.
Turn. 38 [40:42] sts. * *
2nd row 4ch, miss first dtr, leaving last loop of each st on hook, work 1dtr into each of next 3 sts, yrh and draw through all 4 loops – 2dtr dec –, 1dtr into each dtr to last 4 sts, dec 2dtr over next 3 sts, 1dtr into top of turning ch.
Turn. 34 [36:38] sts. Patt 8 rows.
Fasten off.

Front
Work as back from * * to * *.
Shape left neck
1st row 4ch, miss first dtr, dec 2dtr over next 3 sts, 1dtr into each of next 7 [8:9] dtr, dec 2dtr over next 3 sts, 1dtr into next dtr. Turn. Cont on these 11 [12:13] sts for first side of neck.
2nd row 4ch, miss first dtr, dec 2dtr over next 3 sts, 1dtr into each of next 6 [7:8] sts, 1dtr into top of turning ch.
Turn.
3rd row 4ch, miss first dtr, 1dtr into each of next 4 [5:6] dtr, dec 2dtr over next 3 sts, 1dtr into top of turning ch.
Turn. 7 [8:9] sts.
Work in patt for 7 rows.
Fasten off.
Note *There is 1 more row on front than on back, making the shoulder seams fall slightly towards the back.*
Shape right neck
1st row Miss centre 8dtr after right neck and join A to next dtr, 4ch, dec 2dtr over next 3 sts, 1dtr into each of next 7 [8:9] tr, dec 2dtr over next 3 sts, 1dtr into top of turning ch.
Turn.
2nd row 4ch, miss first dtr, 1dtr into each of next 6 [7:8] sts, dec 2dtr over next 3 sts, 1dtr into top of turning ch.
Turn.
3rd row 4ch, miss first dtr, dec 2dtr over next 3 sts, 1dtr into each of next 4

[5:6] dtr, 1dtr into top of turning ch.
Turn.
Work in patt for 7 rows.
Fasten off.

Sleeves (both alike)
Using crochet hook and A, make 39ch.
Work base row as for back. 36 sts.
Work in patt for 4 rows.
Shape top
1st row As first row of armhole shaping of back. 30 sts.
2nd row As 2nd row of armhole shaping of back.
3rd row 4ch, miss first dtr, leaving last loop of each st on hook, work 1dtr into each of next 2 sts, yrh and draw through all 3 loops – 1dtr dec –, 1dtr into each dtr to last 3 sts, dec 1dtr over next 2 sts, 1dtr into top of turning ch.
Turn.
Rep 2nd and 3rd rows twice. 12 sts.
Fasten off.

Welts
With RS facing and using knitting needles, join A to first ch of base row of back. Pick up and K60 [62:64] sts evenly along base edge. Work 4cm in K1, P1 rib. Cast off *very loosely* in rib.
Work other welt to match.

Horizontal stripes
With RS of back facing and using crochet hook, join B to the top of first st of base row.
Stripe row 4ch, 1dtr into top of each st of base row. Fasten off.
Miss the next 2 rows. Rep stripe row into the top of next row.
Cont in this way to shoulders.
Work front and sleeves to match.

Vertical stripes
Note *When working vertical stripes, work through the corresponding sps of horizontal stripe and background tog where appropriate. Work the vertical stripes at a slightly tighter tension than the background to draw the work up and reduce the length slightly.*
1st stripe With RS of back facing and using crochet hook, join C to the sp between the centre 2 sts of base row. Keep yarn at back of work. Fold each horizontal stripe downwards towards

the welt. Yrh, (insert hook into same sp as join, yrh and draw through loop on hook) twice, *insert hook into corresponding sp of next row, yrh and draw through loop on hook, insert hook into same sp, yrh and draw through loop on hook, rep from * to top. Fasten off.

2nd stripe Miss the next 3 sps to the right and join C to the next sp between sts. Fold each horizontal stripe upwards towards the top of the work. Work as for first stripe.

Cont in this way over all the back, missing 3 sps between each stripe and folding horizontal stripes alternately downwards and upwards. Work front

and sleeves to match.

To make up
Join shoulders. Join side and sleeve seams. Set in sleeves.

Neck edging

1st round With RS facing and using crochet hook, join A to neck edge at shoulder. Work dc evenly round neck, working a multiple of 5dc plus 1 extra, ss into first dc.

2nd round 1dc into first dc, *1htr into each dc, 1tr into each of next 2dc, 1htr into next dc, 1dc into next dc, rep from * to end, ss into first dc. Fasten off.

Sleeve edging

Work as for neck edging.

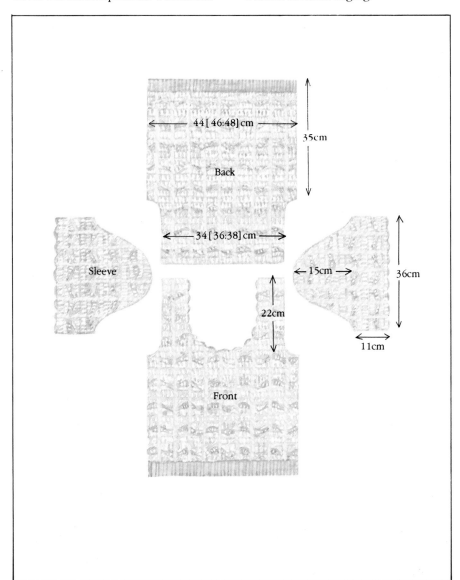

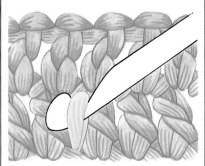

SPECIAL TECHNIQUE
Surface slip stitch

1 To work surface slip stitch into a solid background, begin at the lower edge and, with the yarn at the back of the work, insert the hook into the space between two stitches. Take the yarn round the hook and draw through a loop.

2 Insert the hook into the next space between two stitches. Take the yarn round the hook and draw through a loop. The first surface slip stitch has been anchored to the background fabric. Continue in this way to form the surface chain effects.

3 Work surface slip stitch on to a filet mesh background fabric in the same way, but insert the hook from front to back into the chain space between two treble.

In the diagram:

- 44 [46:48] cm (Back width)
- 35cm (Back height)
- Back
- 34 [36:38] cm
- Sleeve
- 15cm
- 36cm
- 22cm
- 11cm
- Front

FILET CROCHET BLOUSE

This simple blouse can be worn for daytime or evening, depending on how you accessorise it, and requires the minimum of shaping.

Main piece (worked in one piece to armholes)

Make 349 [365:389:409] ch.

Foundation row (RS) 1tr into 7th ch from hook, *1ch, miss 1ch, 1tr into next ch; rep from * to end. 172 [180:192:202] sps.

Next row 4ch, (to count as first 1tr, 1ch), 1tr into next tr, *1ch, 1tr into next tr; rep from * to end of row. Rep this row once more. Work from filet patt chart 1, starting at first [26th:20th:15th] sp/block, rep the first patt row 5 [6:6:6] times complete, then beg rep once more, ending on 27th [2nd:8th:13th] sp/block. Beg the next row on the 27th [2nd:8th:13th] square of chart. Cont straight in filet patt until work measures 30cm.

Divide for armholes

Patt across 44 [46:49:52] sps, turn and cont on these sts for right front. Work 3 [3:5:5] rows more.

Shape sleeve

Inc 1sp at armhole edge at end of next row by working (1ch, 1tr) into same place as the last tr. Inc 1sp at armhole edge on every following 6th row until there are 50 [52:55:57] sps, working extra sts into the filet patt.

4th size only

Work straight for 7 rows, then inc 1sp at armhole edge on next row. 58sps.

All sizes

Work 1 more row, finishing at neck edge. Front now measures 48 [49:50:51] cm.

Shape shoulder

Keeping filet patt correct, shape shoulder as follows:

1st row Work across 49 [51:54:57] sps. Turn.

2nd row Ss over 2sps, patt to end.

3rd row Patt to last 1 [2:2:2] sps. Turn.

4th row Ss over 2 [1:2:2] sps, patt to end.

5th row As 3rd.

6th row Ss over 2 [2:1:2] sps, patt to end.

1st and 2nd sizes only

Next row Work across 40 [41] sps. Turn.

Next row Ss over 2sps, patt to end.

All sizes

Shape neck

Still dec at shoulders, shape neck:

Next row (RS) Ss over 5sps, patt across 32 [32:38:41] sps. Turn.

Next row Ss over 2 [1:2:2] sps, patt to last 4sps. Turn.

Next row Ss over 2sps, patt to last 1 [2:2:2] sps. Turn.

Next row Ss over 2sps, patt to last sp. Turn, leaving last sp unworked.

Next row Ss over sp, patt to last 1 [1:1:2] sps. Turn.

Next row Ss over 2sps, work across 15 [15:20:22] sps. Turn.

Next row Ss over 1sp, patt to last 1 [2:2:1] sp. Turn.

Next row Ss over 2 [1:2:2] sps, patt to last sp. Turn, leaving last sp unworked. Neck shaping is now finished for first, 2nd and 3rd sizes.

Next row Ss over 0 [0:0:1] sp, patt to last 1 [2:2:2] sps. Turn.

Next row Ss over 2 [2:1:2] sps, patt to last 0 [0:0:1] sp. Turn. Neck shaping is now finished for 4th size.

Next row Patt to last 1 [1:2:2] sps. Turn.

Next row Ss over 2sps, patt to end.

Next row Patt over 2 [2:5:6] sps. Turn.

3rd and 4th sizes only

Next row Ss over 2sps, patt to end.

Next row Patt over 2sps.

All sizes Fasten off.

With RS facing, rejoin yarn to last st of right front at underarm, 3ch, work across 84 [88:94:98] sps/blocks, and continue in filet patt across these sts for back. Work straight for 3 [3:5:5] rows more. Inc 1sp each end of next and every following 6th row until there are 96 [100:106:109] sps/blocks, working inc sts into filet patt.

4th size only

Work straight for 7 rows, then inc 1sp at each end of next row. 110sps. Work 1 row more so that back measures same as front to start of shoulder shaping. Keeping filet patt correct, shape shoulders as follows:

1st row (RS) Ss over 1sp, work across 94 [98:104:108] sps. Turn.

2nd row Ss over 2sps, patt to last 2sps. Turn.

3rd row Dec 1 [2:2:2] sps at each end.

4th row Dec 2 [1:2:2] sps at each end.

5th row As 3rd.

6th row Dec 2 [2:1:2] sps at each end.

7th row Dec 1 [1:2:1] sps at each end.

8th row As 2nd.

Sizes

To fit 81 [86:91:96] cm bust
Length 60 [60:61:62] cm

Note *Instructions for larger sizes are in square brackets []; where there is only one set of figures it applies to all sizes.*

Materials

Approx 1150 [1280:1450:1600] m of a No. 5 crochet cotton
1.50mm crochet hook
8 buttons

Tension

18 sps and 19 rows to 10cm over filet patt using 1.50mm hook

To save time, take time to check tension.

9th row As 3rd.
10th row As 4th.
11th row Dec 1 [2:1:2] sps at each end.
12th row As 2nd.
13th row As 7th.
14th row As 2nd.
15th row As 3rd.
16th row Dec 2 [1:1:2] sps at each end.
17th row As 3rd.
18th row As 2nd.
19th row As 7th. 40 [38:38:42] sps.

Shape neck
Next row (WS) Ss over 2sps, work
across 10 [9:9:11] sps. Turn.
Next row Ss over 6 [6:6:7] sps, work
over 2sps. Fasten off. Miss centre 16
sts, (WS facing) rejoin yarn to next st,
4ch, patt to last 2sps. Turn.
Next row Ss over 2 [1:1:2] sps, patt
over 2sps. Turn. Fasten off.

Shape front
With RS of work facing, rejoin yarn to
last st of back at underarm, 3ch, work
in filet patt to end. 44 [46:49:52] sps.
Cont on these sts as for left front and
finish to correspond with right front,
reversing all shapings.

Collar
Make 141 [141:141:153] ch. Work
foundation row as for main part.
68 [68:68:74] sps. Work 10 rows of
filet from chart 2, working the patt rep

11 [11:11:12] times and ending with
2sps at end of row. Fasten off.

To make up
Press very lightly on WS.
Button border
With RS facing, start at beg of neck
shaping and work 1 row of dc down
left front to lower edge.
2nd-4th rows 1ch, 1dc in each st to
end. Fasten off.
Buttonhole border
Work as for button border, beg at
lower edge and working 8 buttonholes
on the 3rd row, the first 1cm above
lower edge, the last at top of border
and the rest spaced evenly between.
To work buttonhole 3ch, miss 3dc, 1dc
into next dc. Work 3dc into each 3ch
sp on following row.
Sleeve borders
With RS facing, work 1 row of dc along
edge of each sleeve. Fasten off.
Lower border
Work as for sleeve borders, beg and
ending at centre front. Place a marker
on neck shaping 2cm from front edge
of front borders. Sew last row of collar
between markers.
Collar and neck border
Work as for sleeve borders, beg and
ending at centre front. Join seams and
sew on buttons.

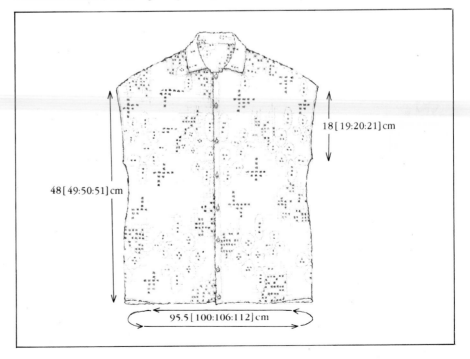

18[19:20:21] cm

48[49:50:51] cm

95.5 [100:106:112] cm

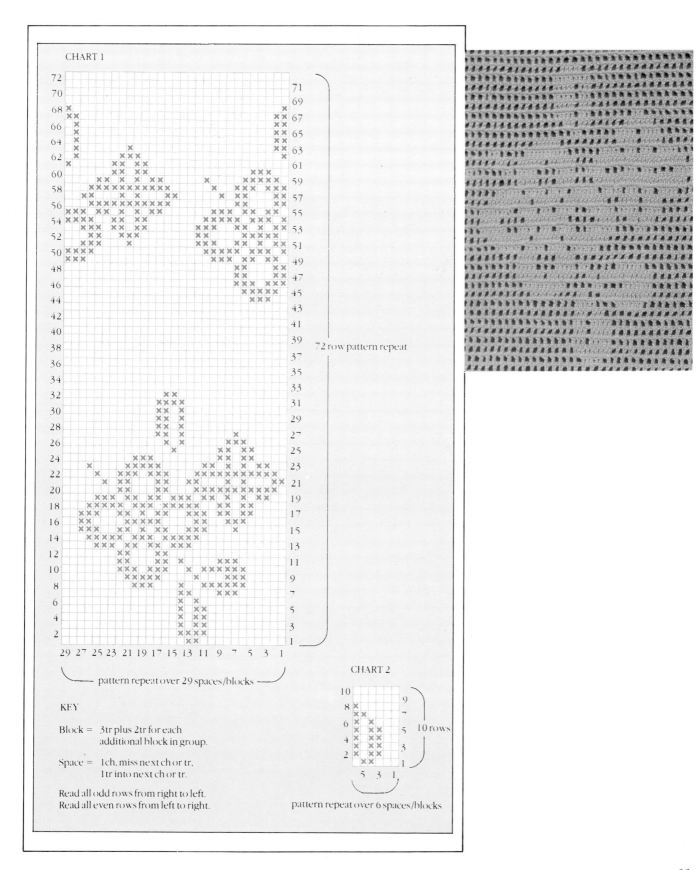

CHART 1

72 row pattern repeat

pattern repeat over 29 spaces/blocks

KEY

Block = 3tr plus 2tr for each
additional block in group.

Space = 1ch, miss next ch or tr,
1tr into next ch or tr.

Read all odd rows from right to left.
Read all even rows from left to right.

CHART 2

10 rows

pattern repeat over 6 spaces/blocks

FLOWER-TRIMMED TOP

Crochet flowers make a pretty trim for a simple blouse like this one.

Back

Using knitting needles, cast on 108 sts.
Rib row * K1, P1, rep from * to end.
Rep rib row until work measures 5cm, ending with WS facing. Cast off loosely in rib until one loop rem. Transfer loop to larger crochet hook.
Next row (RS) 3ch to count as first tr, 1tr into each cast-off st to end. 108tr.
Next row 3ch, 1tr into each tr to end. Rep last row until work measures 33cm from beg.
Next row 4ch, 1tr into 4th ch from hook (2tr inc), 1tr into each tr to end. Turn.
Rep this row once more. 112tr.
Work straight until back measures 46cm.
Shape shoulders
Ss across 7tr, 3ch, work to last 7tr. Turn. Rep last row once more. 84tr.
Shape neck
Ss across 7tr, 3ch to count as first tr, 1tr into each of next 20tr. Turn.
Next row Ss across 7tr, 3ch, 1tr into each of next 6tr.
Fasten off.
With RS facing, miss centre 28tr, rejoin yarn and work across 21tr. Turn leaving 7tr unworked.
Next row Ss across 7tr, 3ch, 1tr into each of next 6tr. Fasten off.

Front

Work as for back until work measures 39cm from beg.
Shape neck
Work across 45tr. Turn. Dec 1tr at neck edge on next and every following row until 35tr rem. Work straight until front measures same as back to beg of shoulder shaping, ending at armhole edge.
Shape shoulders
Ss across 7tr, work in tr to end of row. Turn.
Next row 3ch to count as first tr, 1tr into each of next 20tr. Turn.
Next row Ss over 7tr, work in tr to end of row. Turn.
Next row 3ch, 1tr into each of next 6tr. Fasten off.
Miss centre 20tr, rejoin yarn for 2nd side of neck and work across 45tr.
Work as for first side of neck, reversing all shaping.

Size

To fit *86-96cm bust*
Length *46cm*

Materials

Approx 1120m of a No. 5 crochet cotton in main colour
1 ball of No. 20 crochet cotton in each of five contrasting colours
3.00mm crochet hook
1.50mm crochet hook
1 pair 2mm knitting needles

Tension

22tr and 14 rows to 10cm using 3.00mm hook

To save time, take time to check tension.

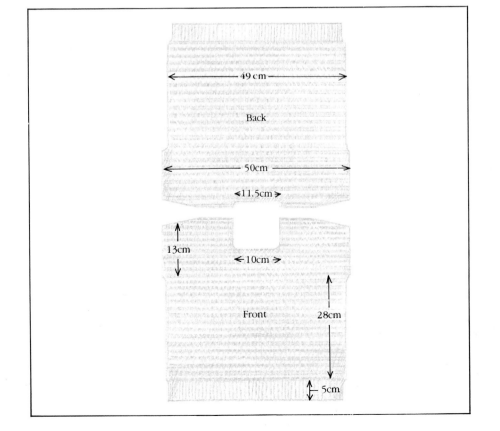

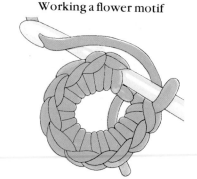

1 *Begin by working the number of chain specified in the pattern and joining them with a slip stitch to form a ring. Work 12 double crochet into the ring. The first and last stitches of each round are joined with a slip stitch.*

To make up
Join shoulder and side seams.
Armhole edging
With RS facing, join yarn to underarm seam, 1dc into same place, miss first row end, * 5tr into next row end, miss next row end, 1dc into next row end, miss next row end, rep from * round armhole, ss to first dc. Fasten off. Rep round 2nd armhole.
Neck edging
Join yarn to left shoulder seam and work shell edging round neck as for armhole, but missing 2tr between sts instead of 1 row end when working across top edge of tr.
Flowers
Using smaller hook, make 9ch, ss to form a ring.

1ch, 18dc into ring, ss to first dc.
2nd round 1dc into same place as ss, *3ch, miss 2dc, 1dc into next dc, rep from *, ending with 3ch, miss 2dc, 1ss into first dc.
3rd round Into each 3ch loop work 1dc, 1htr, 3tr, 1htr, 1dc.
4th round * 5ch, 1dc round first dc of 2nd round inserting hook from back of work, * 5ch, 1dc round next dc of 2nd round, rep from * to end of round.
5th round Into each 5ch loop work (1dc, 1htr, 5tr, 1htr, 1dc), ss to first dc. Fasten off.
Make 26 flowers using different colours as desired. Sew them to blouse as shown.

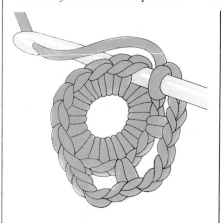

2 *Work one double crochet into the same place as the slip stitch, work three chain, miss one double crochet, work one double crochet into the next stitch. Repeat all the way round.*

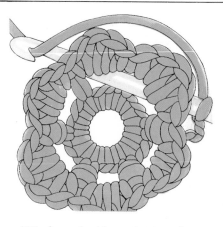

4 *Work one double crochet into the slip stitch of previous round, work five chain, then work one double crochet round the back of the stitch which separated the previous round of loops.*

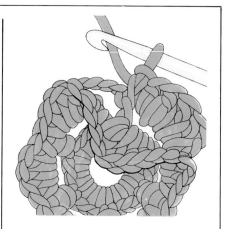

6 *Into the first five-chain loop work one double crochet, one half treble, three trebles, one half treble and one double crochet.*

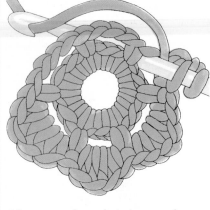

3 *Into every three-chain loop work one double crochet, one half treble, one treble, one half treble and one double.*

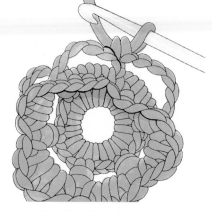

5 *Make a five-chain loop in the same way behind each petal on the previous round.*

7 *Work a petal in the same way into each five-chain loop all round.*

TWO EASY PIECES

. . . make up this checked cotton top. The front fastens with a button; the back forms a low V.

Size
To fit 86 [91] cm bust
Length 45 [50] cm

Note *Instructions for the larger size are in square brackets [ ]; where there is one set of figures it applies to both sizes.*

Materials
Approx 250 [350] g of a medium-weight crochet cotton in main colour (A)
Approx 50 [100] g in each of four contrasting colours (B, C, D and E)
3.50 [4.00] crochet hook
1 pair 3¼mm knitting needles
1 button

Tension
16 [14] tr and 9 [7¾] rows over check patt using 3.50 [400] mm hook; each square measures 3.5 × 3.5 [4 × 4] cm

To save time, take time to check tension.

Right half
Using 3.50 [4.00] mm hook and A, make 38ch *loosely.*
1st row (RS) Using A, 1tr into 4th ch from hook, 1tr into each of next 4tr, changing to B on last st. With B, 1tr into each of next 6ch, weaving A across back of work and changing to A on last tr.. With A, 1tr into each of next 6ch, changing to C on last st. With C, 1tr into each of next 6ch, weaving A across back of work and changing to A on last st. With A, 1tr into each of next 6ch, changing to D on last tr. With D, 1tr into each of next 6ch. Turn. 6 squares, each consisting of 6tr. 36 sts.
2nd row (WS) 3ch to count as first tr, 1tr into each st to end, following chart for colours and working last tr into top of turning ch. Turn.
3rd row As 2nd.
Keeping edges of work as neat as possible cont in tr, working check patt from chart until 66 rows in all have been worked. 22 vertical squares in all. Fasten off.

Left half
Work as for right half, reversing check patt so that first row of chart is WS.

Ribbing
With RS of two halves facing, pin two pieces tog as shown in diagram so that lower edge of right half overlaps lower edge of left half by two squares for front. Pin two pieces in same way for back so that lower edge of left half overlaps lower edge of right half by two squares.
With RS of front facing, using knitting needles and A, pick up and K60 [70] sts along lower edge, taking care to pick up sts through both layers at centre front overlap.
Work firmly in K2, P2 rib until work measures 6cm. Cast off loosely in rib. Pick up and K60 [70] sts on back and work in K2, P2 rib as for front.

To make up
Press lightly on WS, avoiding rib. Count up 5 squares from rib at each side and pin side seams, taking care to match squares. Using finer cotton in a matching colour, join side seams on WS, taking extra care with rib. Count up 6 squares at centre front and sew button to left front on 2nd tr from edge. Use turning ch on right front as button loop. Press seams.

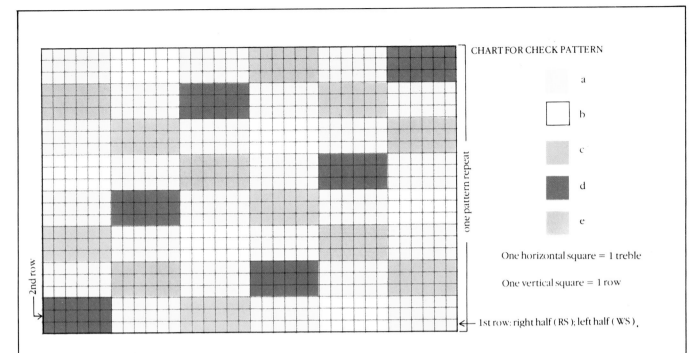

CHART FOR CHECK PATTERN

one pattern repeat

2nd row

a
b
c
d
e

One horizontal square = 1 treble

One vertical square = 1 row

1st row: right half (RS); left half (WS)

Working multicoloured checks

1 *When working a multicoloured check patttern, as for this top, wind a small amount of each colour of yarn (more than one, if the colour is used more than once in the row)on to a small piece of cardboard to prevent the yarns from tangling while you work. Use these small balls for each different square of colour when it occurs in the patttern.*

2 *To work the pattern, follow the diagram above for the colour sequence. The first row represents the right side of the right half, and the wrong side of the left half. One pattern repeat consists of 24 rows (8 coloured squares on the diagram).*
If you prefer, you could devise your own chart, using the same number of squares but different colours. Use a piece of graph paper, mark off the area shown and colour in blocks as desired.

Assembling the top
The diagram on the left shows how the two crochet pieces are assembled. The position of the armholes is 5 coloured squares up from the rib, and the position of the button at the front is 6 squares up. Both the front and the back are overlapped by 2 squares and ribbed together through both thicknesses.

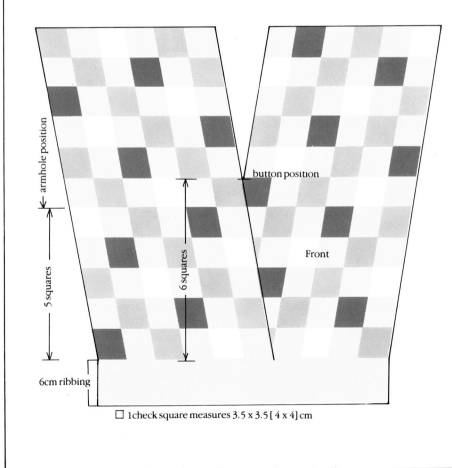

armhole position

button position

Front

5 squares

6 squares

6cm ribbing

□ 1check square measures 3.5 x 3.5 [4 x 4] cm

SKY-BLUE JACKET

Soft chenille yarn is used for this comfortable jacket, which is trimmed with double knitting in a harmonising or contrasting shade.

Back

Using larger hook and A, make 51 [54:57:60] ch.
Base row (RS) 1tr into 4th ch from hook, 1tr into each ch to end. Turn. 49 [52:55:58] sts.
1st row 3ch to count as first tr, 1tr between first and 2nd tr, 1tr between 2nd and 3rd tr, cont to work 1tr between each 2tr to end, 1tr into turning ch. Turn. First row forms patt and is rep throughout. Cont in patt until work measures 41cm from beg, ending with a WS row.
Shape armholes
Next row Ss across first 5 sts, ss into next sp between tr, 3ch, patt to last 6 sts. Turn, leaving rem sts unworked. 39 [42:45:48] sts. Cont straight until work measures 60 [60:61:61] cm from beg, ending with a WS row.
Shape shoulders
1st row Ss across first 4 sts, 1dc into next sp between tr, patt to last 6 sts, miss next tr, 1dc into next tr. Turn. Rep last row once.
3rd row Ss across first 3 [4:5:6] sts, 1dc into next sp between tr, patt to last 5 [6:7:8] sts, miss next tr, 1dc into next tr. 17 [18:19:20] sts. Fasten off.

Pocket linings (make 2)

Using larger hook and A, make 17 ch. Work base row as for back. 15 tr. Work 9 rows in patt as for back on these 15 sts. Fasten off.

Right front

Using larger hook and A, make 30 [32:33:35] ch and work base row as for back. 28 [30:31:33] sts.
Cont in patt as for back, work 10 rows.
Make buttonhole and pocket linings
Next row 3ch, patt 2tr, 2ch, miss next 2 sts (buttonhole formed), patt 6 [7:8:9] tr, patt across 15 pocket lining sts, miss next 15 sts, patt to end. Cont in patt until work measures 41cm.
Shape armhole
Dec 5 sts at side edge on next row. Cont on rem 23 [25:26:28] sts until work measures 5 rows less than back to beg of shoulder shaping, ending at front edge.
Shape neck
Dec 7 [8:8:9] sts on next row, 2 sts at front edge on next row and 1 st at front edge on following 3 rows, ending at armhole edge and working 1dc at front edge to achieve a good curve.
Shape shoulder
Work to match back shoulder shaping, dec 4 sts at armhole edge on following 2 rows. Fasten off, leaving rem 3 [4:5:6] sts as part of shoulder edge.

Left front

Work as for right front, omitting buttonhole, reversing shaping and position of pocket on the front.

Sleeves

Using larger hook and A, work 30 [30:32:32] ch. Work base row as for back. 28 [28:30:30] sts. Cont in patt as for back, inc one st at each end of 4th and every following 4th row 5 times in all, then every following 3rd row twice. 44 [44:46:46] sts. Work straight until work measures 44cm. Place a contrasting marker at each end of last row. Work straight for 3 more rows to fit armhole. Fasten off.

Collar

Using larger hook and A, make 54 [56:58:60] ch. Work base row as for back. 52 [54:56:58] sts. Work 5 rows in patt as for back.
Next row Ss across first 16 [17:17:18] sts, 1sc into next st, patt 18 [18:20:20] tr, 1dc into next st. Fasten off, leaving rem 16 [17:17:18] sts unworked.

To make up

Join shoulder seams. Sew top edges of sleeves to sides of armholes and last rows above markers to armhole shaping. Join side and sleeve seams. Sew shaped edge of collar to neck edges, leaving 5 sts free on each front neck edge.

Borders

Using smaller hook and B, work 5 rows dc across lower edge, taking care not to work too tightly as this will pucker main fabric. Work 5 rounds of dc round lower edge of each sleeve border. Join each round with ss and turn work each time to achieve same effect as lower border.

Sizes

To fit *81* [*86:91:96*] *cm bust*
Length 60 [*60:61:61*] *cm, excluding border*
Sleeve seam 44cm, excluding border

Note: *Instructions for larger sizes are in square brackets* [ ]; *where there is only one set of figures it applies to all sizes.*

Materials

Approx 650 [*700:700:700*] *g of a medium-weight chenille yarn* (A)
Approx 100g of a double knitting yarn (B)
3.50mm crochet hook
5.00mm crochet hook
1 button

Tension

11½ sts and 8 rows to 10cm over patt using 5.00mm hook

To save time, take time to check tension.

SPECIAL TECHNIQUE
Edging the fabric with crochet

1 *One row of double crochet worked along the edge of your fabric makes a firm base on which to work the edging. With the RS of the main fabric facing, join in the yarn at the edge. Work one double crochet into each stitch to produce a firm, even border. Fewer stitches pull the fabric inwards and more stitches create a wavy effect.*

2 *When worked across row ends the number of stitches can vary. A double crochet fabric usually requires only one stitch per row end to maintain a straight edge, whereas longer stitches, such as treble for example, may need two or more stitches worked into each row end to keep the edge flat.*

3 *To shape corners work 3 double crochet into the corner stitch so that the border remains flat. Thicker fabrics or longer stitches may require more stitches to be worked into the corner, but an uneven number should always be worked to make a clearly defined corner.*

Beg at lower edge of lower border, work in dc up right front, across top of revers, all round edge of collar, down left side and across end of lower border. Work 4 more rows in same way, inc at outer edge of revers and collar corners and dec at inner corners to keep work flat. Work 5 rows dc in same way across pocket opening. Sew pocket linings to WS. Sew on button.

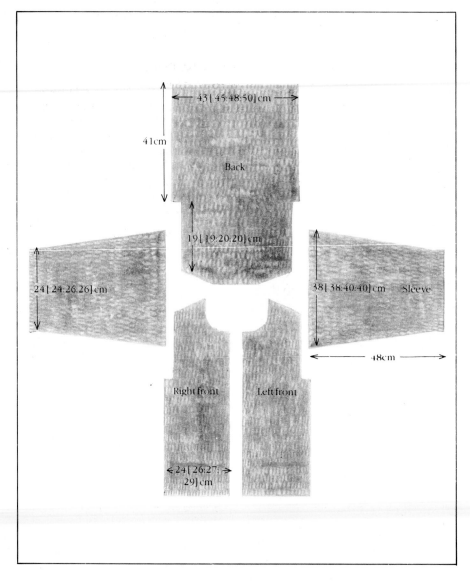

MOSAIC PATTERN SWEATER

This pretty sweater is designed on classic lines with raglan sleeves and a V-neckline. Make it in soft pastel shades, using one of them for the knitted welts and borders.

Sizes

To fit *81 [86:91:96]cm bust*
Length *60 [61:62:63]cm*
Sleeve seam *44cm*

Note *Instructions for the larger sizes are in square brackets [ ]; where there is only one set of figures it applies to all sizes.*

Materials

Double knitting yarn:
Approx 300 [300:350:350]g in main colour (A)
Approx 200 [200:250:250]g in each of contrasting colours (B and C)
4.00mm crochet hook
1 pair 3mm knitting needles

Tension

20 sts and 19½ rows to 10cm over patt using 3.00mm hook

To save time, take time to check tension.

Note *Carry yarns not in use loosely up side of work. Join in new colour by drawing it through last two loops on hook in old colour.*

Back

Using A, make 93[99:105:111] ch.
Base row (RS) Using A, 1dc into 3rd ch from hook, * 1ch, miss next ch, 1dc into next ch, rep from * to end. Turn. 92[98:104:110] sts. Working in colour sequence of 1 row B, 1 row C, 1 row A, cont in patt as follows:
Patt row 1ch to count as first dc, miss first st, * 1dc into next 1ch sp, 1ch, miss next dc, rep from * ending last rep with 1dc into last st. Turn.
Cont in patt until work measures 30cm from beg, ending with a row in A.
Shape raglan armholes
Keeping patt and colour sequence correct:
1st row Ss across first 3 sts, patt to last 2 sts. Turn. 88[94:100:106] sts.
2nd row Work in patt.
3rd row Dec 1 st at each end of row.
Rep last 2 rows 16 times more. 54 [60:66:72] sts.
Rep 3rd row only 11[13:15:17] times more. 32[34:36:38] sts.
Fasten off.

Front

Work as for back until 2[4:4:4] rows less have been worked to beg of raglan, thus ending with a row in B[C:C:C].
Divide for neck
Keeping patt and colour sequence correct:
Next row Patt first 43[46:49:52] sts. Turn and cont on these sts for first side of neck.
Next row Work in patt.
2nd, 3rd and 4th sizes only
Next row Dec 1 st at neck edge. Work 1 row in patt.
All sizes
Shape raglan armhole
Next row Ss over first 3 sts, patt to end. Dec 1 st at armhole edge on next 17 alternate rows and then on the following 8[8:12:16] rows *and at the same time* shape neck edge by dec 1 st at neck edge on 2nd row and every following 4th row until 11[12:13:14] sts in all have been dec at neck edge. 5[7:5:3] sts. Dec 1 st at armhole edge on the next 3[5:3:1] rows.
Fasten off rem 2 sts.
Return to sts left at beg of neck shaping. With RS facing, miss next 6 sts and rejoin appropriate colour to next st, patt to end. 43[46:49:52] sts.
Complete to match first side of neck, reversing all shaping.

Sleeves (both alike)

Using A, make 59 [61:63:65]ch.
Base row Using A, work as for back. 58 [60:62:64] sts.
Work 8 [8:7:7] rows in patt as for back.
Next row Inc 1 st at each end of row.
Inc 1 st at each end of every following 9th [9th:8th:8th] row 6 [6:7:7] times more. 72 [74:78:80] sts.
Work straight in patt until work measures 38cm from beg, ending with a row in A.
Shape raglan top
Keeping patt and colour sequence correct:
1st row Ss over first 3 sts, patt to last 2 sts, turn.
68 [70:74:76] sts.
2nd row Work in patt.
3rd row Dec 1 st at each end of row.
Rep 2nd and 3rd rows 13 [14:14:15] times more, ending with a 3rd row. 40 [40:44:44] sts.
Rep 3rd row only 17 [17:19:19] times more. 6 sts. Fasten off.

Lower welts

With RS facing, using knitting needles and A, pick up and K 79 [83:89:93] sts along lower edge of front and back.
Work 8cm in K1, P1 rib. Cast off in rib.

Cuffs

With RS facing, using knitting needles and A, pick up and K 49[51:53:55] sts along lower edge of sleeve.
Work 6cm in K1, P1 rib.
Cast off in rib.

Raglan borders (make 4)

Using knitting needles and A, cast on 9 sts.
1st row (RS) K2, * P1, K1, rep from * to last st, K1.
2nd row P2, * K1, P1, rep from * to last st, P1.
Rep these 2 rows until strip, when slightly stretched, fits raglan from beg of dec at underarm to neck edge. Cast off in rib.
Sew borders to raglans on front and back. Sew raglan edges of sleeves to borders.

Neck border

Using knitting needles and A, cast on 7 sts and work in rib as for raglan borders until border, when slightly stretched, fits round neck opening, beg and ending at centre front. Cast off in rib.

Sew border to neck edge, lapping the right end over the left at the centre front.

To make up

Do not press.

Join side and sleeve seams, joining ends of raglan borders at underarm. Press seams very lightly.

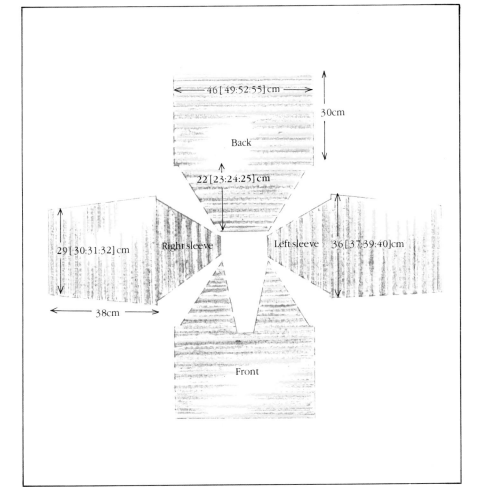

Three-colour mosaic

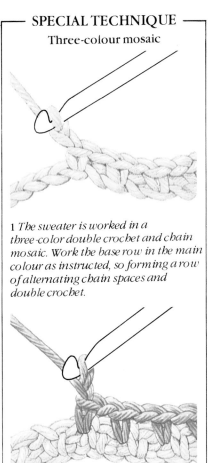

1 *The sweater is worked in a three-colour double crochet and chain mosaic. Work the base row in the main colour as instructed, so forming a row of alternating chain spaces and double crochet.*

2 *Join in the second colour on the last stitch of the base row. On the following row work a double crochet into each chain space and a chain above each double crochet.*

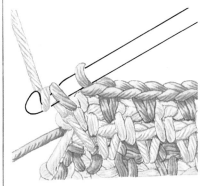

3 *Introduce the third colour for the next row and work as in step 2. Continue in this way using the three different colours in sequence. Do not cut old yarn when changing colour, but leave it at the edge of the work ready for the next row in that colour.*

RIBBON-THREADED TOPS

Satin ribbon provides the finishing touch on these pretty tops worked in filet crochet.

Woman's mesh top

Back

Using crochet hook, make 140 [149:158] ch.
Base row 1tr into 8th ch from hook, (2ch, miss next 2ch, 1tr into next ch) 44 [47:50] times. Turn. 45 [48:51] sps.
Patt row 5ch, miss first tr, 1tr into next tr, *2ch, 1tr into next tr, rep from * to turning ch, 2ch, 1tr into sp formed by turning ch.
Turn.
Rep patt row 44 times more.
Shape sleeves
Next row Make 73ch, 1tr into 8th ch from hook, (2ch, miss next 2ch, 1tr into next ch) 21 times, (2ch, 1tr into next tr) 45 [48:51] times, 2ch, 1tr into sp formed by turning ch, 2ch, 1qtr into same sp, (2ch, 1qtr into sp formed by previous qtr) 22 times.
Turn. 91 [94:97] sps.
Rep patt row 24 times more.
Fasten off.

Front

Work as for back for 60 rows.

Shape neck
1st row 5ch, miss first tr, 1tr into next tr, (2ch, 1tr into next tr) 39 [40:42] times, 1dtr into next tr. Turn.
2nd row 3ch, miss first dtr and tr, 1tr into next tr, * 2ch, 1tr into next tr, rep from * to end, ending with 1tr into sp formed by turning ch. Turn.
3rd row 5ch, miss first tr, 1tr into next tr, (2ch, 1dtr into next tr) 37 [38:40] times, 1dtr into next tr. Turn.
4th row As 2nd row.
5th row 5ch, miss first tr, 1tr into next tr, (2ch, 1tr into next tr) 35 [36:38] times, 1dtr into next tr. Turn.
6th row As 2nd row.
7th row Ch 5, miss first tr, 1tr into next tr, (ch 2, 1tr into next tr) 33 [34:36] times, 1dtr into next tr. Turn.
8th row As 2nd row.
Work straight in patt for 3 more rows.
Fasten off.
Join yarn to first st on other sleeve and work other side of neck to match.

To make up
If necessary, block or press lightly, as appropriate for yarn used.

Woman's mesh top
Sizes
To fit *81 [86:91] cm bust*
Length *54cm*
Sleeve seam *23cm*

Note *Instructions for larger sizes are in square brackets [ ]; where there is only one set of figures it applies to all sizes.*

Materials
Approx 250 [250:300] g of a 3 ply yarn
Approx 4.2 m of 1cm-wide single-faced satin ribbon in each of three colours (A, B and C)
3.50mm crochet hook
1 pair 2¾ knitting needles

Tension
10 sps and 13 rows to 10cm over filet mesh patt using 3.50mm hook

To save time, take time to check tension.

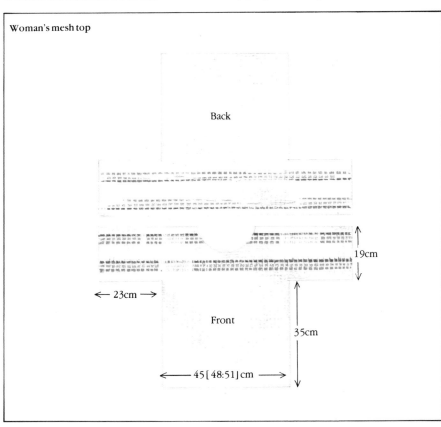

Woman's mesh top

Back

Front

19cm

23cm

35cm

45 [48:51] cm

SPECIAL TECHNIQUE
Ribbon weaving

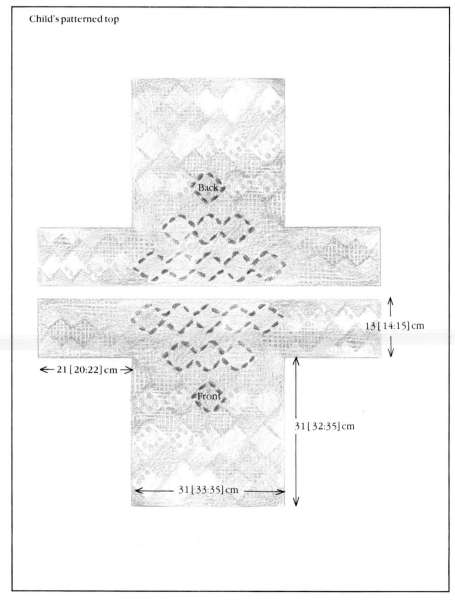

1 To prevent fraying, cut the ribbon diagonally, cutting it 12cm longer than needed. Estimating the length may be difficult, so make a trial weave across the mesh and note the amount required. Using a safety pin, anchor the ribbon to the right-hand edge of mesh, leaving about 12cm of ribbon extending over the edge.

2 Trim the other end of the ribbon diagonally. When using fine ribbon, thread this other end into a large blunt-ended needle. Thicker ribbon must be drawn through the mesh with a safety pin inserted about 3cm from the end.

3 Weave the ribbon through the mesh in your chosen pattern, guiding the ribbon through your fingers to prevent it from twisting. When one row of weaving is complete, remove the safety pin or needle. Fold the ends of ribbon to the wrong side at the side edges and secure with small backstitches, or enclose the ends later when seaming.

Join shoulder seams.
Cuffs (both alike)
Using knitting needles and with RS facing, pick up and K 82 sts from cuff edge. Work in K1, P1 rib for 4cm. Cast off in rib.
Welts
Using knitting needles and with RS facing, pick up and K 110 sts from lower edge of front. Work in K1, P1 rib for 6cm.
Cast off in rib.
Work back welt in the same way.
Neck edging
Using crochet hook and with RS facing, join yarn to centre-back neck.

1st round 1ch, 2dc into each sp all round neck, ss to first ch.
2nd round 1ch, miss first dc, 1dc into each dc to end, ss to first ch.
3rd round Ss into each dc to end.
Fasten off.
Ribbon weaving
Back Beg at RH edge, weave A through each sp on 6th row above sleeve shaping. Using B and C, weave next 2 rows in the same way. Miss next 10 rows and weave next 3 rows as before.
Front Weave A, B and C into same rows as on back, omitting neck opening.
Join side and sleeve seams, enclosing ends of ribbon with side seams.

38

Child's patterned top

Back and front (both alike)
Make 98 [104:110] ch.
Base row 1tr into 8th ch from hook, (2ch, miss next 2ch, 1tr into next ch) 30 [32:34] times. Turn. 31 [33:35] sps.
Next row 5ch, miss first tr, * 1tr into next tr, 2ch, rep from * to end, 1tr into sp formed by turning ch. Turn.
Last row forms mesh patt row.
Rep mesh patt row 2 [1:1] times more.
Next row 5ch, miss first tr, 1tr into next tr, (2ch, 1tr into next tr) 2 [3:4] times, 2tr into next 2ch sp, 1tr into next tr – block formed –, * (2ch, 1tr into next tr) 5 times, 2tr into next 2ch sp, 1tr into next tr, rep from * 3 times more, (2ch, 1tr into next tr) 3 [4:5] times, working last tr into sp formed by turning ch. Turn.
* * Beg with 2nd row, work rem 6 rows of filet diamond patt from chart A.
Work mesh patt row 4 [5:6] times.
Work first row of chart A. * *
Rep from * * to * * twice more.
Work 2nd and 3rd rows of chart A, so that 40 [42:45] rows have been worked from beg.
Shape sleeves
Next row Make 65 [62:68] ch, 1tr into 4th ch from hook, 1tr into next ch – first block formed –, cont working 4th row of chart B to other side edge, remove hook from loop, join a separate length of yarn to base of last tr worked, make 62 [59:65] ch and fasten off, return to main yarn and cont working 4th row of chart B across foundation ch just made.
Turn.
Work 5th-7th rows of chart B.
Work mesh patt row 4 [5:6] times.
Work first-7th rows of chart B.
Work mesh patt row 2 [3:3] times.
Fasten off.

To make up
Join shoulder seams, leaving centre 23 [23:27] sps for neck open.
Ribbon weaving
Beg at RH edge, weave ribbon through sps above and below block diamond patt on front and backs as shown in the measurement diagram, twisting ribbon at corners as necessary.
Join side and sleeve seams; for 8cm above cuff edge place WS tog, so reversing seam.
Lower edge
With RS facing and using crochet hook, join yarn to lower edge at a side seam.
1st round 1ch, 2sc into each sp to end, ss to first ch.
2nd round 1ch, miss first sc, work in crab st (dc worked from left to right) to end, ss to first ch. Fasten off.
Turn back cuffs twice (4cm, then 4cm) and catch to sleeve seam if necessary.

Child's patterned top
Sizes
To fit 55 [60:65] cm chest
Length 44 [46:50] cm
Sleeve seam 21 [20:22] cm

Note *Instructions for larger sizes are in square brackets [ ]; where there is only one set of figures it applies to all sizes.*

Materials
Approx 200 [200:250] g of a 3 ply yarn
Approx 2m of 1cm-wide double-faced satin ribbon
3.50mm crochet hook

Tension
10 sps and 13 rows to 10cm over filet mesh patt using 3.50mm hook

To save time, take time to check tension.

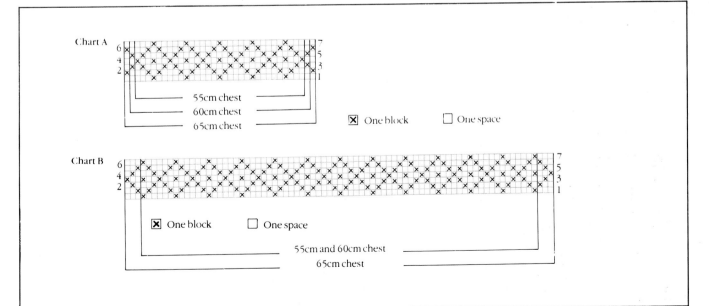

HAIRPIN CROCHET BEDJACKET

This pretty bedjacket is made from strips of hairpin lace crochet worked in three contrasting colours.

Note: Instructions for working hairpin crochet are on pages 164-166. The crochet is worked with yarn double throughout.

Back and fronts

Using yarn double, make 9 strips in colour A, 6 in B and 6 in C, all 51cm long (60 loops along each edge). Then make 1 strip each in A and C to measure 43cm (51 loops on each edge) and 2 strips each in A and C to measure 31cm (36 loops along each edge).

Arrange the strips as shown in the diagram on page 42. Start at the right front edge and join the left side of one 43cm-long strip in C to the other side of a 51cm strip in B, starting at the lower edge and leaving 9 loops free on the longer strip at the top (see page 166). Join the remaining strips in the same way, using the shorter strips for the underarm sections (leaving 24 loops free at the top of the longer strips).

Sleeves

For each sleeve work 12 strips 42cm long (49 loops on each edge), 4 in each of the colours (24 strips in all for both sleeves). Join the strips for each sleeve, alternating colours as on the main body of the jacket.

Join the sleeve seam by looping the first and last strips together, leaving 7 loops open at the top. Cast off these 7 loops by inserting the crochet hook through the first loop and drawing the next loop through it, then continuing to draw successive loops through the preceding loop on the hook. Sew the last loop to finish the cast-off edge.

Edging strips

To make the sleeve edgings take one strand each from two of the colours and make 2 two-tone strips 27cm long (32 loops along each edge); then work 2 more two-tone strips to the same length but using a different colour combination. Loop one strip of each colour together and join them to form a ring. Gather the wrist edge of each sleeve and sew the edgings neatly in place.

For the waist, work 2 two-tone strips 61cm long (72 loops along each edge) or to the desired length, but do not join them to the garment yet. Make two more two-tone strips to measure 44cm (52 loops along each edge) to go from the lower edge up to the neck edge on the right front, and 2 strips 40cm long (48 loops) to go round the neck edge.

To make up

Do not press. Join the shoulder seams,

Size

To fit *81-86cm bust*
Length *approx 58cm*
Sleeve seam *approx 37cm*

Note: The size can easily be adjusted by adding or subtracting strips, by lengthening or shortening the waistband or by lengthening or shortening the vertical strips.

Materials

Approx 480g of a medium-weight mohair in each of 3 colours (A, B and C)
3m narrow ribbon in each of two colours to match yarn
4 press fasteners
40mm hairpin staple (or adjustable staple fixed at this width)
4.00mm crochet hook

Tension

Two strips of hairpin crochet, worked with yarn double and joined with dc measures approx 51cm long (60 loops on each side) and 7.5cm wide

To save time, take time to check tension.

then set in the sleeves, placing the cast-off edges at the underarm edges of the armholes and keeping the free loops along the armholes on the main body to the right side of the work to make a fluffy edge.

Cast off the loops along the neck edge (the 9 loops at each side) and along each front.

Gather the lower edge of the jacket to fit the waist measurement and sew the edging neatly in place. Sew the right front edging in place, fitting it from the neck edge to the lower edge, stitching along the centre of the edging and making sure that it laps over the cast-off edge.

Thread two rows of ribbon through the wrist, neck edge and waist and tie them in bows. Sew four press fasteners at equally spaced intervals down the front.

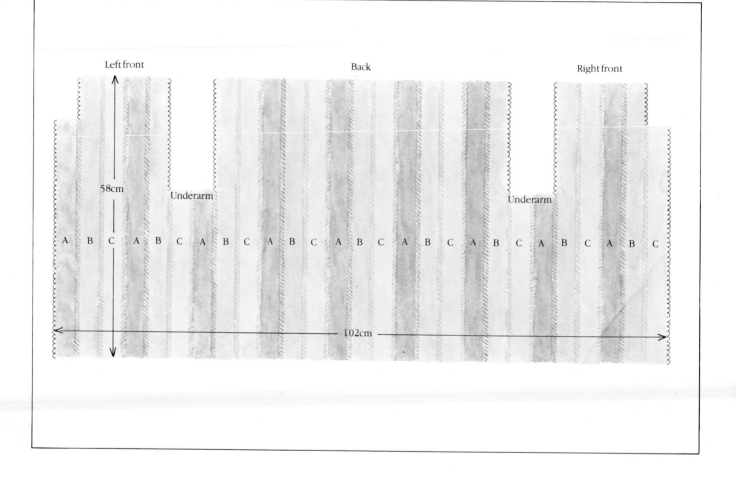

BOBBLES 'N' STRIPES

Subtle pastel colours in stripes and bobbles make an attractive pullover you'll enjoy wearing.

Sizes

To fit 86 [91:96] cm bust
Length 62 [64:65] cm
Sleeve seam 48cm

Note *Instructions for larger sizes are in square brackets [ ]; where there is only one set of figures it applies to all sizes.*

Materials

Approx 300 [300:350] g of a 4 ply yarn in main colour (A)
Approx 250 [300:300] g in each of two contrasting colours (B and C)
3.00mm crochet hook
1 pair 2½mm knitting needles

Tension

22 sts and 12½ rows to 10cm over treble using 3.00mm hook

To save time, take time to check tension.

Back

Using knitting needles and A, cast on 126 [132:138] sts.
1st row (K1, P1) to end.
Rep first row until work measures 7cm. Cast off in rib, transferring last st to crochet hook.
Next row With RS facing and using A, 1ch to count as first dc, miss first st at base of first ch, work 105 [109:113] dc evenly into last row of welt. Turn. 106 [110:114] sts.
Beg patt as follows:
1st row (WS) Using B, 3ch, miss first st, 1tr into each st to end. Turn.
2nd row Using A, as first row.
3rd row Using C, as first row.
4th row Using A, as first row.
5th row Using B, as first row.
6th, 8th, 10th, 12th, 14th, 16th, 18th, 20th and 22nd rows Using A, 1ch to count as first dc, miss first st, 1dc into each st to end. Turn.
7th row Using C, 1ch to count as first dc, miss first st, 1dc into each of next 3 sts, *leaving last loop of each st on hook work 3dtr into next st, yrh and draw through all 4 loops on hook – bobble formed –, 1dc into each of next 3 sts, rep from * to last 2 sts, bobble into next st, 1dc into last st. Turn.
9th row Using B, 1ch to count as first dc, miss first st, 1dc into next st, *bobble into next st, 1dc into each of next 3 sts, rep from * to end. Turn.
11th-22nd rows Rep 7th-10th rows 3 times more.
23rd row Using C, as first row.
24th row Using A, as first row.
25th row Using B, as first row.
26th row Using A, as first row.
27th row Using C, as first row.
28th-44th rows As 6th-22nd rows, reading B for C and C for B.
First-44th rows form patt.
Cont in patt until work measures 41 [42:42] cm, ending with a WS row.
Shape armholes
Next row Keeping patt correct, ss across first 5 [6:7] sts, patt to last 4 [5:6] sts. Turn. 98 [100:102] sts.
Next row Ss across first 3 sts, patt to last 2 sts. Turn. 94 [96:98] sts.
Next 2 rows Work first 2 sts tog, patt to last 2 sts, work last 2 sts tog.

Turn. 90 [92:94] sts.
Work straight in patt until armhole measures 21 [22:23] cm, ending with a WS row.
Shape shoulders and neck
Next row Ss across first 9 sts, patt next 16 sts. Turn.
Next row Patt 8 sts.
Fasten off.
With RS facing, return to sts missed at beg of neck shaping, miss next 42 [44:46] sts, and keeping patt correct, join yarn to next st.
Next row Patt 16 sts. Turn.
Next row Ss across first 9 sts, patt to end. Fasten off.

Front

Work as for back until work measures 61 [63:64] cm from beg.
Shape neck
Next row Patt 37 [38:39] sts. Turn.
Next row Ss across first 4 sts, patt to end. Turn. 34 [35:36] sts.
Next row Patt to last 3 sts. Turn. 31 [32:33] sts.
Rep last 2 rows once more. 25 [26:27] sts.
Next row Ss across first 2 [3:4] sts, patt to end. Turn. 24 sts.
Work straight in patt until armhole matches back armhole to beg of shoulder shaping, ending at armhole edge.
Shape shoulder
Next row Ss across first 9 sts, patt to end. Turn. 16 sts.
Next row Patt first 8 sts.
Fasten off.
With RS facing, return to sts missed at beg of neck shaping, miss next 16 sts and keeping patt correct, join yarn to next st.
Next row Patt to end. Turn. 37 [38:39] sts.
Complete to match first side of neck, reversing all shaping.

Sleeves (both alike)

Using knitting needles and A, cast on 50 [52:54] sts.
Work in K1, P1 rib as for back for 6cm, ending with a RS row.
Cast off in rib, transferring last st to crochet hook.
Next row With RS facing and using A, 1ch to count as first dc, miss first st at

base of first ch, 1dc into each cast-off st to end. Turn. 50 [52:54] sts.
1st-5th rows As 23rd-27th rows of back patt.
Shape sleeve
6th row As 28th row of back patt, inc one st at each end of row. 52 [54:56] sts.
7th-22nd rows As 29th-44th rows of back patt, inc one st at each end of every following 4th row. 60 [62:64] sts. Cont in patt as for back, at the same time inc one st at each end of every following 4th row until there are 64 [66:68] sts.
Work straight in patt as for back until work measures approx 48cm from lower edge, ending with same row as back at beg of armhole shaping.
Shape top
Next row Sl st across first 5 sts, patt to last 4 sts. Turn. 56 [58:60] sts.
Next 3 rows Work first 2 sts tog, patt to last 2 sts, work last 2 sts tog. Turn. 50 [52:54] sts.
Work straight in patt for 5 [6:7] cm.
Next row Work first 2 sts tog, patt to last 2 sts, work last 2 sts tog. Turn. 48 [50:52] sts.
Next row Patt to end. Turn.
Rep last 2 rows until 32 sts rem.
Work straight in patt until work measures 68 [69:70] cm from beg. Fasten off.

Neckband
Join left shoulder seam.
With RS facing, using knitting needles and A, pick up and K 65 sts across back neck and 75 sts across front neck. 140 sts. Work 7 rows of K1, P1 rib.
Cast off in rib.

To make up
Do not press.
Join right shoulder seam.
Set in sleeves, matching stripes.
Join side and sleeve seams, matching stripes.

Note *Use backstitch for shoulder seams and a flat seam for the remaining seams, so as to prevent excess bulk.*

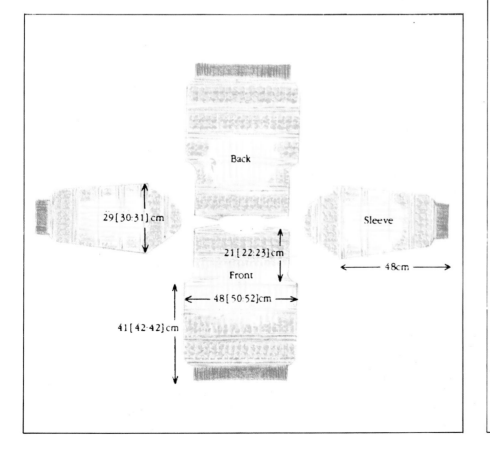

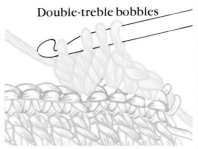

SPECIAL TECHNIQUE
Double-treble bobbles

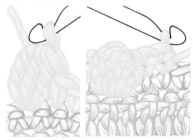

1 *The bobbles on the sweater are formed on the wrong side of the work by bending double-treble clusters. With the right side facing, work a row of double crochet and turn. Change to the first contrasting colour and work in double crochet to the position of the first bobble.*
Leaving the last loop of each stitch on the hook, work three double-trebles into the next stitch.

2 *Wind the yarn round the hook and draw it through all four loops on the hook to form the first double-treble cluster (above left). Work one double crochet into each of the next three stitches to bend the cluster, so forming the first bobble on the right side of the work (above right). If necessary, push the bobble to the right side with the blunt end of the crochet hook.*

3 *Continue in this way to the end of the row. Change back to the first colour and work a row of double crochet. Work another row of bobbles using the second contrasting colour and slightly altering the positions of the bobbles as instructed in the pattern. Continue alternating bobble and double crochet rows for the required length.*

TUNISIAN PULLOVER

Warm colours in Tunisian crochet stripes make this attractive pullover with a boat neck.

Note: *Instructions for working Basic Tunisian stitch (Tst), Tunisian double stitch (Tdc), Tunisian treble (Ttr) and Tunisian purl (Tp) are on pages 161-162.*

Back and front (alike)
Using Tunisian hook and A, make 60 [64:66:70] ch.
1st row Work 1 Ttr into 4th ch from hook, work in Ttr to end.
2nd row With B, work as for 2nd row of Tst – called "return row."
3rd row Tdc in B.
4th row Return row in C.
5th row Work Tp in C.
6th row Return row in A.
7th row Ttr in A.
8th row Return row in C.
9th row Tdc in C.
10th row Return row in B.
11th row Tp in B.
12th row Return row in A.
13th row Ttr in A.
Rows 2-13 form the striped pattern used for the main part of the sweater. Cont in patt until work measures 45 [45:50:50] cm, ending with a Ttr row in A.
To finish the top, work a return row, then 1 row Tp and another return row, all in A. Make 1 row ss from right to left.

Sleeves
Work 52 [54:56:58] ch in A.
1st row Ttr to end of row in A. Change to B and work in patt as for front until work measures 41 [41:45:45] cm, ending with 1 row Ttr in A.
Finish the top of the sleeve in A with 1 row Tdc, a return row and then 1 row ss from right to left.

Waistband
Using ordinary hook and A, make 11ch.
1st row 1dc into 2nd ch from hook, dc to end of row. Turn. 10dc.
2nd row Work dc into the back loops of the dc of the previous row. Turn.
Rep 2nd row to form a crochet rib, which is worked sideways and can be sewn or crocheted onto the garment. Cont until strip measures

72 [76:82:87] cm.
Bring the two ends tog and join the last row to the first 10ch with dc.

Cuffs
Make 15ch in A. Work in dc as for waistband until work measures 16cm. Join last row to first 14ch.

To make up
Darn in all ends and block or press the pieces lightly on WS as appropriate for yarn used.
Place front and back tog with RS facing and sew tog at shoulders for 8cm on each side.
Place centre of sleeve top at shoulder seam, RS facing, and join seam. Join side and sleeve seams. Sew the waistband and cuffs in position.

Sizes
To fit *81 [86:91:96] cm bust*
Length *54 [54:59:59] cm*
Sleeve seam *51 [51:54:54] cm*

Note *Instructions for larger sizes are in square brackets []; where there is only one set of figures it applies to all sizes.*

Materials
Approx 280 [280:320:320] g of a double knitting yarn in main colour (A)
Approx 75 [100:100:100] g in contrasting colour (B)
Approx 80 [120:120:120] g in contrasting colour (C)
7.00mm Tunisian crochet hook
6.00mm crochet hook

Tension
14 sts and 10 rows to 10cm using 7.00mm Tunisian crochet hook

To save time, take time to check tension.

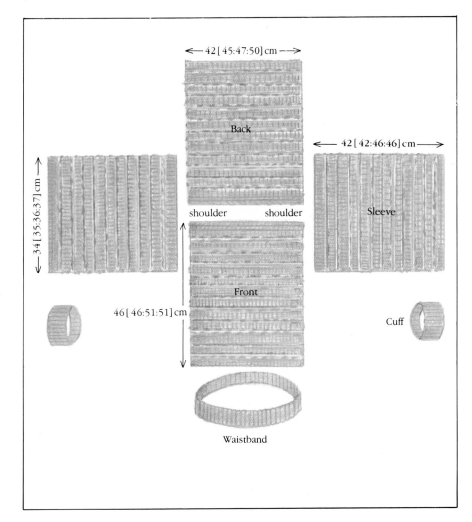

HOT PINK DIAMONDS

Open-work diamond motifs embellished with puff stitches make this pretty pullover.

Size
To fit *81-91cm bust*
Length *57cm*
Sleeve seam *45cm*

Materials
Approx 550g of a 4 ply yarn
3.50mm crochet hook
1 pair 2¾ knitting needles

Tension
*1 patt rep (16 sts) to 8cm and 1 patt rep
(10 rows) to 10cm using 3.50mm hook*

To save time, take time to check tension.

Back
Using knitting needles, cast on 99 sts.
1st row (K1, P1) to last st, K1.
2nd row (P1, K1) to last st, P1.
Rep first and 2nd rows until work measures 6cm, ending with a 2nd row. Cast off loosely in rib, leaving last st on needle.
Transfer last st to crochet hook.
Next row (RS) 1ch to count as first dc, miss first st at base of first ch, 1dc into each cast-off st to end. Turn. 99 sts.
Next row 3ch, miss first st, 1tr into next st, *3ch, miss next 3 sts, (yrh, insert hook into st and draw through a loop) 4 times into next st, yrh and draw through first 8 loops on hook, yrh and draw through rem 2 loops on hook – puff st formed –, (1ch, miss next st, puff st into next st) 4 times, 3ch, miss next 3 sts, 1tr into next st, rep from * to last st, 1tr into last st. Turn.
Beg patt as follows:
1st row (RS) 3ch, miss first st, 1tr into next tr, *1tr into next ch, 3ch, miss next 2ch, (puff st into next ch, 1ch) 3 times, puff st into next ch, 3ch, miss next 2ch, 1tr into next ch, 1tr into next tr, rep from * to last st, 1tr into last st. Turn.
2nd row 3ch, miss first st, 1tr into next tr, *1tr into next tr, 1tr into next ch, 3ch, miss next 2ch, (puff st into next ch, 1ch) twice, puff st into next ch, 3ch, miss next 2ch, 1tr into next ch, 1tr into each of next 2tr, rep from * to last st, 1tr into last st. Turn.
3rd row 3ch, miss first st, 1tr into next st, *1tr into each of next 2tr, 1tr into next ch, 3ch, miss next 2ch, puff st into next ch, 1ch, puff st into next ch, 3ch, miss next 2ch, 1tr into next ch, 1tr into each of next 3tr, rep from * to last st, 1tr into last st. Turn.
4th row 3ch, miss first st, 1tr into next st, *1tr into each of next 3tr, 1tr into next ch, 3ch, miss next 2ch, puff st into next ch, 3ch, miss next 2ch, 1tr into next ch, 1tr into each of next 4tr, rep from * to last st, 1tr into last st. Turn.
5th row 3ch, miss first st, puff st into next tr, * (1ch, miss next tr, puff st into next tr) twice, 3ch, 1tr into next puff st, 3ch, puff st into next tr, (1ch, miss next tr, puff st into next tr) twice, rep from * to last st, 1tr into last st. Turn.
6th row 4ch, miss first 2 sts, * puff st into next ch, 1ch, puff st into next ch, 3ch, miss first 2ch, 1tr into next ch, 1tr into next tr, 1tr into next ch, 3ch, miss next 2ch, (puff st into next ch, 1ch) twice, rep from * to last st, 1tr into last st. Turn.
7th row 3ch, miss first st, puff st into first ch, *1ch, puff st into next ch, 3ch, miss next 2ch, 1tr into next ch, 1tr into each of next 3tr, 1tr into next ch, 3ch, miss next 2ch, puff st into next ch, 1ch, puff st into next ch, rep from * to last st, ending last rep with puff st into 4th turning ch, 1tr into 3rd turning ch. Turn.
8th row 4ch, miss first 2 sts, *puff st into next ch, 3ch, miss next 2ch, 1tr into next ch, 1tr into each of next 5tr, 1tr into next ch, 3ch, miss next 2ch, puff st into next ch, 1ch, rep from * to last st, 1tr into last st. Turn.
9th row 3ch, miss first st, puff st into first ch, *3ch, miss next 2ch, 1tr into next ch, 1tr into each of next 7tr, 1tr into next ch, 3ch, miss next 2ch, puff st into next ch, rep from * to last st, ending last rep with puff st into 4th turning ch, 1tr into 3rd turning ch. Turn.
10th row 3ch, miss first st, 1tr into next puff st, *3ch, (puff st into next tr, 1ch, miss next tr) 4 times, puff st into next tr, 3ch, 1tr into next puff st, rep

from * to last st, 1 tr into last st. Turn.
First-10th rows form patt. Cont in patt
until work measures approx 57cm
from cast-on edge, ending with a 6th
row. Fasten off.

Front
Work as for back until work measures
approx 39cm from cast-on edge,
ending with an 8th row.
Divide for neck
Next row 3ch, miss first st, *puff st into
next ch, 3ch, miss next 2ch, 1tr into
next ch, 1tr into each of next 8tr, 1tr
into next ch, 3ch, rep from * twice
more, ending last rep with 2ch, 1tr into
next puff st. Turn.
Shape left neck
1st row 3ch, puff st into first tr, patt to
end. Turn.
2nd row Work 2 patt reps, 1tr into
next ch, 3ch, miss next 2ch, (puff st
into next ch, 1ch, miss next ch) 3
times, puff st into next ch, 1tr into top
of turning ch. Turn.
3rd row 3ch, puff st into next ch, patt
to end. Turn.
4th row 3ch, work 2 patt reps, 1tr into
each of next 2tr, 1tr into next ch, 3ch,
miss next 2ch, puff st into next ch, 1ch,
puff st into next ch, 1tr into top of
turning ch. Turn.
5th row As 3rd row.
6th row 3ch, work 2 patt reps, (1ch,
miss next tr, puff st into next tr) twice,
1tr into top of turning ch. Turn.
7th row As 3rd row.
8th row 3ch, work 2 patt reps, 1ch, puff
st into next ch, 1tr into top of turning
ch. Turn.
9th row As 3rd row.
10th row 3ch, work 2 patt reps, puff st
into next st, 1tr into top of turning ch.
Turn.
11th row 3ch, miss first st, 1tr into first
puff st, patt to end. Turn.
12th row 3ch, work 2 patt reps, 1tr
into 3rd turning ch. Turn.
13th row 3ch, miss first st, 1tr into
next st, patt to end. Turn.
14th row Work 2 patt reps, omitting
1tr from end of last rep. Turn.
15th row As 13th row.
Keeping patt correct, work straight in
patt until work matches back to
shoulder, ending with a 6th row.
Fasten off.

With RS facing and using crochet hook,
return to sts left at beg of neck shaping
and rejoin yarn to next puff st.
Next row 5ch, miss first 2ch, 1tr into
next ch, patt to end.
Turn.
Shape right neck
1st row Work 3 patt reps, ending last
rep with puff st into last tr, 1tr into 3rd
turning ch. Turn.
2nd row 3ch, miss first st, puff st into
first ch, patt to end.
Turn.
Complete to match left side of neck,
reversing shaping as shown.

Sleeves (both alike)
Using knitting needles, cast on 45 sts.
Rep first and 2nd rib rows as for back
for 5cm, ending with a 2nd row.
Cast off loosely in rib, leaving last st on
needle. Transfer last st to crochet
hook.
Next row (RS) 1ch to count as first dc,
miss first st at base of first ch, work
82dc into cast-off edge. 83 sts. Cont as
for back until work measures approx
45cm from cast-on edge, ending with a
9th row.
Fasten off.

To make up
Do not press. Join right shoulder seam,
matching patts.
Neckband
With RS facing, using knitting needles
and beg at top of left neck, pick up and
K 60 sts down left neck, one st from ch
lying between 2 puff sts at beg of V,
(mark this st with contrasting yarn) 60
sts up right neck and 46 sts across back
neck. 157 sts.
Next row (WS) (K1, P1) to within 2
sts of marked st, K2 tog, P1, K2 tog,
(P1, K1) to end.
Next row (P1, K1) to within 2 sts of
marked st, P2 tog, K1, P2 tog, (K1, P1)
to end.
Rep last 2 rows for 3cm.
Cast off loosely in rib, dec one st at
each side of marked st as before. Place
contrasting markers 20cm from
shoulders on both side edges of back
and front, i.e. on a 5th patt row.
Set in sleeves between markers, easing
top edges to fit.
Join side and sleeve seams.

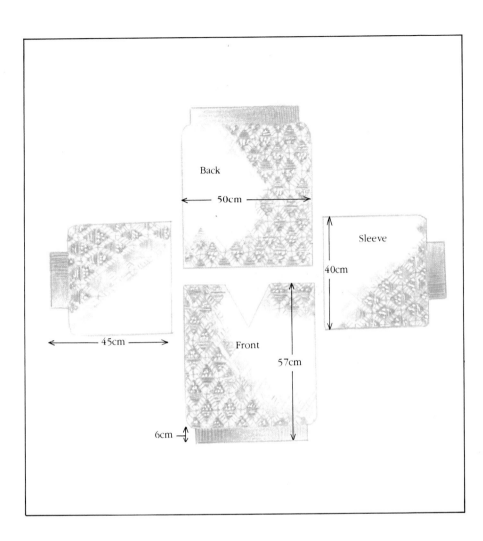

Back

50cm

45cm

Sleeve

40cm

Front

57cm

6cm

Working an approximate foundation

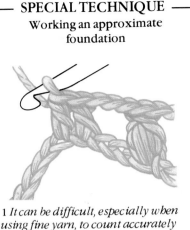

1 *It can be difficult, especially when using fine yarn, to count accurately the number of chain required for the base row. This problem can be avoided by working an approximate foundation chain. Work roughly the required number of chain plus about 25 more. Work the base row as instructed, leaving a length of unworked chain.*

2 *Using sharp scissors, cut across the first chain worked, so removing the beginning slip loop. Discard the short piece of yarn now caught in the second foundation chain. Insert the point of the crochet hook into the loop at the end of the chain and draw through the loose length of yarn.*

3 *Continue drawing through yarn and undoing chain in this way until one loop remains. Do not draw through the yarn, but instead pull it firmly to tighten the last chain. The remaining end of yarn can now be used for seaming or can be darned into the edge of the work as usual.*

51

CROSS-STITCH SWEATER

Contrasting patterns of crossed stitches give an interesting texture to this two-tone pullover.

Back (See chart, page 54.)

Using A, make 90 [94:98] ch.
Base row 1dc into 2nd ch from hook, 1dc into each ch to end. Turn. 89 [93:97] dc.
1st row (WS) 3ch, miss first dc, (miss next dc, 1tr into next dc, working behind last tr work 1tr into missed dc – 1 pair of crossed tr or Xtr worked) 7 [8:9] times, 1tr into each of next 22dc, miss next 3dc, 1dtr into each of next 3dc, working behind dtr work 1dtr into each of 3 missed dc – back cable worked – 1tr into each of next 3dc, miss next 3dc, 1dtr into each of next 3dc, working in front of dtr work 1dtr into each of 3 missed dc – front cable worked – 1tr into each of next 22 dc, (1 pair Xtr into next 2dc) 7 [8:9] times, 1tr into last dc. Turn.
2nd row 3ch, miss first st, (1 pair Xtr into next 2 sts) 7 [8:9] times, 1tr into next st, inserting hook from front of work, from right to left, work 1tr round stem of next st – 1tr front worked – * (miss next 2 sts, inserting hook from front of work, from right to left, work 1dtr round stem of next tr – 1dtr front worked – working behind dtr work 1tr into each of 2 missed sts, miss next st, 1tr into each of next 2 sts, 1dtr front round stem of missed tr) 3 times – dtr V pat worked* – 1tr front round stem of next tr, (1tr into next st, 1dc into each of next 6 sts, 1tr into next st, 1tr front round stem of next st) twice, rep from * to * once, 1tr front round stem of next tr, 1tr into next st, (1 pair Xtr into next 2 sts) 7 [8:9] times, 1tr into top of turning ch. Turn.
3rd row 3ch, miss first tr, (1 pair Xtr into next 2 sts) 7 [8:9] times, 1tr into next st, inserting hook from back of work, from right to left, work 1tr round stem of next st – 1tr back worked – 1tr into each of next 18 sts, 1tr back round stem of next st, 1tr into next st, work front cable over next 6 sts, 1tr into next st, 1tr back round stem of next st, 1tr into next st, work back cable over next 6 sts, 1tr into next st, 1tr back round stem of next st, 1tr into each of next 18 sts, 1tr back round stem of next st, 1tr into next st, (1 pair Xtr into next 2 sts) 7 [8:9] times, 1tr into turning ch. Turn.
4th row As 2nd row.

5th row As 3rd row working back cable in place of front cable and front cable in place of back cable.
Rep 2nd-5th rows for patt.
Cont in patt until a total of 62 [63:64] rows have been worked in patt.
Shape neck
1st row Patt across 27 [29:31] sts. Turn.
2nd row Keeping patt correct, patt to end. Fasten off.
2nd side: 1st row Miss centre 35 sts, rejoin yarn to next st and patt to end. Patt 1 row. Fasten off.

Front

Work as for back until a total of 44 rows of patt have been worked.
Shape neck
1st row Patt across 44 [46:48] sts. Turn. Keeping patt correct cont on these sts only for first side.
2nd row 3ch, miss first tr, 1dc into each of next 6 sts, 1tr into next st, 1tr front round stem of next st, miss next 2 sts, 1dtr round stem of next st, working behind dtr and leaving last loop of each st on hook, work 1tr into each of 2 missed sts – 1tr dec worked –, patt to end. Turn.
3rd row Work in patt to last 2 sts of dtr V patt, dec 1tr over next 2 sts, patt to end. Turn.
4th row Work in patt to first 2 sts of dtr V patt, dec 1tr over next 2 sts, patt to end. Turn. Cont to dec 1tr in this way on every row until 27 [29:31] sts rem. Patt 2 [3:4] rows straight. Fasten off.
2nd side: 1st row Miss center st, rejoin yarn to next st and complete to match first side, reversing shaping.

Sleeves (both alike)

Using A, make 52 [56:60] ch.
Base row Work as for back. 51 [55:59] dc.
1st row (WS) 3ch, miss first dc, (1 pair Xtr into next 2 sts) 7 [8:9] times, 1tr into each of next 3 sts, work back cable over next 6 sts, 1tr into each of next 3 sts, work front cable over next 6 sts, 1tr into each of next 3 sts, (1 pair Xtr into next 2 sts) 7 [8:9] times, 1tr into last dc. Turn.
2nd row 3ch, miss first st, (1 pair Xtr into next 2 sts) 7 [8:9] times, 1tr into next st, 1tr front round stem of next st,

Sizes

To fit 86 [91:96] cm bust
Length 63 [64:65] cm
Sleeve seam 42 [44:46] cm

Note *Instructions for larger sizes are in square brackets [ ]; where there is only one set of figures it applies to all sizes.*

Materials

*Approx 700 750:800] g of a double knitting yarn in main colour (A)
Approx 200g in contrasting colour (B)
4.00mm crochet hook*

Tension

20 sts and 11 rows to 10cm over Xtr (crossed dc) patt using 4.00mm hook

To save time, take time to check tension.

(1 tr into next st, 1dc into each of next 6 sts, 1tr into next st, 1tr front round stem of next tr) twice, 1tr into next tr, (1 pair Xtr into next 2 sts) 7 [8:9] times, 1tr into top of turning ch. Turn. With sts as set, inc 1 st at end of every row until there are 63 [67:71] sts, working inc sts into patt. Work straight until a total of 42 [44:46] rows has been worked in patt.
Fasten off.

To make up
Join shoulder seams. With centre of sleeve to shoulder seam, sew sleeves to front/back section. Join side and sleeve seams.

Cuffs
With RS facing join B to lower edge of sleeve at seam and work into other side of foundation ch as follows:
1st round 3ch, 1tr into each ch, ss to top of 3ch. Turn. 52 [56:60] sts.
2nd round 3ch, miss turning ch, 1tr back round stem of first tr, *1tr front round stem of next tr, 1tr back round stem of next tr, rep from * to end, ss to top of 3ch. Turn.
3rd round 3ch, miss turning ch, 1tr front round stem of first tr, *1tr back round stem of next tr, 1tr front round stem of next tr, rep from * to end, ss to top of 3ch. Turn.
Rep 2nd and 3rd rounds twice.
Fasten off.

Welt
Work round lower edge of back and front as for cuffs on 180 [188:196] sts.
Rep 2nd and 3rd rounds 3 times.

Pockets (make 2)
Using B, make 27ch.
Base row Work as for back. 26 dc.
1st row 3ch, miss first dc, *1 pair Xtr into next 2 sts, rep from * to last st, 1tr into last st. Turn.
Rep last row 13 times but do not turn at end of last row.
Edging
1st round 1ch, *work dc evenly along row ends to corner, 1ch*, 1dc into each ch along other side of foundation ch, 1ch, rep from * to *once, 1dc into each st along top edge, ss to first ch. Turn.
2nd round 1dc into each st to end, ss to first dc.
Fasten off.
Press or block and sew to front as shown.

Collar
With RS facing, join C to centre front st of V neck.
1st row 1ch, work in dc evenly round neck edge working an odd number of sts, ss to first ch. Turn.
2nd row 3ch, miss first 2dc, missing 1dc at each shoulder seam, work 1tr into each dc to last 2dc, miss next dc, 1tr into last dc. Turn.

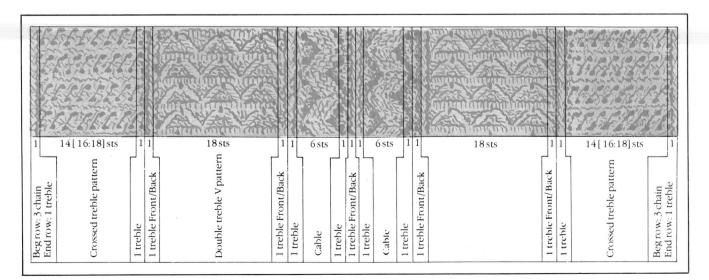

1	14[16:18] sts	1	1	18 sts	1	1	6 sts	1	1	1	6 sts	1	1	18 sts	1	1	14[16:18] sts	1

Beg row: 3 chain End row: 1 treble — 1 treble — Crossed treble pattern — 1 treble — 1 treble Front/Back — Double treble V pattern — 1 treble Front/Back — 1 treble — Cable — 1 treble — 1 treble Front/Back — 1 treble — Cable — 1 treble — 1 treble Front/Back — 1 treble Front/Back — 1 treble — Crossed treble pattern — Beg row: 3 chain End row: 1 treble

3rd row 3ch, miss first 2tr, *1tr front round stem of next tr, 1tr back round stem of next tr, missing 1tr at each shoulder seam, rep from * to last 3 sts, 1tr front round stem of next tr, miss next tr, 1tr into top of turning ch. Turn.
4th row 3ch, miss first 2tr, rib as set to last 2 sts, miss next tr, 1tr into top of turning ch. Turn.
Rep 4th row 3 times.
Next row 3ch, miss first st, rib as set to last st, 1tr into top of turning ch. Turn. Rep last row once.

Next row 3ch, 1tr into first tr, rib as set to last st, 2tr into top of turning ch. Turn.
Working extra sts into ribbing, rep last row 9 times but do not turn at end of last rep.
Edging
Next row 1ch, work 1 row of dc evenly down shaped edge of collar to centre, miss 1 st at centre, work dc evenly up other edge of collar to corner. Fasten off.
Press seams lightly.

1 'Cable' panels are formed by slanting blocks of stitches to the right or left. After a base row of double crochet, the cables begin on the next (WS) row. To cable to the right, miss the next three stitches and work one double-treble into each of the next three stitches.

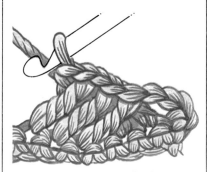

2 Then, working behind the three double-treble, work one double-treble into each of the three stitches just missed. You will find these stitches easier to work if you fold the first three double-treble towards you.

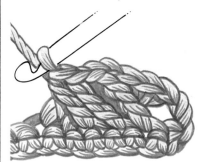

3 Cable to the left by missing three stitches and working three double-treble as in step 1. Then, from the front of the work, work one double-treble into each of the three missed stitches. This will be easier if you fold the first three double-treble away from you.

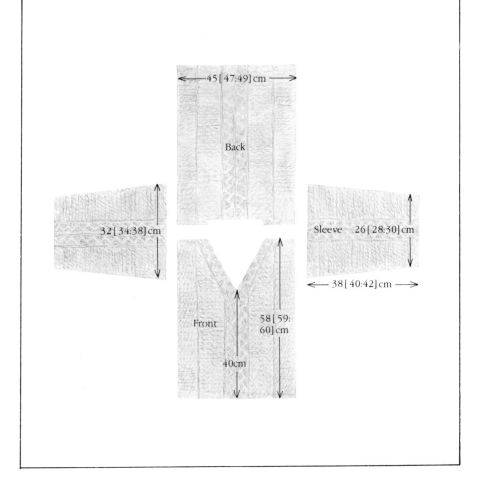

← 45[47:49] cm →

Back

32[34:38] cm

Sleeve   26[28:30] cm

← 38[40:42] cm →

Front

58[59: 60] cm

40cm

SKI SWEATER AND CAP

The Yugoslavian province of Bosnia is the home of firmly-textured, multicoloured crochet. Use the simple technique shown here to make this striking pullover and matching hat.

Sizes
Sweater
To fit *81-86 [91-96] cm bust*
Length *63 [66] cm*
Sleeve seam *42 [45] cm*
Hat *To fit average head*

Note *Instructions for larger size are in square brackets []; where there is only one set of figures it applies to both sizes.*

Materials
Sweater
Approx 550 [600] g of a double knitting yarn in main colour (A)
Approx 50g in each of two contrasting colours (B and C)
3.50mm crochet hook
Set of four 3¼mm double-pointed knitting needles
Hat
Approx 50g of a 4 ply yarn in main colour (A)
Approx 25g in each of two contrasting colours (B and C)
2.50mm crochet hook
Set of four 2¾ double-pointed knitting needles

Tension
Sweater 20 sts and 20 rows to 10cm over tubular dc patt using 3.50mm hook
Hat 24 sts and 32 rows to 8cm over tubular ss patt using 2.50mm hook

To save time, take time to check tension.

Sweater
Note *Sweater is worked in three tubes —one for body and one each for sleeves —joined at the yoke. Work into back loop only of each stitch and with RS facing throughout the work. (See page 59.)*

Body
Using larger hook and A, make 180 [204] ch, join with a ss to first ch to form a ring.
1st round 1ch, 1dc into each ch to end, ss into first ch, making sure that ch is not twisted. 180 [204] sts.
Mark end of round with a contrasting thread.
Patt round 1ch, working into back loop only of each st work 1dc into each dc to end, ss to first ch.
Patt 2 more rounds in A.
Cont in patt, work 12 rounds of Chart A (page 58).
Break off B and C and, using A, cont in patt until work measures 34cm.
Fasten off.
Shape back armholes
Miss first 4 [5] sts of round and rejoin A to next st.
* * **Next row** 1ch to count as first dc, miss st at base of first ch, 1dc into back loop of each of next 81 [91] dc. Fasten off and do not turn. 82 [92] sts.
Next row Return to beg of row and rejoin A to 2nd st, 1ch to count as first dc, miss st at base of first ch, 1dc into back loop of each st to within last st. Fasten off. 80 [90] sts.
Rep last row 3 [5] times more. 74 [80] sts.
Fasten off. * *
Shape front armholes
Return to end of first row of back armholes, miss next 8 [10] sts and rejoin A to next st.

Work from * * to * * once more.

Sleeves (both alike)
Using larger hook and A, make 58 [70] ch.
Work base row and patt row as for body until 3 rounds have been worked.
Inc round 1ch, working into back loop of each st, work 1dc into first st, 2dc into next st, 1dc into each st to last 2 sts, 2dc into next st, 1dc into last st, ss to first ch. 60 [72] sts. Cont in patt, working 12 rounds of Chart A (page 58).
Break off B and C and cont with A only.
Next round Work as for inc round. Work straight in patt for 6 rounds.
Rep last 7 rounds until there are 72 [80] sts. Work straight in patt until work measures 36 [39] cm. Fasten off.
Shape armhole
Miss first 4 [5] sts and rejoin A to next st.
Next row 1ch to count as first dc, miss st at base of first ch, 1dc into back loop of each of next 63 [71] sts. Fasten off. 64 [72] sts.
Next row Return to beg of row and rejoin yarn to 2nd st, 1ch to count as first dc, miss st at base of first ch, patt to within last st. Fasten off. 62 [70] sts.
Rep last row 3 [5] times more. 56 [60] sts. Fasten off.

Yoke
With RS facing, rejoin A to first st on last row of back.
Next round 1ch, patt 74 [80] sts of back, patt 56 [60] sts of first sleeve, patt 74 [80] sts of front, patt 56 [60] sts of 2nd sleeve. 260 [280] sts. Patt 2 more rounds.
Next round 1ch, patt first 11 [12] sts, work next 2dc tog, * patt next 11 [12] sts, work next 2dc tog, rep from * to

end, sl st to first ch. 240 [260] sts.
2nd size only
Work even in pat for 3 more rounds.
Next round Ch 1, pat first 11 sts, work
next 2sc tog, * pat next 11 sts, work
next 2sc tog, rep from * to end, sl st to
first ch. 240 sts.
Both sizes
Cont in pat, working 12 rounds of
Chart B (below), working decs on 4th
and 8th rounds as shown. 200 sts.
Break off B and C and cont in A only.
Next round Ch 1, pat first 8 sts, work
next 2sc tog, * pat next 8 sts, work
next 2sc tog, rep from * to end, sl st to
first ch. 180 sts.
Work even for 4 rounds.
Next round Ch 1, pat first 7 sts, work
next 2sc tog, * pat next 7 sts, work
next 2sc tog, rep from * to end, sl st to
first sc. 160 sts.
Work even in pat for 4 rounds.
Next round Ch 1, pat first 6 sts, work
next 2sc tog, * pat next 6 sts, work
next 2sc tog, rep from * to end, sl st to
first ch. 140 sts.
Cont in pat, working 12 rounds of

Chart C (below), working decs on 4th
and 8th rounds as shown. 100 sts.
Break off B and C and, using A only,
work even in pat for one round.
Fasten off.

To finish
Do not press.
Join underarm seams.
Waistband
With RS facing and using size 3
double-pointed needles and A, pick up
and K 180 [204] sts from lower edge of
body.
Work in rounds of K2, P2 ribbing for
2½in.
Bind off loosely.
Cuffs (alike)
With RS facing, using size 3
double-pointed needles and A, pick up
and K 40[48] sts evenly from lower
edge of sleeve.
Complete cuffs as instructed for
waistband.
Turtleneck collar
With RS facing, using size 3
double-pointed needles and A, pick up

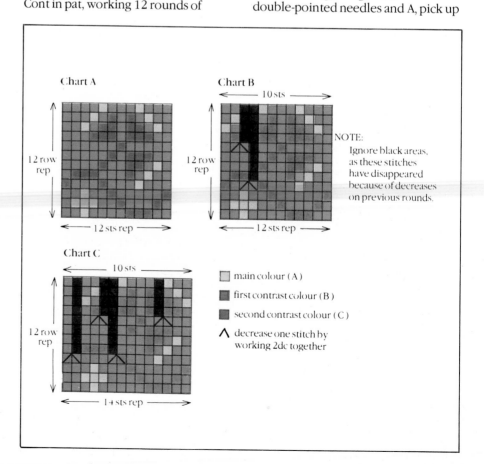

Chart A

Chart B
← 10 sts →

12 row rep

12 row rep

← 12 sts rep →

← 12 sts rep →

NOTE:
Ignore black areas,
as these stitches
have disappeared
because of decreases
on previous rounds.

Chart C
← 10 sts →

12 row rep

← 14 sts rep →

☐ main colour (A)
■ first contrast colour (B)
■ second contrast colour (C)
∧ decrease one stitch by
working 2dc together

100 sts evenly round neck edge. Work in rounds of K2, P2 rib for 18cm.

Hat

Note *Hat is worked in continuous rounds. Work into back loop only of each stitch and with RS facing as shown in the Special Technique at right.*

To make

Using smaller hook and A, make 132ch, ss to first ch to form a ring.
1st round Ss into each ch to end, making sure that ch is not twisted. Mark end of round with a contrasting thread.
Patt round Working into back loop of each st, work 1 ss into each ss to end. Patt 8 more rounds in A.
Cont in patt, work 12 rounds of Chart A (page 58).
Break off B and C and, using A, cont in patt for 4 more rounds.
Cont in patt, work 12 rounds of Chart

A. Break off B and C and, using A, cont in patt.
Shape crown
Next round * Ss into each of next 10 sts, miss next st, rep from * to end. Patt one round without shaping.
Next round * Ss into each of next 9 sts, miss next st, rep from * to end. Work straight in patt for one round. Cont in this way, dec 12 sts on every alternate round until 12 sts rem.
Next round * Ss into next st, miss next st, rep from * to end, ss into first st. Fasten off, leaving a long end of yarn.

To make up

Run end of yarn through last round and draw up tightly to close hole. Secure yarn firmly on WS of work.
Brim
With RS facing, using 2¾mm double-pointed needles and A, pick up and K 132 sts from lower edge of hat.
Work in K2, P2 rib for 10cm.
Cast off loosely.
Turn up brim as desired.

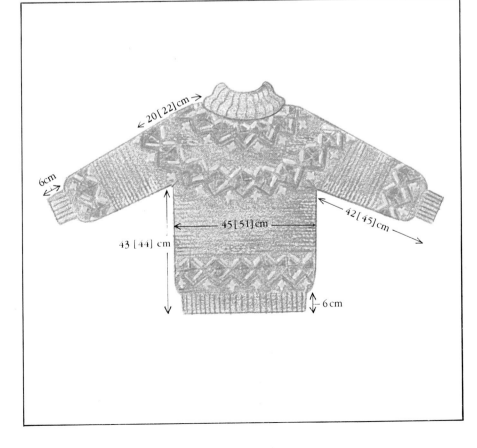

SPECIAL TECHNIQUE
Yugoslavian crochet

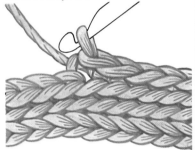

1 *The ridges of Yugoslavian crochet are formed by working into the back loop of each stitch. When working in rounds of double crochet as on the sweater, begin each round with one chain. Work one double crochet into the back loop of the first and every following stitch. Slip stitch the last stitch to the first chain.*

2 *When working in slip stitch, as on the basic hat, work in continuous rounds. Work one slip stitch into the back loop of each stitch as instructed. To make it easier to work the hat, mark the beginning of each round with a contrasting thread.*

3 *Traditional Yugoslavian crochet is always worked with the right side facing. This is easy in tubes or continuous rounds, but more difficult in rows, as for the armhole shaping on this sweater. Work the first row and fasten off. Do not turn, but with the right side facing, rejoin the yarn to the beginning of the row and pattern to the end. Repeat as required.*

STRIPED EVENING SWEATER

This glamorous striped evening sweater is very simple to make. The glitter yarn gives it extra sparkle.

Size
To fit *86-91cm*
Length *55cm*
Sleeve seam *47cm*

Materials
Approx 180g of a fine glitter yarn in main colour (A)
Approx 20g in contrasting colour (B)
3.00mm crochet hook
1 pair 2¾mm knitting needles
Set of 4 double-pointed 2¾mm knitting needles

Tension
18tr and 14 rows to 10cm using 3.00mm hook

To save time, take time to check tension.

Back
Using knitting needles and A, cast on 108 sts.
Work 5cm in K1, P1 rib.
Cast off *loosely* until 1 loop rem. Place loop on crochet hook.
1st row 3ch, 1tr into each st to end. Turn. Rep last row 4 times, join in B at end of last row.
6th row 1ch, 1dc into each st to end, join in A. Turn.
7th row 3ch, 1tr into each st to end. Turn.
8th-15th rows Rep 7th row 8 times, join in B at end of last row.
16th-47th rows Rep rows 6-15 three times, then rep rows 6 and 7 once more.

Shape armholes
48th row Ss into first 9 sts, 3ch, work 2tr tog as follows: yrh, insert hook into next st and draw loop through, yrh and draw through 2 loops on hook, yrh, insert hook into next st and draw loop through, yrh and draw through 2 loops, yrh and draw through all 3 loops; work in patt to last 11 sts, tr 2tog, 1tr into next st. Turn.
49th row 3ch, tr 2tog, 1tr into each st to last 3 sts, tr 2tog, 1tr into last st. Turn.
50th-53rd rows Rep last row 4 times. 80 sts.

Shape neck
54th row 3ch, 1tr into next 19 sts, tr 2tog, 1tr into next st. Turn.
55th row 3ch, tr 2tog, 1tr into each st to end, join in B. Turn.
56th row 1ch, 1dc into each st to end, join in A. Turn
57th row As 55th.
58th row 3ch, 1tr into each st to last 3 sts, tr 2tog, 1tr into last st. Turn.
59th row As 55th. 18 sts. Work straight in tr for 6 more rows, then work 1 row dc in B, and then 3 rows tr in A.

Fasten off.
Return to 53rd row, miss 34 sts at centre, rejoin A with ss to next st.
54th row 3ch, tr 2tog, 1tr into each st to end. Turn.
Cont to match other side, reversing shaping.

Front
Work as for back to 53rd row, then work straight in patt for 6 rows more. Shape neck as for back on next (60th) row, i.e. work rows 60-64 as for rows 54-58 of back. Work straight until 69 rows are complete. Complete other side to match.

Sleeves (both alike)
Using A and pair of knitting needles, cast on 60 sts. Work 5cm of K1, P1 rib as for back, cast off *loosely,* insert crochet hook in rem loop. Work 4 rows as for back.
5th row 3ch, 2tr into next st, tr into each st to last 2sts, 2tr into next st, 1tr into last st, change to B. Turn.
6th-14th rows Work as for rows 6-14 of back.
15th row Work as for 5th row of sleeve.
16th-45th rows Rep rows 6-15 three times more. 70 sts.
46th-55th rows Work straight for 10 rows, keeping colour sequence.
Work 1 row dc in B, then work 1 row tr in A.

Shape top
58th row Ss into first 9 sts, 3ch, tr 2tog, 1tr into each st to last 11 sts, tr 2tog, 1tr into next st. Turn.
59th row 3ch, tr 2tog, 1tr into each st to last 3 sts, tr 2tog, 1tr into last st. Turn.
60th-68th rows Rep 59th row 6 times, then work 1 row dc in B, then work 59th row twice more.

SPECIAL TECHNIQUE
Working crochet into knitting

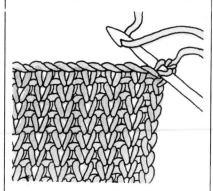

1 *Knitted rib welt and cuffs give a closer fit than crocheted rib. The crochet can be worked directly on to the rib. Complete the knitting and cast off. When changing colours for the crochet, break the yarn. Insert the hook into the knitted edge, one row below cast-off edge.*

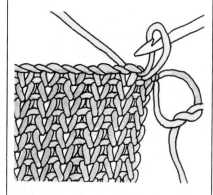

2 *Draw the yarn through and knot the loose end of crochet yarn to the knitting yarn to secure it.*

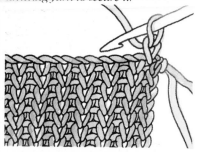

3 *Holding the knitting in the left hand, take the yarn round the hook and draw through a loop to form one chain to count as the first double crochet (2ch for htr, 3ch for tr, etc).*

69th row Ss into 2nd st, 3ch, tr 2tog, 1tr into each st to last 4 sts, tr 2tog, 1tr into next st. Turn.
70th and 71st rows Rep row 69 twice. 22 sts.
72nd row Ss into first 5 sts, 1ch, 1dc into next 3 sts, 1tr into next 6 sts, 1dc into next 4 sts. Fasten off.

To make up
Join shoulder, side and sleeve seams. Set in sleeves. Using set of 4 double-pointed needles, pick up and K 210 sts evenly round neck. Work 20 rows in K1, P1 rib, cast off *loosely* and turn under and sew cast-off edge to base of rib.

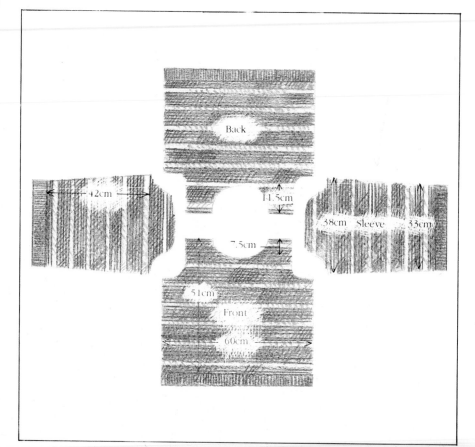

4 *Insert the hook into the next stitch, and work a double crochet (or the stitch required by your pattern). Repeat to the end for the required number of stitches.*

When the knitted rib and the crochet are to be worked in the same yarn, do not break off the yarn as in step 1. Instead cast off the rib until one loop remains. Insert the hook into this loop and work from step 3.
In some cases — depending on the relative tensions of the knitted and the crocheted stitches — the pattern may instruct you to work fewer crochet stitches (which tend to be larger) into the knitted ribbing. For example, you might need to work into every other stitch as shown here.

CHEVRON CARDIGAN AND SCARF

For your most glamorous nights – an elegant cardigan and scarf in a glittery yarn.

Sizes

Cardigan *to fit 86 [91:96] cm bust*
Length from shoulder 64cm approx
Sleeve seam 48cm
Scarf 150cm approx by 20cm

Note *Instructions for larger sizes are in square brackets [ ]; where there is only one set of figures it applies to all sizes.*

Materials

Cardigan *Approx 300 [350:400] g of a fine glitter yarn in main colour (A)*
Approx 275 [325:375] g in contrasting colour (B)
Scarf *Approx 100g in main colour (A)*
Approx 100g in contrasting colour (B)
3.00mm crochet hook
6 buttons

Tension

26tr and 13 rows to 10cm over patt using 3.00mm hook

To save time, take time to check tension.

Note *To keep the edges of the work straight, one stitch has been increased at the end of a row where the zigzag points downwards at the edge, and one stitch has been decreased where the zigzag points upwards. When shaping the fronts or sleeves, count the stitches carefully, so that the correct number is increased or decreased. Count the 3 treble worked into one stitch as 3, and the 3 treble worked together as 1.*

Note *When measuring the work, measure between its farthest points — that is, between a downwards-pointing zigzag on the lower edge and an upwards-pointing zigzag on the top edge.*

Scarf

Using A, make 55ch.
Base row 1tr into 4th ch from hook, 1tr into each of next 3ch, * 3tr into next ch, 1tr into each of next 5ch, (yrh, insert hook into next ch, yrh, draw through a loop, yrh, draw through 2 loops on hook) 3 times, yrh, draw through all 4 loops on hook – called work 3tr tog –, 1tr into each of next 5ch*, rep from * to * twice more, 3tr into next ch, 1tr into each of last 5ch. Turn. 55 sts.
Patt row 3ch, miss first 2tr, 1tr into each of next 4tr, **3tr into centre tr of 3tr group, 1tr into each of next 5tr, work 3tr tog, 1tr into each of next 5tr**, rep from ** to ** twice more, 3tr into next tr, 1tr into each of next 4tr, miss next tr, 1tr into top of turning ch. Turn.
Rep patt row throughout, working 1 more row in A and cont in stripe sequence as follows: 2 rows B, 2 rows A, 1 row B, 1 row A, 3 rows B, 2 rows A, 2 rows B, 1 row A, 1 row B, 3 rows A.
Cont in patt, working stripe sequence, until work measures approx 150cm from beg, ending with 3 rows in A. Fasten off.

Cardigan
Back

Using A, make 123 [127:137] ch.
Base row 1tr into 4th ch from hook, 1tr into each of next 2 [4:2]ch, work from * to * as for base row of scarf 8 [8:9] times, 3tr into next ch, 1tr into each of last 4 [6:4]ch. Turn. 123 [127:137]sts.

Patt row 3ch, miss first 2tr, 1tr into each of next 3 [5:3]tr, **3tr into centre tr of 3tr group, 1tr into each of next 5tr, work 3tr tog, 1tr into each of next 5tr**, rep from ** to ** 7 [7:8] times more, 3tr into next tr, 1tr into each of next 3 [5:3] tr, miss next tr, 1tr into top of turning ch. Turn.
Rep patt row throughout, working 1 more row in A, and working stripe sequence as set for scarf until work measures 43cm. Mark both ends of last row with contrasting threads.
Cont in patt in stripe sequence until work measures 69cm from beg, ending with a row in A.
Straighten top edge
Using A, 3ch, 1tr into each of next 1 [3:1] tr, 1htr into each of next 2tr, *1dc into next tr, ss into centre tr of 3tr group, 1dc into next tr, 1htr into each of next 2tr, 1tr into each of next 2tr, 1dtr into each of next 3tr, 1tr into each of next 2tr, 1htr into each of next 2tr, rep from *7 [7:8] times more, 1dc into next tr, ss into centre tr of 3tr group, 1dc into next tr, 1htr into each of next 2tr, 1tr into each of next 1 [3:1] tr, 1tr into top of turning ch. Fasten off.

Left front

Using A, make 67 [70:73] ch.
Base row 1tr into 4th ch from hook, 1tr into each of next 2 [4:4] ch, work from * to * as for base row of scarf 4 times, 3tr into next tr, 1tr into each of last 4 [5:8] tr. Turn. 67 [70:73] sts. Working in patt and stripe sequence as for back, cont until work measures 43cm from beg.
Mark beg of last row for armhole.
Shape neck edge
Keeping armhole edge straight, dec 1 st at neck edge on every row until 40 [42:44] tr rem.
Work straight in patt until work measures same as back, ending with a row in A.
Straighten top edge
Using A, straighten edge as for back, working ss into centre of 3tr group and working 3dtr over 3tr worked tog. Fasten off.

Right front

Work as for left front, reversing shaping.

Sleeves (both alike)

Using A, make 55ch.
Work base row and patt row as for scarf. 55sts.
Cont in patt and stripe sequence as for scarf, inc 1tr at each end of every alternate row until there are 111sts.
Work straight until work measures 48cm from beg, ending with a row in A.
Straighten top edge as for back.
Fasten off.

Front band

Join shoulder seams.
With RS facing, join A to right front at the inner corner of the lower edge.
Work 2dc into each row end up right front, across back neck and down left front. Work 5 more rows of dc, ending at lower right front. Turn.
Buttonhole row 1ch, miss first dc, 1dc into each of next 3dc, * 3ch, miss next 3dc, 1dc into each of next 16dc, rep from * 4 more times, 3ch, miss next 3dc, 1dc into each dc to end. Turn.
Next row Ch 1, miss first dc, 1dc into each st to end, working 3dc into 3ch sp of previous row.
Work 5 more rows in dc.
Fasten off.

To make up

Set in sleeves. Sew side and sleeve seams. Sew on buttons.

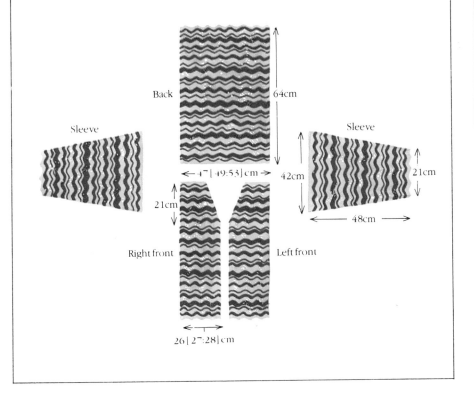

Back 64cm

Sleeve

Sleeve

← 47 [49:53] cm →

42cm

21cm

21cm

Right front

Left front

48cm

26 [27:28] cm

SPECIAL TECHNIQUE
Working chevrons

1 *The zigzag effect of chevrons is produced by alternately increasing and decreasing stitches at intervals along row. The zigzags point upwards where stitches have been increased and downwards where stitches have been decreased.*

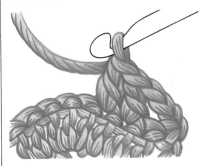

2 *When working some chevron patterns it can be difficult to keep the edges straight. Patterns will therefore suggest that you increase one stitch where the zigzag points downwards at the end of a row and decrease one stitch at the side edge where the zigzag points upwards.*

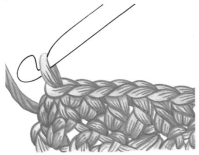

3 *To straighten top edges, work gradually longer stitches to the lowest point of the zigzag, working the longest stitch into the top of the decreased stitches, and then work shorter stitches to the highest point, working the shortest stitch into the centre stitch of the increasing.*

PINEAPPLE LACE BLOUSE

Made as two semicircles joined at the shoulders, this glamorous top can be enlarged to fit any size by continuing to work more of the pattern. The knitted ribs can be adjusted as required.

Size
Total width from cuff to cuff 22cm

Materials
Approx 500g of a 3 ply yarn
2.50mm crochet hook
1 pair 2¼mm knitting needles
Matching sewing thread

Tension
One pineapple measures 7cm × 6cm

To save time, take time to check tension.

Back
Make 84ch.
1st row 1dc into 2nd ch from hook, 1dc into each ch to end. Turn.
2nd row 3ch, miss first dc, (2tr, 2ch, 2tr) into next dc, * 6ch, miss 3dc, (2tr, 2ch, 2tr) into next dc, rep from * to last dc, 1tr into last dc. Turn. 21 groups.
3rd row 3ch, (2tr, 2ch, 2tr) into next 2ch sp, * 3ch, 13dtr into next 2ch sp, 3ch, (2tr, 2ch, 2tr) into next 2ch sp, rep from *, ending with 1tr into top of turning ch. Turn.
4th row 3ch, (2tr, 2ch, 2tr) into next 2ch sp, * 3ch, (1dtr into next dtr, 1ch), 12 times, 1dtr into next dtr, 3ch, (2tr, 2ch, 2tr) into next 2ch sp, rep from *, ending with 1tr into top of turning ch. Turn.
5th row 3ch, (2tr, 2ch, 2tr) into next 2ch sp, * (3ch, 1dc into next 1ch sp) 12 times, 3ch, (2tr, 2ch, 2tr) into next 2ch sp, rep from *, ending with 1tr into top of turning ch. Turn.
6th row 3ch, (2tr, 2ch, 2tr) into next 2ch sp, * miss next 3ch sp, (3ch, 1dc into next 3ch sp) 11 times, 3ch, (2tr, 2ch, 2tr) into next 2ch sp, rep from *, ending with 1tr into top of turning ch. Turn.
7th row 3ch, (2tr, 2ch, 2tr) into next 2ch sp, * miss next 3ch sp, (3ch, 1dc into next 3ch sp) 10 times, 3ch, (2tr, 2ch, 2tr) into next 2ch sp, rep from * ending with 1tr into top of turning ch. Turn.
8th row 3ch, (2tr, 2ch, 2tr, 2ch, 2tr) into next 2ch sp, * miss 3ch, (3ch, 1dc into next 3ch sp) 9 times, 3ch, (2tr, 2ch, 2tr, 2ch, 2tr) into next 2ch sp, rep from *, ending with 1tr into top of turning ch. Turn.
9th row 3ch, (2tr, 2ch, 2tr) into first 2ch sp, 1ch, (2tr, 2ch, 2tr) into next 2ch sp, * miss next 3ch sp, (3ch, 1dc into next 3ch sp) 8 times, 3ch, (2tr, 2ch, 2tr) into next 2ch sp, 1ch, (2tr, 2ch, 2tr) into next 2ch sp, rep from *, ending with 1tr into top of turning ch. Turn.
10th row 3ch, (2tr, 2ch, 2tr) into next 2ch sp, 1ch, (2tr, 2ch, 2tr) into next 1ch sp, 1ch, (2tr, 2ch, 2tr) into next 2ch sp, * miss next 3ch sp, (3ch, 1dc into next 3ch sp) 7 times, 3ch, (2tr, 2ch, 2tr) into next 2ch sp, 1ch, (2tr, 2ch, 2tr) into next 1ch sp, 1ch, (2tr, 2ch, 2tr) into next 2ch sp, rep from *, ending with 1tr into top of turning ch. Turn.
11th row 3ch, (2tr, 2ch, 2tr) into next 2ch sp, 2ch, (2tr, 2ch, 2tr) into next 2ch sp, 2ch, (2tr, 2ch, 2tr) into next 2ch sp, * miss next 3ch sp, (3ch, 1dc into next 3ch sp) 6 times, 3ch, (2tr, 2ch, 2tr) into next 2ch sp, 2ch, (2tr, 2ch, 2tr) into next 2ch sp, 2ch, (2tr, 2ch, 2tr) into next 2ch sp, rep from *, ending with 1 tr into top of turning ch. Turn.
12th row 3ch, (2tr, 2ch, 2tr) into next 2ch sp, 3ch, miss next 2ch sp, (2tr, 2ch, 2tr) into next 2ch sp, 3ch, miss next 2ch sp, (2tr, 2ch, 2tr) into next 2ch sp, * miss next 3ch sp, (3ch, 1dc into next 3ch sp) 5 times, 3ch, (2tr, 2ch, 2tr) into next 2ch sp, miss next 2ch sp, 3ch, (2tr, 2ch, 2tr) into next 2ch sp, 3ch, miss next 2ch sp, (2tr, 2ch, 2tr) into next 2ch sp, rep from *, ending with 1tr into top of turning ch. Turn.
13th row 3ch, (2tr, 2ch, 2tr) into next 2ch sp, 4ch, (2tr, 2ch, 2tr) into next 2ch sp, 4ch, (2tr, 2ch, 2tr) into next 2ch sp, * miss next 3ch sp, (3ch, 1dc into next 3ch sp) 4 times, 3ch, (2tr, 2ch, 2tr) into next 2ch sp, 4ch, (2tr, 2ch, 2tr) into next 2ch sp, 4ch, (2tr,

2ch, 2tr) into next 2ch sp, rep from *, ending with 1tr into top of turning ch. Turn.

14th row 3ch, (2tr, 2ch, 2tr) into next 2ch sp, 5ch, (2tr, 2ch, 2tr) into next 2ch sp, 5ch, (2tr, 2ch, 2tr) into next 2ch sp, * miss next 3ch sp, (3ch, 1dc into next 3ch sp) 3 times, 3ch, (2tr, 2ch, 2tr) into next 2ch sp, 5ch, (2tr, 2ch, 2tr) into next 2ch sp, 5ch, (2tr, 2ch, 2tr) into next 2ch sp, rep from *, ending with 1tr into top of turning ch. Turn.

15th row 3ch, (2tr, 2ch, 2tr) into next 2ch sp, 6ch, (2tr, 2ch, 2tr) into next 2ch sp, 6ch, (2tr, 2ch, 2tr) into next 2ch sp, * miss next 3ch sp, (3ch, 1dc into next 3ch sp) twice, 3ch, (2tr, 2ch, 2tr) into next 2ch sp, 6ch, (2tr, 2ch, 2tr) into next 2ch sp, 6ch, (2tr, 2ch, 2tr) into next 2ch sp, rep from *, ending with 1tr into top of turning ch. Turn.

16th row 3ch, (2tr, 2ch, 2tr) into next 2ch sp, * 3ch, 13dtr into next 2ch sp, 3ch, (2tr, 2ch, 2tr) into next 2ch sp, miss next 3ch sp, 3ch, 1dc into next 3ch sp, 3ch, (2tr, 2ch, 2tr) into next 2ch sp, rep from *, ending with 3ch, 13dtr into next 2ch sp, 3ch, (2tr, 2ch, 2tr) into last 2ch sp, 1tr into top of turning ch. Turn.

17th row 3ch, (2tr, 2ch, 2tr) into next 2ch sp, * 3ch, (1dtr into next dtr, 1ch) 12 times, 1dtr into next dtr, 3ch, (2tr, 2ch, 2tr) into next 2ch sp, 3ch, (2tr, 2ch, 2tr) into next 2ch sp, rep from *, ending with 3ch, (1dtr into next dtr, 1ch) 12 times, 1dtr into next dtr, 3ch, (2tr, 2ch, 2tr) into last 2ch sp, 1tr into top of turning ch. Turn.

18th row 3ch, (2tr, 2ch, 2tr) into next 2ch sp, * (3ch, 1dc into next 1ch sp) 12 times, 3ch, (2tr, 2ch, 2tr) into next 2ch sp, 2ch, (2tr, 2ch, 2tr) into next 2ch sp, rep from *, ending with (3ch, 1dc into next 1ch sp) 12 times, 3ch, (2tr, 2ch, 2tr) into last 2ch sp, 1tr into top of turning ch. Turn.

19th row 3ch, (2tr, 2ch, 2tr) into next 2ch sp, * miss next 3ch sp, (3ch, 1dc into next 3ch sp) 11 times, 3ch, (2tr, 2ch, 2tr) into next 2ch sp, 1ch, miss next 2ch sp, (2tr, 2ch, 2tr) into next 2ch sp, rep from *, ending with miss next 3ch sp, (3ch, 1dc into next 3ch sp) 11 times, 3ch, (2tr, 2ch, 2tr) into

last 2ch sp, 1tr into top of turning ch. Turn.

20th row 3ch, (2tr, 2ch, 2tr) into next 2ch sp, *miss next 3ch sp, (3ch, 1dc into next 3ch sp) 10 times, 3ch, (2tr, 2ch, 2tr) into next 2ch sp, (2tr, 2ch, 2tr) into next 2ch sp, rep from * ending with miss next 3ch sp, (3ch, 1dc into next 3ch sp) 10 times, 3ch, (2tr, 2ch, 2tr) into last 2ch sp, 1tr into top of turning ch. Turn.

21st row 3ch, (2tr, 2ch, 2tr, 2ch, 2tr) into next 2ch sp, *, miss next 3ch sp, (3ch, 1dc into next 3ch sp) 9 times, 3ch, (2tr, 2ch, 2tr) into next 2ch sp, (2tr, 2ch, 2tr) into next 2ch sp, rep from *, ending with miss next 3ch sp, (3ch, 1dc into next 3ch sp) 9 times, 3ch, (2tr, 2ch, 2tr, 2ch, 2tr) into last 2ch sp, 1tr into top of turning ch. Turn.
Rep rows 9-21 until a total of 63 rows have been worked, ending with a 12th row.
Fasten off.

Front
Work as for back.

To make up
Block the pieces, if necessary.
Using matching sewing thread, join the two semicircles tog at straight edges, forming the sleeve/shoulder seams.

Cuffs
Mark a distance of 28cm along the outer edge (with one seam in the centre), and using knitting needles with RS facing, pick up and K 72 sts. Work in K1, P1 rib for 4cm. Cast off. Rep for other cuff.

Welt
Mark a distance of 36cm along the centre of the lower edge of each semicircle, and similarly pick up and K 112 st on each section. Work in K1, P1 rib for 6cm. Cast off.
Join the two underarm seams from cuffs to waist.

Neck edging
Using crochet hook with WS facing, join yarn to either shoulder seam.
1st round 1dc into each foundation ch all round.
2nd round 1dc into each dc of first round.
Fasten off.

SPECIAL TECHNIQUE
Working a pineapple motif

1 *Start with a base of four chain, then work one treble, two chain and two treble all into the fourth chain from the hook.*

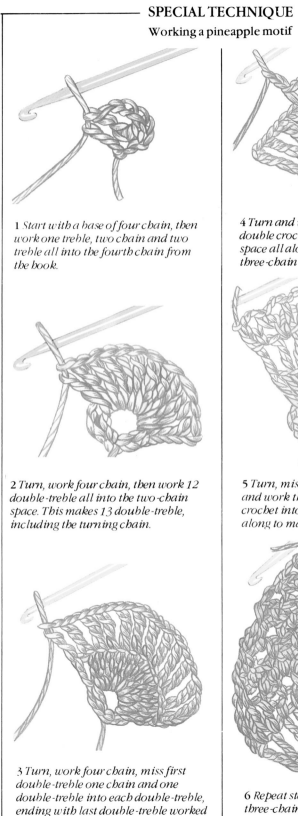

2 *Turn, work four chain, then work 12 double-treble all into the two-chain space. This makes 13 double-treble, including the turning chain.*

3 *Turn, work four chain, miss first double-treble one chain and one double-treble into each double-treble, ending with last double-treble worked into top of turning chain.*

4 *Turn and work three chain and one double crochet into the next one-chain space all along. This makes 12 three-chain spaces.*

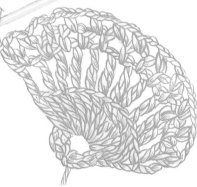

5 *Turn, miss first three-chain space, and work three chains and one double crochet into next three-chain space all along to make 11 three-chain spaces.*

6 *Repeat step 5 until the number of three-chain spaces in the row is reduced to one. Fasten off.*

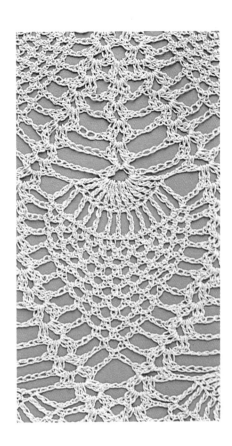

69

BEADED CARDIGAN

This elegant cardigan, made in a mohair yarn and worked with beads, is the perfect light wrap for an evening out.

Sizes
To fit 76 [81:86:91] cm bust
Length 50 [50:53:53] cm
Sleeve seam 42cm

Note: *Instructions for larger sizes are in square brackets [ ]; where there is only one set of figures it applies to all sizes.*

Materials
Approx 380 [380:400:420] g of a light-weight mohair
Approx 2000 [2000:2200:2200] small pearl beads
4.50mm crochet hook
10 small buttons

Tension
13tr and 8 rows to 10cm over patt using 4.50mm hook

To save time, take time to check tension.

Back
Before beg each new ball of yarn, thread approx 200 beads on to it.
Make 56 [60:60:64] ch.
Base row 1tr into 4th ch from hook, *bring forward a bead to lie at RS of work, 1tr into each of next 2ch, rep from * to end. Turn. 54 [58:58:62] tr.
1st row 3ch, *bring forward a bead to lie at RS of work, 1tr into each of next 2tr, rep from * to last tr, bring forward a bead, 1tr into last tr. Turn.
2nd row 3ch, 1tr into next tr, *bring forward a bead to lie at RS of work, 1tr into each of next 2tr, rep from * to end. Turn.
Rep first and 2nd rows 11 times more.
Shape armholes
Next row Ss over 3tr, 2ch, miss next tr, still working in bead patt, work 1tr into each of next 46 [50:50:54] tr, 1htr into next tr. Turn.
Next row Ss over first htr, 2ch, miss next tr, 1tr into each of next 44 [48:48:52] tr, 1htr into next tr. Turn.
Next row Ss over first htr, 2ch, miss next tr, 1tr into each of next 42 [46:46:56] tr, 1htr into next tr. Turn.
Next row 3ch, miss htr, 1tr into each tr to end. Turn, leaving htr unworked. 42 [46:46:50] tr.
Work straight for 11 [11:13:13] rows in tr bead patt.
Shape shoulders
Next row 2ch, 1htr into each tr to end.
Next row Ss across 11 [12:12:13] htr, 2ch, miss next htr, 1htr into each of next 19 [21:21:23] htr.
Fasten off.

Left front
Make 29 [31:31:33] ch. Work base row as for back. 27 [29:29:31] tr. Cont in patt as for back until front measures same as back to underarm, ending at armhole edge.
Shape armhole
Next row Ss over 2tr, 2ch, miss next tr,
1tr into each tr to end. Turn.
Next row 3ch, 1tr into each of next 23 [25:25:27] tr. Turn.
Next row Ss over first tr, 2ch, miss next tr, 1tr into each tr to end. Turn.
Next row 3ch, 1tr into each of next 20 [22:22:24] tr, 1htr into next tr. Turn.
Next row 3ch, 1tr into each tr to end. Turn. 21 [23:23:25] tr.
Work 5 [5:7:7] rows in tr bead patt without shaping, ending at armhole edge.
Shape neck
Next row 3ch, 1tr into each of next 12 [13:13:14] tr, 1htr into next tr. Turn and leave rem sts unworked.
Next row Ss into htr, 1htr into next tr, 1tr into each tr to end. Turn.
Next row 3ch, 1tr into each of next 10 [11:11:12] tr, 1htr into next tr. Turn.
Next row 3ch, miss htr, 1tr into each tr to end. Turn. 11 [12:12:13] tr. Work 1 more row in patt on these sts.
Next row 2ch, 1htr into each tr to end. Fasten off.

Right front
Work as for left front, making sure beads lie on RS of fabric, reversing shaping.

Sleeves
Make 28 [28:32:32] ch and work in patt as for back for 3 rows. 26 [26:30:30] tr.
Next row Inc 1tr at each end of next row, working extra sts into patt. 28 [28:32:32] tr.
Work straight for 4 rows. Rep last 5 rows once more. 30 [30:34:34] sts.
Next row Inc 1tr at each end of next row. Work 3 rows without shaping. Rep last 4 rows once more. 34 [34:38:38] tr.
Next row Inc 1tr at each end of next row. Work even for 2 rows. 36 [36:40:40] sts.

SPECIAL TECHNIQUE
Treble crochet with beads

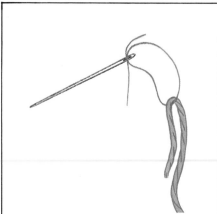

1 *Beads are worked into the fabric of the mohair cardigan. Begin by threading the number of beads specified on to the ball of yarn. Use a fine sewing needle that will slip through the beads. Make a loop of cotton through the needle so that both ends pass through the eye as shown. Loop the working yarn through the cotton.*

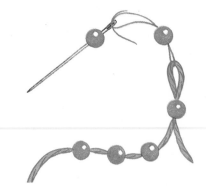

2 *Slip the first bead over the needle, along the cotton and on to the doubled end of yarn. Thread each bead on to the yarn in the same way. Keep one bead over the doubled yarn at all times to keep the yarn in place over the loop of the cotton.*

3 *With the right side of the fabric facing work in treble crochet to the position for the first bead. Slip the bead up close to the hook. Take the yarn round the hook, taking the yarn beyond the bead, and holding the bead at the front.*

4 *Insert the hook into the next stitch and complete the treble in the usual way, keeping the bead at the front of the work.*

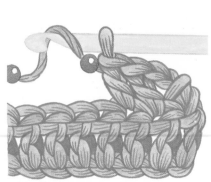

5 *Smaller beads sometimes have a tendency to slip to the back of the work. To prevent this, slip the bead up close to the hook and begin the next treble by taking the yarn over the hook from front to back.*

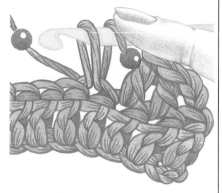

6 *Hold the bead and yarn on the hook at the front of the work with the forefinger of the right hand to prevent the yarn from becoming too tight. Insert the hook into the next stitch and pull the yarn through.*

7 *Complete the treble in the usual way. In order to maintain an even tension it is important to hold the yarn and bead on the hook each time while working the stitch.*

Next row Inc 1tr at each end of next row. Work 1 row without shaping. Rep last 2 rows once. 40 [40:44:44] sts. Inc 1tr at each end of next 4 rows. 48 [48:52:52] tr. Work 1 row without shaping.

Shape sleeve top

Next row Ss over 2tr, 1htr into next tr, 1tr into each of next 42 [42:46:46] tr. 1htr into next tr. Turn and leave rem sts unworked.

Next row Ss into htr, 1htr into next tr, 1tr into each of next 40 [40:44:44] tr, 1htr into next tr. Turn.

Next row Ss into htr and first tr, 1htr into next tr, 1tr into each of next 36 [36:40:40] tr, 1htr into next tr. Turn.

Next row Ss into htr, 1htr into next tr, 1tr into each tr to last tr, 1htr into last tr. Turn. Rep last row until there are 14 sts. Fasten off.

To make up

Join shoulder, side and sleeve seams. Set in sleeve, gathering sleeve top to form puff.

Edging With RS facing join yarn at lower side seam. Work in hdc along lower edge, up right front, round neck, back down left front and back along lower edge. Join with a ss.
Fasten off.

Sew on buttons down left front, spacing evenly and using spaces between htr as buttonholes.

Gently brush mohair to raise pile.

Press seams lightly, taking care to avoid beads.

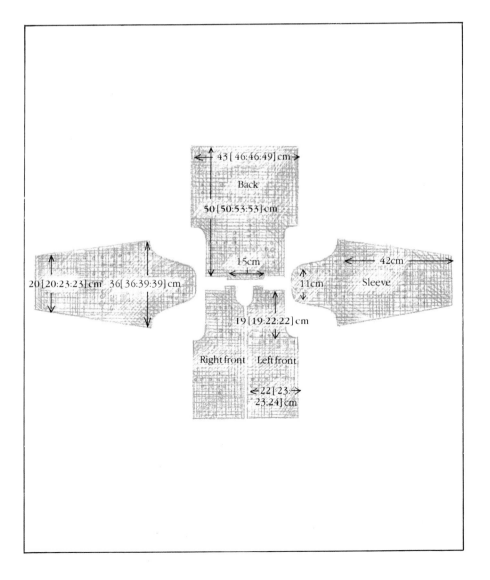

STRIPED CARDIGAN

Glitter yarn adds a bit of sparkle to this versatile striped cardigan.

Sizes
To fit 86 [91:96] cm bust
Length 60cm
Sleeve seam 43cm

Note *Instructions for larger sizes are in square brackets [ ]; where there is only one set of figures it applies to all sizes.*

Materials
Approx 150 [200:200] g of a double knitting yarn in main colour (A)
Approx 100 [150:150] g in each of 4 contrasting colours (B, C, D and E)
Approx 60g of a fine metallic yarn
4.50mm crochet hook
1 pair 3mm knitting needles
5 buttons

Tension
16dc to 10cm using 4.50mm hook and A

To save time, take time to check tension.

Pocket linings (make 2)
Using crochet hook and A, make 17ch.
Base row (RS) 1dc into 2nd ch from hook, 1dc into each ch to end. Turn. 16 sts.
Next row 1ch to count as first dc, miss first st, 1dc into each st to end. Turn.
Rep last row until work measures 10cm from beg. Fasten off.

Back and fronts (worked in one piece to armholes)
Using knitting needles and A, cast on 194 [206:216] sts.
Rib row *K1, P1, rep from * to end.
Rep rib row until work measures 10cm from beg.
Cast off in rib.
Using crochet hook, join B to last cast-off st.
Next row 1ch to count as first dc, miss st at base of joining, work 153 [161:169] dc evenly into cast-off edge. Turn. 154 [162:170] sts.
Beg stripe patt
1st row (WS) Using C and F tog, 2ch, miss first st, 1htr into each st to end. Turn.
2nd row Using E, 3ch, miss first st, 1tr into each st to end. Turn.
3rd row Using 3 strands of F, 1ch to count as first tr, miss first st, 1dc into each st to end. Turn.
4th row Using D, as first row.
5th row Using A, as 2nd row.
6th row Using B, as 3rd row.
First-6th rows form stripe patt. Cont in stripe patt until work measures 18cm from cast-on edge, ending with a RS row.
Place pockets
Next row Patt first 8 sts, miss next 16 sts, patt across 16 sts of first pocket lining, patt to last 24 sts, miss next 16 sts, patt across 16 sts of second pocket lining, patt last 8 sts. Turn. Cont in stripe patt until work measures 41cm from cast-on edge, ending with a WS row.

Divide for back and fronts
Next row Ss across first 2 sts, patt next 35 [37:39] sts. Turn. 35 [37:39] sts.
Shape right armhole and front
1st row (WS) Ss across first 2 sts, patt to end. Turn. 34 [36:38] sts.
2nd row Patt to last st. Turn, leaving last st unworked. 33 [35:37] sts.
3rd row Ss across first 2 sts, patt to last st. Turn, leaving last st unworked. 31 [33:35] sts.
4th row As 2nd row. 30 [32:34] sts.
5th row As first row. 29 [31:33] sts.
6th row As 3rd row. 27 [29:31] sts.
Rep first and 2nd rows once more. 25 [27:29] sts.
Keeping armhole edge straight, dec one st at front edge as before on every following 3rd row until 18 [21:24] sts rem.
Work straight in stripe patt shaping until right front measures 60cm from cast-on edge, ending at armhole edge.
Shape shoulder
Next row Ss across first 7 [8:9] sts, patt to end. Turn. 12 [14:16] sts.
Next row Patt to end.
Rep last 2 rows once more. 6 [7:8] sts.
Patt one row.
Fasten off.

Back
With RS facing, miss next 6 sts left unworked at beg of right front and using crochet hook and keeping stripe patt correct, join yarn to next st.
Next row Patt into same place as joining, patt next 71 [75:79] sts. Turn. 72 [76:80] sts.
Shape armholes
Next row Ss across first 2 sts, patt to last st. Turn, leaving last st unworked. Rep last row 8 [7:6] times more. 54 [60:66] sts.
Work straight in stripe patt until back matches right front at armhole edge, ending with a RS row.
Shape shoulders
Next row Ss across first 7 [8:9] sts, patt

Inserting a horizontal pocket

1 *The cardigan has a horizontal pocket on each front. Before beginning the back and fronts, work two pocket linings as instructed in the pattern. After working the knitted rib, work in the stripe pattern until the work is the required length, ending with a right-side pattern row.*

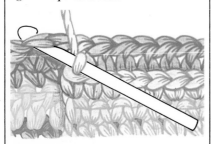

2 *Work to the pocket as instructed. Bring the top of the pocket lining up to the front of the work (i.e. on the wrong side) and pattern across the 16 stitches of the pocket lining. Miss the next 16 stitches on the front. Pattern to the position of the other pocket and place the lining as before. Pattern to the end of the row.*

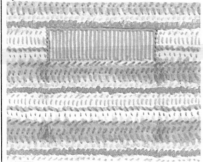

3 *When making up the cardigan, pick up the stitches at the top of the pocket as instructed and work the pocket tops in knit-one, purl-one rib. Sew the row ends of the pocket tops invisibly to the right side of the fronts. Using slipstitch, sew the pocket linings in place on the wrong side of each front.*

to last 6 [7:8] sts. Turn.
Next row Patt to end. Rep last 2 rows once more. Fasten off.

Left front

With RS facing, miss next 6 sts left unworked at beg of back and using crochet hook and keeping stripe patt correct, join yarn to next st.
Next row Patt into same place as joining, patt next 34 [36:38] sts. Turn. 35 [37:39] sts.
Keeping stripe patt correct, work as for right front, reversing all shaping.

Sleeves (both alike)

Using knitting needles and A, cast on 54 sts. Work in K1, P1 rib as for back and fronts for 9cm.
Cast off in rib.
Using crochet hook, join B to last cast-off st.
Next row 1ch to count as first dc, miss st at base of joining, 1dc into each bound-off st to end. 54 sts.
Cont in stripe pat as for back and fronts until work measures 43cm from cast-on edge, ending with same row as back and fronts to 'Divide for armholes'.

Shape top

Next row Ss across first 4 sts, patt to last 3 sts. Turn. 48 sts.
Next row Ss across first 2 sts, patt to last st. Turn. 46 sts.
Rep last row 11 times more. 24 sts.
Fasten off.

To make up

Block the work. Join shoulder seams.

Button band

Mark positions of 5 buttonholes on right front edge, the first 4 rows from the cast-on edge, the last at the beg of front neck shaping and the rem 3 evenly spaced in between.
Using knitting needles and A, cast on 11 sts.
1st row K1, (P1, K1) to end.
2nd row P1, (K1, P1) to end.
Rep last 2 rows once more.
1st buttonhole row Rib 4, cast off 3 sts, rib to end.
2nd buttonhole row Rib 4, cast on 3 sts, rib to end.
** Cont in rib to position of next buttonhole.
Work buttonhole as before over next 2 rows. **
Rep from ** to ** 3 times more.
Cont in rib until button band, slightly stretched, fits up right front, round back neck and down left front.
Bind off in rib.
Set in sleeves, matching stripes at armhole. Join sleeve seams, matching stripes at edges.
Sew border neatly to fronts and back neck. Sew buttons to left front to correspond with buttonholes.

Pocket tops (both alike)

With RS facing, using knitting needles and A, pick up and K 32 sts from sts at top of pocket opening.
Work in K1, P1 rib for 3cm.
Bind off in rib.
Sew pocket linings neatly in place on WS. Sew row ends of pocket tops to RS.

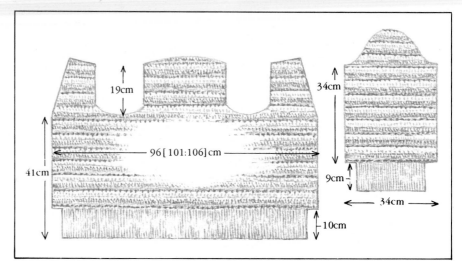

BOBBLE CARDIGAN

This pretty cotton cardigan is easier than it looks. The bobbles are worked in three different colours using a simple technique to create an interesting variation in colour and texture.

Size

To fit *81-86cm bust*
Length *50cm*
Sleeve seam *40cm*

Materials

Approx 275g of a fine cotton yarn in main colour (A)
Approx 50g in contrasting colour (B)
1 ball each in contrasting colours (C and D)
7 buttons
3.50mm crochet hook

Tension

16 sts and 9 rows to 10cm over patt using 3.50mm hook

To save time, take time to check tension.

Note *Use one contrasting colour, along with main colour A, for each bobble row, alternating colours as instructed and carrying yarn not in use across back of work. Break off each contrasting colour at end of row.*

Back

Using A, make 75ch.
1st row 1tr into 4th ch from hook, 1tr into each ch to end. Turn. 73tr.
2nd row (RS) 3ch to count as first tr, 1tr into each of next 8tr joining in B on last tr, (5tr into next tr, drop working loop and re-insert hook from front to back through top of first tr of 5tr group, then back through working loop, drop B, using A draw yarn through and pull 5tr tog – called Bl –, 1tr into each of next 10tr) 5 times, Bl, 1tr into each tr to end, 1tr into top of turning ch. Turn.
3rd row Using A, 3ch, 1tr into each tr to end. Turn.
4th row 3ch, 1tr into each of next 3tr, (using C, Bl, 1tr into each of next 10tr) 6 times, Bl, 1tr into tr to end. Turn.
5th row As 3rd row.
6th row As 2nd row, using D for bobbles.
These 6 rows form patt. Cont in patt, maintaining colour sequence on bobble rows throughout, until 26 rows in all have been worked.
Shape armholes
27th row Ss over first 4tr, 2ch to count as first htr, 1htr into next st, 1tr into each of next 61tr, htr into next st. Turn and leave rem sts unworked.
28th row 2ch, 1htr into next st, 1tr into each of next 8tr, (B1, 1tr into each of next 10tr) 4 times, B1, 1tr into each of next 7tr. Turn.
29th row 3ch, 1tr into each of next 61tr. Turn. 62tr.
30th row 3ch, 1tr into each of next 3tr, (B1, 1tr into each of next 10tr) 5 times, B1, 1tr into each of last 2tr. Turn. Keeping patt correct work straight for another 14 rows.
Shape shoulders
Next row Ss over first 16 sts, 2ch, 1htr into each of next 29 sts. Turn and leave rem sts unworked. Fasten off.

Right front

Using A, make 37ch. Work first row as for back. 35tr.
2nd row 3ch to count as first tr, 1tr into each of next 9tr, (using B, B1, 1tr into each of next 10tr) twice, B1, 1tr into each of next 2tr. Turn.
3rd row 3ch, 1tr into each tr to end. Turn. 35tr.

4th row 3ch, 1tr into each of next 4tr, (using C, B1, 1tr into each of next 10tr) twice, B1, 1tr into each st to end. Turn.
5th row As 3rd row.
6th row As 2nd row, using D for bobbles.
Cont in patt as set, maintaining correct colour sequence for bobble rows until 26 rows in all have been worked from beg.
Shape armhole
27th row Ss over first 3 sts, work 1htr into next st, 1tr into each st to end. Turn.
28th row 3ch, 1tr into each of next 4tr, (B1, 1tr into each of next 10tr) twice, B1, 1tr into each of next 2tr, 1htr into next st. Turn.
29th row 3ch, miss htr, 1tr into each tr to end. Turn.
Keeping patt correct work straight for 9 rows more.
Shape front neck
39th row 3ch, 1tr into each of next 15 sts. Turn and leave rem sts unworked. Keeping patt correct work 6 rows more on these sts. Fasten off.

Left front

Using A, make 37ch. Work first row as for right front. 35tr.
2nd row 3ch, to count as first tr, 1tr into next tr, (using B, B1, 1tr into each of next 10tr) 3 times. Turn.
3rd row 3ch, 1tr into each st to end. Turn.
4th row 3ch, 1tr into each of next 6tr, (using C, B1, 1tr into each of next 10tr) twice, B1, 1tr into each tr to end.
Cont in patt following colour sequence as for right front until 26 rows in all have been worked from beg.
Shape armhole
27th row 3ch, 1tr into each of next 29tr, 1htr into next st. Turn.
28th row 2ch, 1htr into next st, 1tr into next st, (B1, 1tr into each of next 10 sts) twice, B1, tr to end. Turn.
29th row 3ch, 1tr into each of next 29tr. Turn. 30tr.
Cont in patt as set, work straight for 9 rows more.
Shape front neck
39th row Ss over first 14 sts, 3ch, 1tr into each tr to end. Turn. 16 sts.

40th row 3ch, 1tr into next tr, B1, 1tr into each of next 10tr, B1, 1tr into each of last 2tr. Turn.
Keeping patt correct work straight for 5 rows more on these sts.
Fasten off.

Sleeves

Using A, make 40ch.
1st row 1tr into 4th ch from hook, 1tr into each ch to end. Turn. 38tr.
2nd row 3ch to count as first tr, 1tr into each of next 2tr, (B1, 1tr into each of next 10tr) 3 times, B1, 1tr into last tr. Turn.
3rd row 3ch, 1tr into each st to end. Turn.
4th row 3ch, 1tr into each of next 8tr, (B1, 1tr into each of next 10tr) twice, B1, 1tr into each st to end. Turn. These 4 rows form patt. Cont in patt until 13 rows have been worked, alternating colours for bobbles as before.
14th row 3ch to count as first tr, 1tr into first (edge) st, 1tr into each of

next 2tr, (B1, 1tr into each of next 10tr) 3 times, B1, 1tr into next tr, 2tr into last st. Turn. 40tr.
15th row 3ch, 1tr into each tr to end. Turn.
16th row 3ch, 1tr into each of next 9tr, (B1, 1tr into each of next 10tr) twice, B1, 1tr into each st to end. Patt 2 rows more on these sts.
19th row 3ch, 1tr into first (edge) st, 1tr into each st to last st, 2tr into last st. Turn. 42tr.
Keeping bobble patt correct cont increasing one st at each end of row in this way on 22nd, 26th and 32nd row. 48tr. Work straight for 3 rows more.
Shape sleeve top
36th row 1ch, ss over next 2 sts, 1htr into next st, patt to last 4 sts, 1htr into next st. Turn and leave rem 3 sts unworked.
37th row 2ch, 1htr into next st, 1tr into each of next 39tr, 1htr into next st. Turn.
38th row 2ch, 1htr into next st, 1tr

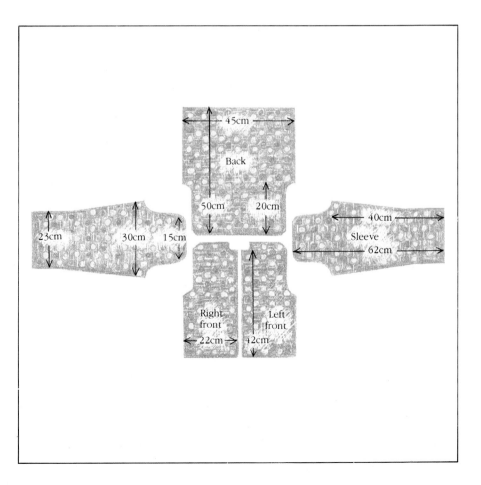

into each of next 3tr, (B1, 1tr into each of next 10tr) 3 times, B1, 1tr into next st, 1htr into next st. Turn.

39th row 3ch, 1tr into each of next 39tr. Turn. 40tr.

40th row 3ch, 1tr into each of next 9tr, (B1, 1tr into each of next 10tr) 3 times, 1tr into each of next 3tr. Turn.

41st row As 39th.

42nd row 3ch, 1tr into each of next 3tr, (B1, 1tr into each of next 10tr) 3 times, 1tr into each of next 2tr. Turn.

43rd row As 39th.

44th row 1ch, 1tr into next st, 1tr into each of next 8tr, (B1, 1tr into each of next 10tr) twice, B1, 1tr into each of next 5tr, 1htr into next st. Turn.

45th row 2ch, 1htr into next st, 1tr into each of next 34tr, 1htr into next st. Turn.

46th row 2ch, 1htr into next st, 1tr into each of next 11tr, B1, 1tr into each of next 10tr, B1, 1tr into each of next 9tr, 1htr into next st. Turn.

47th row 2ch, 1htr into next st, 1tr into each of next 30tr, 1htr into next st. Turn.

48th row 2ch, 1htr into next st, 1tr into each of next 4tr, (B1, 1tr into each of next 10tr) twice, B1, 1tr into next st, 1htr into next st. Turn.

49th row 2ch, 1htr into next st, 1tr into each of next 26tr, 1htr into next st. Turn.

50th row 2ch, 1htr into next st, 1tr into each of next 7tr, B1, 1tr into each of next 10tr, B1, 1tr into each of next 5tr, 1htr into next st. Turn.

51st row As 49th, working 22tr instead of 26.

52nd row 2ch, 1tr into each of next 2 sts, B1, 1tr into each of next 10tr, B1, 1tr into each of next 10tr. Turn.

53rd row 2ch, 1tr into each of next 22tr. Turn.

54th row 2ch, 1htr into next st, 1tr into each of next 4tr, B1, 1tr into each of next 10tr, B1, 1tr into each of next 3tr, 1htr into next st. Turn.

55th row As 51st, working 19tr instead of 23.

56th row 2ch, 1htr into next st, 1tr into each of next 19tr, 1htr into next st. Fasten off.

To make up
Block the work if necessary, but do not press.
Join shoulder, side and sleeve seams.
Set in sleeves, gathering excess on sleeve top to form puff.

Border
Using D, join yarn to edge of centre front at lower corner, 3ch, work 67tr up front edge to neck, 3ch, turn work 90 degrees and work 16tr to first inside corner of neck, * 3ch, rep 90-degree turn, ss through 3rd tr * to make corner, work 12tr to back neck, rep from * to *, work 28tr across back neck, rep from * to *, work 10tr down side of neck, rep from * to *, work 12tr across front neck, 3ch, turn 90 degrees and work 67tr down left front to lower corner, 3ch, turn and work 144tr along lower edge to beg of edging, join with a ss. Fasten off. Sew buttons to border, spacing them evenly down right front. Use spaces between tr in opposite border as buttonholes.

Sleeve border
Using D, rejoin yarn at sleeve seam, 3ch, work 27tr round sleeve edge, join with a ss to 3rd of first 3ch. Fasten off. Press seams.

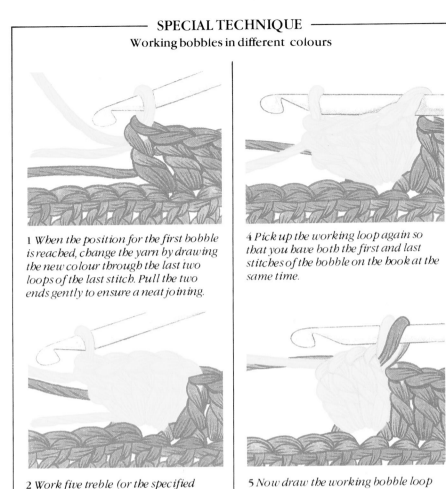

1 *When the position for the first bobble is reached, change the yarn by drawing the new colour through the last two loops of the last stitch. Pull the two ends gently to ensure a neat joining.*

4 *Pick up the working loop again so that you have both the first and last stitches of the bobble on the hook at the same time.*

2 *Work five treble (or the specified number) into the next stitch, working over the free end of the bobble yarn to avoid having to darn in too many ends when the crochet has been completed.*

5 *Now draw the working bobble loop together with a loop of the main colour through the first stitch to complete the bobble. The main colour is now ready for use.*

3 *Drop the working yarn and re-insert the hook from front to back through the top of the first treble of the bobble. Make sure that the working loop does not slip back through the top of the last stitch.*

6 *Drop the bobble colour and continue to work with the first or main colour only. Pull the colour used for the bobble gently at the back of the work to make a good shape. Break off the yarn.*

WOVEN CROCHET JACKET

Strands of a contrasting mohair blend yarn are woven into the fabric of this attractive, comfortable jacket.

Sizes

To fit *86 [91:96] cm bust*
Length 58 [59:60] cm
Sleeve seam 48cm

Note *Instructions for larger sizes are in square brackets []; where there is only one set of figures it applies to all sizes. Measurements given are for completed jacket pieces* before *weaving, since weaving tends to make pieces shorter and wider.*

Materials

Approx 500g of a double knitting yarn (A)
Approx 80g of a medium-weight mohair (B)
3.50mm crochet hook
4 buttons

Tension

10 spaces and 10 rows to 10cm over filet mesh using 3.50mm hook

To save time, take time to check tension.

Back

Using A, make 102 [106:110] ch.
Base row 1tr into 6th ch from hook, *1ch, miss 1ch, 1tr into next ch, rep from * to end of ch. Turn. 49 [51:53] 1ch sps – called sp(s).
1st row 4ch to count as first tr and sp, * 1tr into next tr, 1ch, rep from *, ending with 1tr into top of turning ch. Turn.
First row forms basic filet mesh patt and is rep throughout. Cont in patt until work measures 36cm from beg, ending with a WS row.
Shape armholes
Next row Ss across first 6 sps, 4ch, patt across 39 [41:43] sps. Turn and leave rem sps unworked.
Work straight until work measures 58 [59:60] cm, ending with a WS row.
Shape shoulders
Next row Ss across first 5 sps, 4ch, patt across 31 [33:35] sps. Turn and leave rem sps unworked.
Next row Ss across first 5 sps, 4ch, patt across next 23 [25:27] sps. Turn and leave rem sps unworked.
Next row Ss across first 6 [6:7] sps, 4ch, patt across next 13 [15:15] sps. Fasten off leaving rem sps unworked.

Left front

Using A, make 50 [52:54] ch. Work base row as for back. 23 [24:25] sps. Cont in patt as for back for 17 more rows. Break off yarn.
Make pocket lining
Using A, make 34ch. Work base row as for back. 15 sps. Cont in patt as for back for 17 more rows.
Next row 4ch, 1tr into next tr, (1ch, 1tr into next tr) twice, 1ch, work next tr through first tr on front section and next tr of pocket lining tog, now cont working mesh across front section

only to end of row. 27 [28:29] sps.
Cont in patt until work measures 36cm, ending at same side as pocket opening (armhole edge).
Shape armhole
Next row Ss across first 6sps, 4ch, 1tr into next tr, patt to end of row. 22 [23:24] sps. Work straight until work measures 50 [51:52] cm, ending at armhole edge.
Shape neck
Next row Patt across 18 [19:20] sps, turn and leave rem 4sps unworked. Dec one sp at neck edge on next and every following row until 13 [13:14] sps rem. Work straight until front measures 58 [59:60] cm, ending at armhole edge.
Shape shoulder
Dec 4 sps at armhole edge on next 2 rows. Fasten off.

Right front

Make pocket lining as for left front. Break off yarn.
Work as for left front for first 8 rows of filet mesh, ending with RS of work facing.
Buttonhole row 4ch, 1tr into next tr, 1ch, 1tr into next tr, 3ch, miss next tr, 1tr into next tr, patt to end of row.
Next row Patt to buttonhole, 1ch, 1tr into 2nd of 3ch, 1ch, 1tr into next tr, patt to end of row.
Complete as for left front, reversing all shaping. Insert pocket lining after 18 rows of mesh and work 2 more buttonholes 12 rows apart.

Sleeves (both alike)

Using A, make 62ch. Work base row as for back. 29sps. Cont in patt as for back. Work 3 more rows.
Next row (inc) 4ch, 1tr into tr at base of 4ch, patt to end of row working 1tr

SPECIAL TECHNIQUE
Placing a vertical pocket

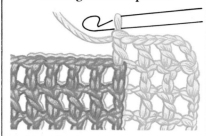

1 *The pocket linings for the woven jacket are made as separate pieces which must be incorporated on to the wrong side of the work while making the front. Hold the pocket at back of the work where indicated in the pattern and work into the stitch on the front piece and on the pocket simultaneously, thus joining the pocket to the front of the garment.*

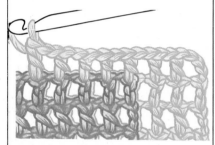

2 *Because of the weaving, the jacket pocket has been joined in only one place, but generally all pocket stitches are worked together with front stitches to hold the pocket in place across the top edge.*

3 *Using matching yarn, sew the pocket lining in place on the wrong side of the garment, making sure that the stitches do not show on the right side of the work. Overcast firmly, but do not pull too tightly or the fabric may pucker.*

into last tr, 1ch, 1tr into same place as last tr. Turn.
Work 5 [4:4] rows in patt.
Rep last 6[5:5] rows until there are 43 [45:47]sps. Work straight until sleeve measures 48cm. Fasten off.

Weaving
Using 3 strands of A or B tog, weave in and out of mesh holes vertically, alternating the first stitch each time and making sure that weaving is worked evenly. Work colour sequence as follows:
Back 5 rows B, 5 rows A, starting by weaving 5 rows B down centre of work, then working towards the sides.
Sleeves Work as for back.
Fronts Beg by working 5 rows B down centre front, making sure sides match back section.
Pocket lining Use A throughout.

To make up
Join shoulder seams.
Collar
Using A and with RS facing, work 2dc into each sp round neck edge.
Turn.

Work another 9 rows dc on these sts. Fasten off.
Cuffs
Using A and with RS facing, work 40dc along cuff edge, working *2dc into first sp, 1dc into each of next 2 sps, rep from * to end. Work 12 more rows dc on these sts. Fasten off.
Pocket edges
Using A and with RS facing, work 2dc into each sp along pocket edge.
Work 4 more rows dc on these sts.
Fasten off.
Waistband
Join side seams. Using A and with RS facing, work *2dc into first sp, 1dc into next sp, rep from * to end. Work 6 rows dc, ending at right front edge.
Buttonhole row 1dc into each of first 2dc, 4ch, miss 4dc, 1dc into next dc, work in dc to end.
Work 5 more rows dc, working 1dc into each of 4ch of buttonhole.
Fasten off.
Set in sleeves. Join sleeve seams. With RS of work facing and A, work 1 row dc up centre front, round collar and down other front. Fasten off. Sew down pocket linings.

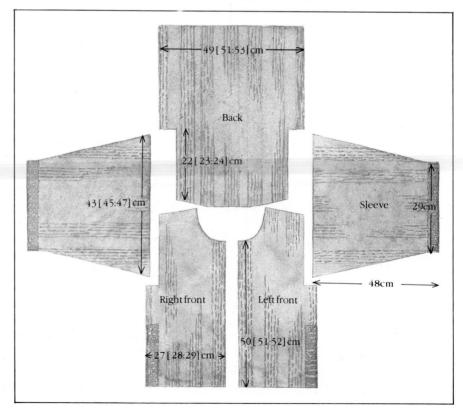

CLASSIC WAISTCOAT

Two textured patterns – a butterfly crossed stitch and single rib – have been used to make this waistcoat with deep V-neck and adjustable half belt.

Sizes

To fit *86* [*91:96*] *cm bust*
Length *43* [*46:48*] *cm*

Note *Instructions for larger sizes are in square brackets [ ]; where there is only one set of figures it applies to all sizes.*

Materials

Approx 200 [*200:225*] *g of a 4 ply yarn*
3.00mm crochet hook
5 small buttons
Small buckle to fit completed strap

Tension

20 sts and 9 rows to 10cm over front patt using 3.00mm hook
20 sts and 18 rows to 10cm over back patt using 3.00mm hook

To save time, take time to check tension.

Left front

Make 9 [**11:11]ch.
Base row 2tr into 5th ch from hook, 1tr into each of next 3 [5:5]ch, (2tr, 1dtr) into last ch. Turn. 9 [11:11] sts.
1st row (RS) 4ch, 2tr into first dtr, 1tr into each of next 1 [2:2] sts, inserting hook from front to back and leaving last loop of each st on hook work 2dtr round stem of tr on row below and 3 sts to left, yrh and draw through all 3 loops on hook – called cluster front –, miss next st behind cluster front, 1tr into each of next 3 sts, cluster front round same st now 3 sts to right, miss next st – called butterfly st over 5 sts or b st over 5 –, 1tr into each of next 1 [2:2] sts, (2tr, 1dtr) into top of turning ch. Turn. 13 [15:15] sts.
2nd row 4ch, 2tr into first dtr, 1tr into each st to turning ch, (2tr, 1dtr) into top of turning ch. Turn. 17 [19:19] sts.
3rd row 4ch, 2tr into first dtr, 1tr into each of next 1 [2:2] sts, b st over 5, 1tr into each of next 3 sts, b st over 5, 1tr into each of next 1 [2:2] sts, (2tr, 1dtr) into top of turning ch. Turn. 21 [23:23] sts.
4th row As 2nd row. 25 [27:27] sts.
5th row 4ch, 2tr into first dtr, 1tr into each of next 1 [2:2] sts, * b st over 5, 1tr into each of next 3 sts, rep from * once more, b st over 5, 1tr into each of next 1 [2:2] sts, (2tr, 1dtr) into top of turning ch. Turn. 29 [31:31] sts.
6th row As 2nd row. 33 [35:35] sts.
7th row 4ch, 2tr into first dtr, 1tr into each of next 1 [2:2] sts, * b st over 5, 1tr into each of next 3 sts, rep from * to end, ending last rep with 1tr into each of next 1 [2:2] sts, (2dtr, 1dtr) into top of turning ch. Turn. 37 [39:39] sts.
8th row As 2nd row. 41 [43:43] sts.
3rd size only
9th row As 7th row. 47 sts.
10th row 3ch, miss first st, 1tr into each st to end. Turn.
All sizes
Beg patt as follows:
1st row (RS) 3ch, miss first st, 1tr into each of next 1 [2:8] sts, * b st over 5, 1tr into each of next 3 sts, rep from * to end, ending last rep with 1tr into each of next 1 [2:8] sts, 1tr into top of turning ch. Turn.
2nd row 3ch, miss first st, 1tr into each st to end. Turn.

3rd row 3ch, miss first st, 1tr into each of next 5 [6:4] sts, * b st over 5, 1tr into each of next 3 sts, rep from * to end, ending last rep with 1tr into each of next 5 [6:4] sts, 1tr into top of turning ch. Turn.
4th row As 2nd row.
Last 4 rows form patt.**
Shape side
Next row 3ch, miss first st, 2tr into next st – called inc one –, patt to end. Turn. 42 [44:48] sts.
Keeping patt correct, inc one st at beg of following 3 alternate rows. 45 [47:51] sts.
Work straight in patt until *front* edge measures 15 [18:18] cm from last row of point, ending at front edge.
Shape front
Next row Patt to last 3 sts, work next 2 sts tog, 1tr into top of turning ch. Turn. 44 [46:50] sts.
Next row 3ch, miss first st, work next 2 sts tog, patt to end. Turn. 43 [45:49] sts.
Rep last 2 rows twice more. 39 [41:45] sts.
Shape armhole
Next row Ss across first 7 sts, 3ch, miss st at base of 3ch, work next 2 sts tog, patt to last 3 sts, work next 2 sts tog, 1tr into top of turning ch. Turn.
Cont to dec one st at front edge on every following row, *at the same time* dec one st at armhole edge on every row until 21 [23:25] sts rem. Keeping armhole edge straight, cont to dec one st at front edge on next and every following alternate row until 17 [19:20] sts rem.
Work straight in patt until armhole measures 21 [21:23] cm, ending at armhole edge.
Shape shoulder
Next row Ss across first 6 [7:7] sts, 3ch, miss st at base of 3ch, patt to end. Turn.
Next row Patt to last 5 [6:6] sts. Turn. Fasten off.

Right front

Work as for left front from ** to **.
Shape side
Next row Patt to last 2 sts, inc one, 1tr into top of turning ch. Turn. 42 [44:48] sts.
Keeping patt correct, inc one st at end

of following 3 alternate rows. 45 [47:51] sts. Work straight in patt until front edge matches left-front edge, ending at front edge.

Shape front

Next row 3ch, miss first st, work next 2 sts tog, patt to end. Turn. 44 [46:50] sts.

Next row Patt to last 3 sts, work next 2 sts tog, 1tr into top of turning ch. Turn. 43 [45:49] sts.

Rep last 2 rows twice more. 39 [41:45] sts.

Shape armhole

Next row 3ch, miss first st, work next 2 sts tog, patt to last 9 sts, work next 2 sts tog, 1tr into next st. Turn. 31 [33:37] sts.

Work as for left front from *** to ***

Work straight in patt until armhole measures 21 [21:23] cm, ending at front edge.

Shape shoulder

Next row Patt to within last 5 [6:6] sts. Turn.

Next row Ss across first 6 [7:7] sts, 3ch, miss st at base of 3ch, patt to end. Turn. Fasten off.

Back

Make 87 [91:97]ch.

Base row (RS) 1tr into 4th ch from hook, 1tr into each ch to end. Turn. 85 [89:95] sts.

Next row 1ch to count as first dc, miss first st, 1dc into each st to end. Turn.

Next row 2ch, miss first st, inserting hook from front to back and from right to left work 1tr round next tr on base row – raised tr formed –, *miss next dc behind raised tr, 1tr into next dc, miss next tr on base row, raised tr round next tr on base row, rep from * to end, ending with 1htr into last dc. Turn. 42 [44:47] raised tr.

Beg patt as follows:

1st row (WS) 1ch to count as first dc, miss first htr, 1dc into next raised tr, *1dc between next tr and next raised tr, 1dc into next raised tr, rep from * to end, ending with 1dc into top of turning ch. Turn. 85 [89:95] dc.

2nd row 2ch, miss first st, raised tr round next raised tr, *miss next dc behind raised tr, 1tr into next dc, raised tr round next raised tr, rep from * to end, ending with 1htr into last dc. Turn.

First and 2nd rows form patt. Cont in patt until work matches fronts at side edges, ending with a first row.

Shape armholes

Next row Ss across first 7 sts, 2ch, miss first st at base of 3ch, work next 2 sts

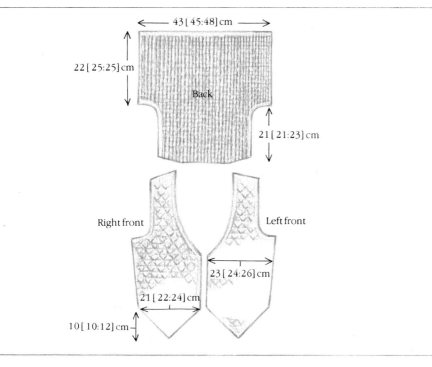

43 [45:48] cm

22 [25:25] cm

Back

21 [21:23] cm

Right front

Left front

23 [24:26] cm

21 [22:24] cm

10 [10:12] cm

tog, patt to last 9 sts, work next 2 sts tog, 1htr into next st. Turn.
Keeping patt correct, dec one st at each end of every following alternate row until 61 [65:71] sts rem.
Work straight in patt until work matches fronts to shoulder shaping, ending with a first row at armhole edge.

Shape shoulders
Next row Ss across first 6 [7:7] sts, 2ch, miss st at base of 2ch, patt to last 6 [7:7] sts, 1htr into next st. Turn.
Next row Patt to end.
Rep last 2 rows once more.
Next row Ss across first 8 [8:9] sts, 2ch, miss st at base of 2ch, patt to last 8 [8:9] sts, 1htr into next st. Turn.
Next row Patt to end. 27 [27:31] sts. Fasten off.

To make up
Join side and shoulder seams. Mark position of 5 buttonholes on left front, one 1cm from end of point, one at beg of front neckline shaping and rem 3 evenly spaced in between.

Edging
With RS facing join yarn to side seam on lower edge.
1st round Work a round of dc into outer edge of work, ss to first dc.

Buttonhole round Work 1dc into each dc to end, working 2dc into each dc at corners and working buttonholes at markers as follows: 2ch, miss next 2dc, 1dc into next dc, ss into first dc. Turn.
3rd round Work 1dc into each dc to end, working 2dc into each dc at corners and 2dc into each buttonhole, ss into first dc.
Fasten off.

Armhole borders (both alike)
With RS facing join yarn to side seam.
1st round Work a round of dc into armhole edge, ss into first dc. Turn.
2nd round 1dc into each dc to end, ss into first dc. Fasten off.

Strap
Make 36 [40:44]ch.
Base row 1dc into 2nd ch from hook, 1dc into each ch to end. Turn. 35 [39:43]dc.
Next row 1ch to count as first dc, miss first st, 1dc into each st to end. Turn.
Rep last row twice more. Fasten off.

Buckle strap
Make 22 [26:30]ch.
Work as for Strap.
Sew on buckle.
Sew straps to back approx 6cm from lower edge and 8cm from side seams.
Sew on buttons to correspond with buttonholes.

SPECIAL TECHNIQUE
Alternating rib

1 *The back of the waistcoat has been worked in a form of crochet rib which can also be used to make cuffs and welts. This alternating rib is worked on an odd number of stitches. Work the base row in treble crochet and the next row in double crochet as usual. Begin the next row with two chain and miss the first stitch.*

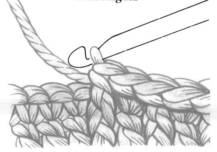

2 *Work a raised treble round the stem of the next treble on the base row, inserting the hook from front to back and from right to left. Miss the next double crochet lying behind the raised treble and work one treble into the next single crochet. Miss the next treble on the base row. Continue in this way to the last stitch, ending with a half treble crochet into the top of the turning chain.*

3 *Begin the next row with one chain to count as the first double crochet and miss the first stitch. Work one double crochet into the next raised treble. Work the next double crochet between the next treble and the next raised treble. Continue in this way, working one double crochet into the top of the turning chain. Work the next row as in step 2, this time working raised treble round the stems of the previous raised treble.*

REVERSIBLE TOP

This reversible waistcoat – fluffy on one side and smooth on the other – is made from two rectangular strips of Tunisian crochet, joined at the centre back and sides. The buttons are sewn to a separate strip.

Back and front (both alike)
Using Tunisian hook and A, make 106 [112] ch.
Base row (RS) 1 Ttr into 4th ch from hook, 1 Ttr into each ch to end. Join in B.
1st row Yrh, draw through first st, *yrh, draw through 2 sts, rep from * to end of row.
2nd row Tdc to end of row, join in A.
3rd row As first row.
4th row 1ch, Ttr to end of row, join in B.
5th row As first row.
Rep first–5th rows 4 [5] times more.
Work first row once more. Fasten off.
Make another piece in the same way.

Right front edging
Using ordinary crochet hook and A, make 15ch, working first ch into last Tst (RS).
Base row Work 1dc into second st from hook, 1dc into each ch and along the long side of the Tunisian crochet rectangle. Turn.
1st row 1ch, miss first st, 1dc into each dc of previous row. Turn.
2nd row (buttonhole row) 1ch, 2dc into 2dc of previous row, * 2ch, 1dc into third dc, 4dc*. Rep from * to * twice more and work 1dc into each dc of previous row to end. Turn.
3rd row 1ch, 1dc into each dc and ch of previous row. Turn.
4th row 1ch, 1dc into each dc of previous row.
Fasten off.

Left front edging
Using ordinary hook and A, make 15ch, working first ch into last Tst (RS) of

Sizes
To fit *81-86 [91-97] cm bust*
Length *51 [54] cm*

Note *Instructions for the larger size are in square brackets []; where there is only one set of figures it applies to both sizes.*

Materials
Approx 400g of a medium-weight mohair in main colour (A)
Approx 100g in a contrasting colour (B)
7.00mm Tunisian crochet hook
6.00mm crochet hook
3 brass or plastic rings, approximately 2.5cm in diameter

Tension
13 sts and 10 rows to 10cm over patt using 7.00mm Tunisian hook

To save time, take time to check tension.

Note *Instructions for working Tunisian double crochet (Tdc) Tunisian treble (Ttr) and Tunisian crochet st (Tst) are on pages 161 and 162.*

lower front corner of left front. Fasten off.

Starting at the centre back of the lower edge of the left front rectangle, work dc along to the centre front and along the 15ch. Turn.

Complete left front edging to match right front edging including the three buttonholes (to make the waistcoat completely reversible).

Fasten off.

To make up

Block the work if necessary.

Armhole edging and side seams

Using ordinary hook and A, work one row of dc along the other long side of the rectangle. Fold rectangle in half. Picking up one dc from each side, work 30 [33] dc through two sts at a time, starting at the opposite end from the fold.

Fasten off.

Join centre back seam from lower edge up to about half-way from shoulder.

Waistband

Using ordinary hook and A, work one dc into every dc of the 15dc on right front edging, picking up the back loop of every dc of previous row. Make the waistband 69 [77] cm long. Join it to left front edging with a row of dc. Sew rest of waistband invisibly to main body.

Buttons

Using B, make three Dorset crosswheel buttons as shown below left.

Button strip

Using ordinary hook and A, make 16ch.
Base row 1dc into second ch from hook, 1dc into each ch to end, 6dc into last ch, dc along other edge to first ch. Fasten off.

Sew buttons to the strip, 6cm apart. To fasten waistcoat, lap right front edge over left and pull buttons through both sets of buttonholes from wrong side.

SPECIAL TECHNIQUES

Dorset crosswheel buttons

1 *Hand-worked buttons, using a traditional technique, are used to fasten the waistcoat. Use a metal curtain ring for the base. Cut a piece of yarn about two metres long; tie it to the top of the ring and work buttonhole stitch all round in a clockwise direction. (Use a blunt-ended needle so as not to split the yarn.) Conceal the loose end of the knot under the first few stitches.*

2 *Turn the outer edge of the buttonhole stitches to the inside of the ring. To make the spokes, take the ring to the top. Carry the thread round from south-east to north-west, then from east to west and so on round the ring. Finish with a cross in the centre as shown to hold the spokes in place.*

3 *Working from the centre with the same thread, backstitch over each spoke as shown. Continue around the spokes, turning the ring counter-clockwise with each stitch. To make a multicoloured wheel, change to another colour, fastening the thread at the back. Continue until the wheel is filled.*

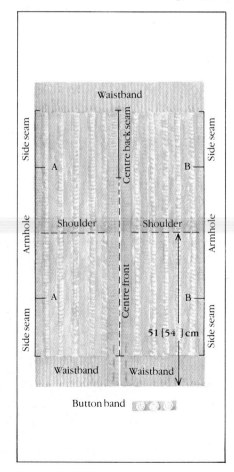

Button band

PUFF STITCH SLIPOVER

Make this attractive slipover in shades to co-ordinate with a favourite skirt or pair of trousers.

Sizes
To fit *81 [86:91:96]cm bust*
Length *53 [56:58:61]cm*

Note *Instructions for larger sizes are in square brackets [ ]; where there is only one set of figures it applies to all sizes.*

Materials
Approx 100 [100:150:150]g of a double knitting yarn in each of two colours (A and B)
Approx 100g in each of two colours (C and D)
4.00mm crochet hook
1 pair 3¾mm knitting needles

Tension
16 sts and 16 rows to 10cm over patt using 4.00mm hook

To save time, take time to check tension.

Back
Using A, make 61 [65:69:73] ch.
1st row 1dc into 2nd ch from hook, 1dc into each ch to end. Turn.
2nd row (RS) 1ch to count as first dc, * 2dc into next st, miss next st, rep from * to last st, 1dc into last st changing to A. Turn.
3rd row 1ch, 1dc into each of next 2 sts, * yrh, insert hook into next st and pull loop through loosely, (yrh, insert hook into same st and pull loop through loosely) twice, yrh and pull through 6 loops on hook, yrh and pull through rem 2 loops – 1 puff st formed –, 1dc into each of next 3 sts, rep from * to last st, 1dc into last st, changing to C. Turn.
4th row 1ch, 1dc into next st, * insert hook into sp between sts on row below next st and pull loop through to height of row being worked, insert hook into next st as usual and pull loop through, yrh and pull through 3 loops on hook – 1 spike st formed –, 1dc into each of next 3 sts, rep from * to last st, 1dc into last st changing to D. Turn.
5th row 1ch, * (1dc, 1tr) into next st, miss next st, rep from * to last st, 1dc into last st changing to A. Turn.
6th row 1ch, 1dc into same place as ch, * miss 1dc, (1dc, 1tr) into next dc, rep from * to last 2 sts, 1dc into each st, changing to B on last st. Turn.
7th row 1ch, * 1dc into next dc, 1 puff st into next tr, rep from * to last st, 1dc into last st, changing to C. Turn.
8th row 1ch, * 1dc into top of puff st, 1 spike st over next dc, rep from * to last st, 1dc into last st, changing to D. Turn.
9th row 1ch, * 2dc into next st, miss next st, rep from * to last st, 1dc into last st, changing to A. Turn.
Rep 2nd-9th rows throughout for stitch and colour patt.

Work straight until 47 [49:51:53] rows have been completed.
Shape armholes
Next row Miss 5 [5:6:6] sts, join new colour with a ss to next st, 1ch, work in patt to last 6 [6:7:7] sts, 1dc into next st. Fasten off.
Next row Join next colour with a ss to 2nd st, 1ch, work in patt to last 2 sts, 1dc into next st, changing colour. Turn.
Next row Work in patt to end. Fasten off.
Rep last 2 rows 2 [3:3:4] times, then work straight until 27 [29:31:33] rows from beg of armhole shaping have been completed.
Shape shoulder
Next row Join new colour with a ss to 6th [7th:7th:7th] st, 1ch, patt to last 6 [7:7:7] sts, 1dc into next st. Fasten off.
Next row Join next colour to 7th [7th:7th:8th] st, 1ch, patt to last 7 [7:7:8] sts, 1dc into next st. Fasten off.

Front
Work as for back to armhole.
Shape neck and armhole
Next row Miss 5 [5:6:6] sts, join next colour with ss to next st, 1ch, work in patt for 24 [26:28:30] sts, changing colour on the last st. Turn.
Next row Work in patt to last 2 sts, 1dc into next st, changing colour. Turn.
Rep last row 4 [6:6:8] more times, then cont keeping armhole edge straight and dec one st as before at neck edge on every 2nd row until 11 [12:12:13] sts rem.
Work straight until 27 [29:31:33] rows from beg of armhole shaping have been completed.
Shape shoulder
Next row Join in new colour to 6th [7th:7th:7th] st, 1ch, work in patt to end. Fasten off.

Return to first row of neck shaping and rejoin yarn with a ss to next st at centre of neck, 1ch, work in patt to last 6 [6:7:7] sts, 1dc into next st. Fasten off. Complete to correspond with first side, reversing all shapings.

To make up

Using knitting needles and A, pick up and K 60 [64:68:72] sts along foundation ch of back. Work in K1, P1 rib for 10 rows. Cast off loosely in rib. Rep for front. Darn in all ends at the back of the work.
Join shoulder and side seams.

Armhole edging

With RS facing, join in A with a ss to seam at underarm. 1ch, work in dc all round armhole, working 1dc into each row end, join with a ss to first ch. Turn.
Next round 1ch, 1dc into each dc all round, join with a ss to first ch. Turn.
Next round Ss into each st to end, join with a ss to first ss. Fasten off. Rep on other armhole.

Neck edging

With RS facing, join in A with a ss to edge of first neck row, work in dc all round neck edge. Turn.
Next row 1ch, leaving last loop of each st on hook work 1dc into each of next 2 sts, yrh and pull through all loops on hook – called dc2tog –, 1dc into each st to last 3 sts, dc2tog, 1dc into last st. Turn. Rep this row twice more.
Next row Ss into each st all round. Fasten off.
Join short seam at point of neck.

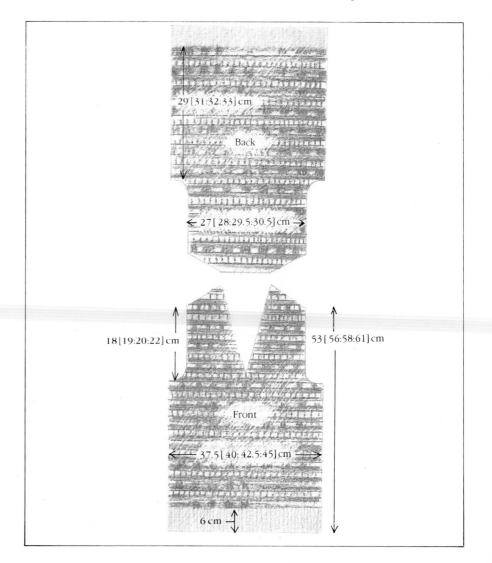

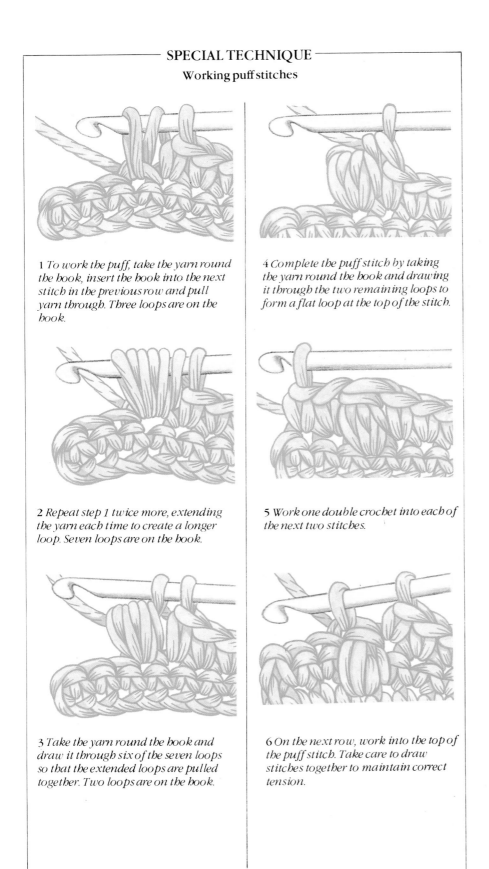

1 *To work the puff, take the yarn round the hook, insert the hook into the next stitch in the previous row and pull yarn through. Three loops are on the hook.*

2 *Repeat step 1 twice more, extending the yarn each time to create a longer loop. Seven loops are on the hook.*

3 *Take the yarn round the hook and draw it through six of the seven loops so that the extended loops are pulled together. Two loops are on the hook.*

4 *Complete the puff stitch by taking the yarn round the hook and drawing it through the two remaining loops to form a flat loop at the top of the stitch.*

5 *Work one double crochet into each of the next two stitches.*

6 *On the next row, work into the top of the puff stitch. Take care to draw stitches together to maintain correct tension.*

PATCHWORK WAISTCOAT

This unusual waistcoat is made of hexagons and half hexagons crocheted together.

Size
To fit 86-91cm bust

Materials
Approx 150g of a double knitting yarn in main colour (A)
Approx 100g in each of two contrasting colours (B and C)
Approx 50g of a medium-weight mohair (D)
4.00mm crochet hook
3 buttons

Tension
Each motif measures 8cm between two opposite sides using 4.00mm hook

To save time, take time to check tension.

Hexagon motifs (make 43)
1st round Using B, make 4ch. Join into a ring with a ss.
2nd round 3ch to count as first tr, work 11tr into ring. Join with a ss to 3rd of first 3ch. 12tr.
3rd round Using C, 3ch to count as first tr, * 3tr into next tr, 1tr into next tr, rep from * 4 more times, 3tr into next tr. Join with a ss to 3rd of first 3ch.
4th round 3ch to count as first tr, * 1tr into next tr, 3tr into next tr (centre tr of 3tr group worked in previous round), 1tr into each of next 2tr, rep from * 4 more times, 1tr into next tr, 3 tr into next tr, 1tr into next tr. Join with a ss to 3rd of first 3ch. Fasten off. To make motif larger, work each round in same way, working two more tr between each 3tr group each time.

Make 42 more motifs in same way, using B, C and D at random for each motif.

Half hexagon motif (make 12)
1st round Using C, make 4ch. Join into a ring with a ss.
2nd round Using C, 3ch to count as first tr, 1tr into st at base of ch, * 1tr into next tr, 3tr into next tr, rep from * once more, 1tr into next tr, 2tr into top of turning ch. Turn.
3rd round Using B, 3ch to count as first tr, 1tr into st at base of ch, *1tr into each of next 3tr, 3tr into next tr, rep from * once more, 1tr into each of next 3tr, 2tr into top of turning ch. Turn.
4th round Using C, 3ch to count as first tr, 1tr into st at base of ch, * 1tr into each of next 5tr, 1tr into next tr, rep

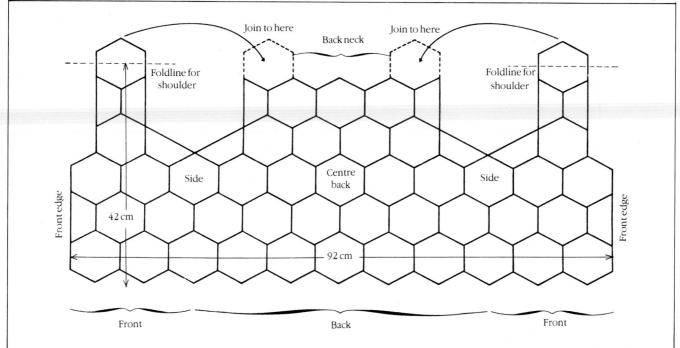

Front   Back   Front

from * once more, 1tr into each of next 5tr, 2tr into top of turning ch. Fasten off.

To make motif larger cont working in same way, working 2 extra tr between 3tr groups and 2tr into st at each end of row.

Make 11 more motifs in same way, using B, C and D at random on each motif.

To make up

Block or press motifs, as appropriate for yarn used. Using A and with RS tog, join motifs and half motifs into horizontal strips with dc as in diagram. Then fold shoulder motifs and join to back as indicated.

Using A and with RS facing, work 5 rows dc round back neck, then down one front and round lower edges, and then up the other front. On every round at lower edge work 3dc into motif points and omit 2dc where motifs join.

Mark positions for 3 buttonholes, spaced evenly, on right front, and make buttonholes on 3rd row of dc as markers are reached by working 2ch, miss next 2tr, cont working in tr until next marker is reached. On the next row work 1tr into each ch worked in previous row to complete buttonholes.

Sew buttons to left front edge to correspond with buttonholes. Work armhole edging in same way, starting at underarm.

SPECIAL TECHNIQUE

Working a half hexagon motif

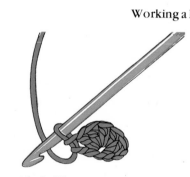

1 The half hexagons used at the armholes of this waistcoat are essentially the same as the whole hexagon motifs, but, of course, use fewer stitches. Make four chain, slip stitch to the first chain to form a ring. Work three chain and six treble into the ring, turn.

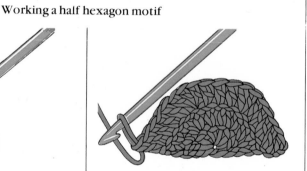

*3 Chain three, work one treble into the stitch at the base of the chain. *One treble into each of the next three treble, three treble into the next treble*. Repeat from * to *. Work one treble into each of the next three treble, two treble into the top of the turning chain, turn.*

*2 Work three chain, work one treble into the stitch at the base of the chain. * Work one treble into the next treble and three treble into the next treble*. Repeat from * to * once. Work one treble into the next treble and two treble into the top of the turning chain, turn.*

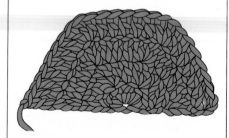

4 Continue to work as for step 3, working 2 extra treble between each group of three treble (or two treble at the ends of the row) until the motif is the required size.

MULTI-TEXTURED JACKET

A subtle blending of yarns and Tunisian crochet stitches give this jacket real fashion flair.

Sizes

To fit *81-86* [*91-96*] *cm bust*
Length 54 [*60*] *cm*
Sleeve seam 48 [*51*] *cm*

Note Instructions for the larger size are in square brackets [ ]*; where there is only one set of figures it applies to both sizes.*

Materials

Approx 200g of chunky-weight yarn (A)
Approx 100g of medium-weight mohair (B)
Approx 150 [*200*] *g of a medium-weight mohair with glitter (C)*
Approx 100 [*150*] *g of light-weight mohair (D)*
Approx 100g of a double knitting yarn (E)
Approx 300 [*350*] *g of a medium-weight mohair (F)*
8.00mm Tunisian crochet hook
7.00mm crochet hook

Tension

12 Ttr to 10cm using 8.00mm Tunisian hook

To save time, take time to check tension

Note: Instructions for working Basic Tunisian crochet stitch (Tst), Tunisian double crochet (Tdc), Tunisian treble (Ttr), Tunisian triple treble (Ttrtr), Tunisian purl (Tp) and Tunisian bobble stitch (Tb) are on pages 161-163.

Note Cut off each colour as it is used and run ends in. The colour is always changed on the left side of the work for the return row.

Back and fronts (Jacket is worked in one piece to armholes)

Using Tunisian hook and A, make 111 [119]ch.

1st row Tdc, work first st into 2nd ch.
2nd row With B, work as for row 2 of Tst – called "return row."
3rd row Ch 3, Ttr into 2nd st, Ttr to end of row.
4th row With C, work return row.
5th row * 1Ttrtr into vertical loop of 2nd row. 1Tdc into 4th row *. Rep from * to * to end.
6th row With D, return row.
7th row Tp.
8th row With E, return row.
9th row Tdc.
10th row With F, return row.
11th row 3ch, Ttr into 2nd st, Ttr to end.
12th row With A, return row.
13th row Into 2nd st 1Tdc, * 1Tp, 1Tdc*.
Repeat from * to * to end of row.
14th row With E, return row.
15th row Working into 2nd loop, 3 [7] Tdc, * 5Tdc, 1Tb*. Repeat from * to * to end of row, finishing with 4 [8]Tdc.
16th row With B, return row.
17th row Ttr into 2nd loop, Ttr to end of row.
18th row With D, return row.
19th row 1Tdc into 2nd loop, 3 [7] Tdc, *yrh 3 times, place hook into loop 2 rows down and 3 sts to right, complete Ttrtr, 1dc, yrh 3 times, hook into loop 2 rows down and 3sts to left, complete Ttrtr, yrh, and pull through 1Ttrtr, 1Tdc, 1Ttrtr, making an inverted V from Tdc, 5Tdc, rep from * to end of row, finishing with 4 [8] Tdc.
20th row With A, return row. Slip last row on to a hook and leave while pockets are worked.

Pockets (make 2)
Using Tunisian hook and B, make 15 [17] ch.
1st row Ttr.
2nd row With C, return row.
3rd row Tdc.
4th row With D, return row.
5th row Tdc.
6th row With E, return row.
7th row Tdc.
8th row With F, return row.
9th row Tdc.
10th row With A, return row.

11th row Tdc.
12th row With E, return row.
13th row Tdc.
14th row With B, return row.
15th row Tdc.
16th row With D, return row.
17th row Tdc.
18th row With A, return row.
19th row Tdc.
Place both pockets on hooks and return to the main garment.
21st row 1Tdc into 2nd st, 11Tdc, ss over 15 [17] Tdc, 57 [61] Tdc, ss over 15 [17] Tdc, 12Tdc.
22nd row Pin pocket linings into place behind 15 [17] ss. With F, work a return row over 11Tdc of garment, 15 [17] Tdc of right pocket, 57 [61] Tdc across back, 15 [17] Tdc of left pocket and finish with 12Tdc to left front.
23rd row Tdc.
24th row With C, return row.
25th row 1 [2] Tdc, *1Tdc, 3ch, 2Tdc* to end of row, finishing with 2Tdc.
26th row With E, return row.
27th row Tp.
28th row With B, return row. 3rd-28th rows form patt. Using either rows 3 to 28 or any preferred combination of colours and rows, cont until work measures 33 [36] cm from beg, ending with a return row.
Divide for back and fronts: 1Tdc into 2nd st, 21 [23] Tdc, ss 8 [9] sts, Tdc 49 [51] sts, ss 8 [9] sts, Tdc 23 [25] sts.

Back yoke

The centre 49 [51] sts form back. Work in sequence already selected for 19 [22] cm. End with 1 row of ss, working from right to left.
Fasten off.

Right front

Work on right front for 10 [12] cm. Ss along 6sts. Cont on rem sts until right front is the same length as back. Work left front to match right front, but leave 6sts at end of row to shape neck instead of ss as on right front. Place right front shoulder against back. With ordinary hook and F, crochet tog with 1 row of sc. Complete left shoulder in the same way.

Sleeves

With Tunisian hook and A, make 28

[32] ch.

Work in patt to match main garment,
starting with row 1. Inc 1 st each side,
every 5cm, until there are 44[52] sts.
Work in chosen sequence until sleeve
measures 46[49] cm. End with a row
of ss. Fasten off.

Pocket edging
With ordinary hook and F, work 2
rows of dc on front edge of pocket. Join
D to left front. Inserting hook into
front loop only of each st, work a row
of crab st (dc worked from left to
right).
4th row With F, work 1 row dc on back
loops of dc of 2nd row. Fasten off. Sew
down each side of facing. Sew pocket
linings in place.

Jacket edging
With RS facing, join F to neck edge.
1st row With ordinary hook and F,
work dc down left front, across bottom
and up right front to neck edge.
Turn.
2nd row Work in dc to neck edge of
left front, inc 2sts at each front corner.
Turn.
3rd row As row 2, but ending at right
neck edge. 2ss on each side of dc.
4th row Work along neck to first row
of dc, making 1tr in each neck curve.

Turn.
5th row 1 row dc. Turn.
Rep 5th row 4 times. Fasten off.
Next row Join D to centre back of
neckband and from left to right work
crab st on front loop of sts along
neckband, and all round jacket,
finishing off at centre back of neck.
Next row Join F to centre back on back
loop of dc, behind crab st, and work all
the way round jacket on back loops of
dc.

Sleeve and armhole edgings
Join F to corner of armhole and work
44[52] dc along straight armhole
edge.
Pin top of sleeve to armhole edge.
Work 1 row of dc, taking hook through
ss on top of sleeve and dc of jacket for
each st.
With F, sew 2 sides of sleeve to lower
edge of armhole. Sew sleeve seams.

Sleeve band
With F, work 2 rows of dc, 1 row of
crab st and 1 row dc to match band on
jacket.

To make up
Lightly press seams, using a dry cloth
on wrong side of garment.

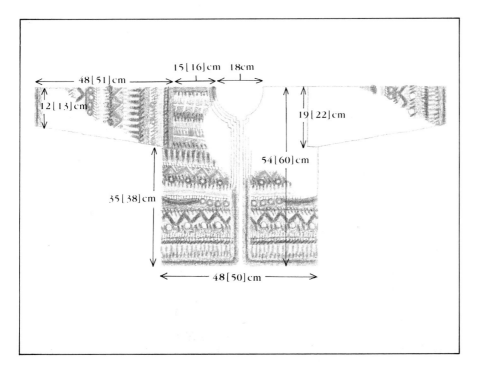

CASUAL PLAID CARDIGAN

This attractive plaid cardigan is made by weaving different colours through a striped filet background.

Sizes
To fit 86 [91:96] cm bust
Length 21 [55:57] cm
Sleeve 45 [47:49] cm

Note *Instructions for larger sizes are in square brackets [ ]; where there is only one set of figures it applies to all sizes.*

Materials
Double knitting yarn:
500 [525:525] g in main colour (A)
250 [275:275] g in contrasting colour (B)
25g in each of contrasting colors (C and D)
4.00mm crochet hook
5.00mm crochet hook
8 buttons
Large wool needle

Tension
10 sps and 10 rows to 10cm over patt using 5.00mm hook

To save time, take time to check tension.

Note: *Weaving tends to shorten the garment pieces. The sleeve and body lengths on diagram indicate measurements before weaving has been worked.*

Back
Using smaller hook and A, make 23ch.
1st row 1dc into 2nd ch from hook, 1dc into each ch to end. Turn. 22 sts.
2nd row 1ch to count as first dc, working into back loop only of each st, work 1dc into each st to end. Turn.
Rep 2nd row 88 [92:96] more times to complete rib.
Beg patt as follows:
Turn rib sideways. Using larger hook, cont working along side edge of rib.
Next row Using A, 4ch to count as first tr and 1ch sp, 1tr into top of 2nd row end, * 1ch, miss 1 row end, 1tr into top of next row end, rep from * to end of rib, working last tr into edge of last row end. 45 [47:49] 1ch sps.
2nd row Using A, 4ch to count as first tr and 1ch sp, 1tr into next tr, * 1ch, 1tr into next tr, rep from * to end of row working last tr into 3rd of first 4 turning ch and joining in C at end of row. Turn.
3rd row Using C, 1ch to count as first dc, *1dc into next 1ch sp, 1dc into next tr, rep from * to end of row, working last dc into 3rd of 4 turning ch and changing to A at end of row. Turn.
4th row Using A, 4ch to count as first tr and 1ch sp, miss next dc, 1tr into next dc, *1ch, miss one dc, 1tr into next dc, rep from * to end of row, working last tr into turning ch. Turn.
5th-16th rows Work as for 2nd row, working in colour sequence of 1 row A, 1 row B, 1 row A, 2 rows B, 1 row A, 2 rows B, 1 row A, 1 row B, 2 rows A.
17th row Using D, as third row.
4th-17th rows These form patt and are rep throughout, noting that C and D are used alternately when dc row is reached.
Cont working in patt and colour sequence until 31 [33:35] rows in all

have been worked from waistband. Fasten off.
Shape armholes
Next row With RS facing, rejoin correct colour in sequence to 9th [11th:11th] st from side edge, patt to last 8 [10:10] sts. Turn and leave rem sts unworked. Cont in patt on rem sts for 22 [23:24] rows. Fasten off.

Right front
Using smaller hook and A, make 23ch. Work 45 [47:49] rows rib as for back waistband.
Beg patt as follows:
Using larger hook and A. Turn rib and work in patt as for back across edge of rib. 22 [23:24] 1ch sps. Cont in patt as for back until 31 [33:35] rows have been worked from waistband.
Shape armholes
Next row Patt to last 8 [10:10] sts. Turn and leave rem sts unworked. Cont in patt on these sts for 14 rows. Fasten off.
Shape neck
Next row With RS facing, rejoin correct colour to 10th [10th:12th] st at front edge, counting each tr and each 1ch sp as one st, patt to end. Cont in patt on rem sts, work 7 [8:9] rows from beg of neck. Fasten off.

Left front
Work as for right front, reversing armhole and neck shaping.

Sleeves
Using smaller hook and A, make 23ch. Work in rib as for back for 45 [49:53] rows.
Beg patt as follows:
Turn rib sideways. Using larger hook, cont working along side edge of rib.
Next row Using A, 4ch to count as first tr and 1ch sp, 1tr into first row end,

SPECIAL TECHNIQUE
Weaving a filet crochet fabric

1 The basic fabric used for the cardigan is a 1 treble, 1 chain mesh. To begin the weaving, cut lengths of yarn equivalent to the length of the background, plus at least 10cm. You can use two or more strands together, depending on the thickness of the yarn.

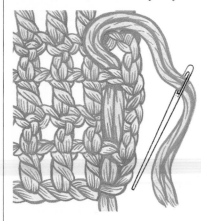

2 Thread the strands on to a large wool needle, making sure that they are exactly the same length. Pull yarn through the middle of the foundation chain, leaving a short end. Take the yarn under the first bar of the background mesh, then weave the strands up the vertical line of spaces, weaving in and out of each space. Do not pull the strands too tightly. If the yarn is too thick for a needle, use a crochet hook to pull the strands through.

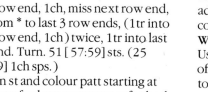

1ch, (1tr into next row end, 1ch) twice, miss next row end, * 1tr into next row end, 1ch, miss next row end, rep from * to last 3 row ends, (1tr into next row end, 1ch) twice, 1tr into last row end. Turn. 51 [57:59] sts. (25 [27:29] 1ch sps.)
Cont in st and colour patt starting at 4th row of colour sequence as for back, using C for first dc stripe and inc one sp at each end of 4th and every following 4th row by working (1tr, 1ch) into first sp at beg of row and last sp at end of row, until there are 83 [87:91] sts. (41 [43:45] 1ch sps.) Cont in patt until 45 [47:49] rows have been worked from cuff.
Fasten off.

Neckband
Using smaller hook and A, make 8ch. Work in rib as for back until strip measures 33 [35:37] cm. Fasten off.

To work the weaving
Weave each piece separately before sewing pieces tog. Work weaving vertically with the yarn used double, working 2 lines of weaving into each ch sp. Measure length of yarn needed for each vertical row, adding 20cm, then cut several lengths at once. When

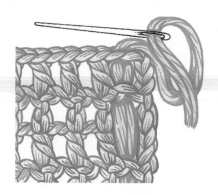

3 To secure the yarn at the top, take it through the centre of the top chain. Leave a short end, as at the bottom.

working weaving, leave a loop of 6cm at edge so that fabric and checks can be adjusted once weaving has been completed.

Weaving sleeves
Using C, start at cuff and centre 1ch sp of sleeve. Weave in and out of 1ch sp to top of sleeve. Work another line of weaving into same 1ch sp. (2 lines of weaving up centre of sleeve.) Cont working out to each side of centre, working 2 lines of weaving into each vertical row of 1ch sps and using colours as follows: 2 lines A, 1 line B, 1 line A, 2 lines B, 1 line A, 1 line B, 2 lines A, 1 line D, cont weaving to side of sleeve on each side of centre stripe in this way, noting that you should alternate C and D when they occur in weaving as in crochet stripe patt.

Weaving back and fronts
Join shoulder seams. Beg at centre sp at centre of back and using C double work 2 lines weaving from rib to top of back. Using yarn double throughout and working 2 lines of weaving up each vertical row of 1ch sps, work weaving in colour sequence as given for sleeve, working from centre back to each side and working back and fronts tog by taking weaving across shoulder seam and down fronts to waistband.

4 On the next row, alternate the weaving so that the yarn is taken over the first bar of the background fabric. Work the lines of weaving alternately across the mesh fabric until all the spaces have been filled. If necessary, adjust weaving by pulling gently at the top or bottom so that the fabric lies smoothly.

To make up
Block garment to size, then press lightly if appropriate for yarn used. Darn all loose ends to WS. Set in sleeves along straight edge. Join sleeve and side seams, working from cuff, up sleeve, along bodice to waistband. Sew neckband in place.

Button band
Using smaller hook and A, work as for neck edging until strip is long enough to fit from neck to hem, slightly stretched. Sew to left front.

Buttonhole band
Mark positions for 8 buttons on button band, the first 1cm from beg, another 1cm from the top, and the rest evenly spaced between. Work buttonhole band as for button band, making buttonholes as markers are reached as follows:

Next row 1ch, 1dc into back loop of next st, 3ch, miss next 3 sts, 1dc into back loop of each st to end. Turn.

Next row Work in dc, working into back loop of each st and 1dc into each ch made in previous row. Turn.

Sew buttonhole band to right front. Sew on buttons to correspond with buttonholes.

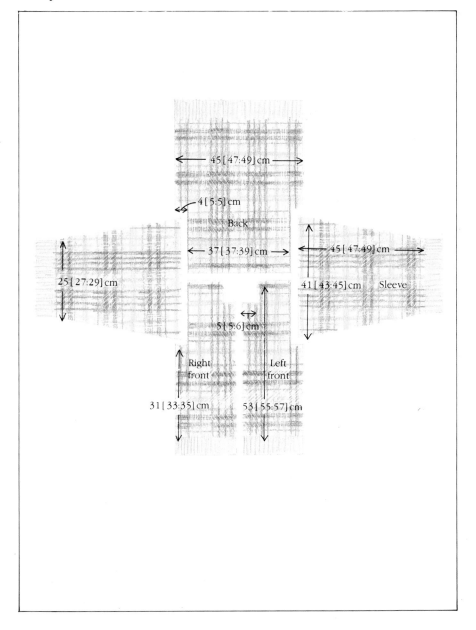

ARAN-STYLE CARDIGAN

Inspired by knitted Aran garments, this crocheted cardigan is a classic style you'll enjoy wearing for years.

Sizes
To fit 96 [107] cm bust
Length 64 [66] cm
Sleeve seam 46cm

Note: *Instructions for the larger size are in square brackets [ ]; where there is only one set of figures it applies to both sizes.*

Materials
Approx 1000 [1100] g of a chunky yarn
6.00mm crochet hook
5.50mm crochet hook
6 buttons

Tension
12 sts and 16 rows to 10cm over patt using 6.00mm hook

To save time, take time to check tension.

Back
Using smaller hook, make 7ch for welt.
1st row 1dc into 3rd ch from hook, 1dc into each ch to end. Turn. 6dc.
2nd row 1ch, * 1dc into horizontal loop below next dc, rep from * to end. Turn.
Rep 2nd row 59 [65] times more. 61 [67] rows. Do not break off yarn.
Change to larger hook, turn and work along long edge of welt: 1ch, 1dc into each row end. Turn. 61 [67] sts.
Next row (WS) 1ch, (1htr into next dc, ss into next dc) 4 [5] times, 1dc into each of next 10dc, 1ss into next dc, (1htr into next dc, ss into next dc) 11 [12] times, 1dc into each of next 10 dc, ss into next dc, (1htr into next dc, ss into next dc) 4 [5] times. Turn.
Next row 2ch, (ss into htr, 1htr into ss) 4 [5] times, 1dc into each of next 10dc, 1htr into next ss, (ss into htr, 1htr into ss) 11 [12] times, 1dc into each of next 10dc, 1htr into next ss, (ss into htr, 1htr into ss) 4 [5] times. Turn.
Next row 1ch, (1htr into ss, ss into htr) 4 [5] times, 1dc into each of next 10dc, 1ss into htr, (1htr into ss, 1ss into htr) 11 [12] times, 1dc into each of next 10dc, 1ss, into htr, (1htr into ss, ss into htr) 4 [5] times. Turn.
Rep last 2 rows until work measures 42cm from beg, ending with a WS row.
Shape armholes
Next row Ss over first 5 sts, 2ch, patt to last 4 sts. Turn.
Keeping patt correct, dec one st at each end of next 3 [4] rows. 47 [51] sts.
Work straight until armholes measure 22 [24] cm, ending with a WS row.
Shape neck and shoulders
Next row Ss over first 6 sts, 1ch, patt over next 10 [11] sts. Turn.

Complete this side first.
Next row Ss over first 3 sts, 1ch, patt over next 3 [4] sts. Turn. 4 [5] sts. Fasten off.
Return to where work was left, miss first 15 [17] sts, using larger hook rejoin yarn into next st, 1ch, patt to last 5 sts. Turn.
Next row Ss over first 6 sts, 1ch, patt to last 2 sts. Turn. 4 [5] sts. Fasten off.

Left front
Using smaller hook, make 7ch for welt and work first 2 rows as for back. 6 sts.
Rep 2nd row 27 [30] times more. 29 [32] rows.
Change to larger hook, turn and work along top of welt as for back. 29 [32] sts. * *.
Next row (WS) 2ch, [1ch, 1htr into next dc], 1ss into next dc, (1htr into next dc, 1ss into next dc) 4 times, 1dc into each of next 10dc, 1ss into next dc, (1htr into next dc, 1ss into next dc) 4 [5] times. Turn.
Cont in patt as set until work measures same as back to underarm, ending at armhole edge.
Shape armhole and front edge
Next row Ss over first 5 sts, 2ch, patt to last st. Turn.
Dec one st at armhole edge on next 3 [4] rows and *at the same time* cont to dec one st at front edge on every 4th row 7 [8] times more. 14 [15] sts.
Work straight until armhole measures same as back to shoulder, ending at armhole edge.
Shape shoulder
Next row Ss over first 6 sts, 1ch, patt to end. Turn.
Next row Patt to last 5 sts. Turn. 4 [5] sts. Fasten off.

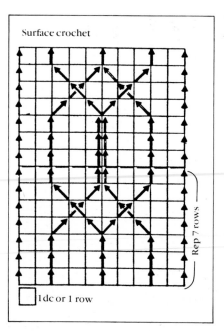

Surface crochet

Rep 7 rows

☐ 1dc or 1 row

Right front

Work as for left front to * *.
Next row (WS) 1ch, (1htr into next dc, 1ss into next dc) 4[5] times, 1dc into each of next 10dc, 1ss into next dc, (1htr into next dc, 1ss into next dc) 4[5] times, 1htr into last st on first size only. Turn.
Complete to match left front, reversing all shaping.

Sleeves

Using smaller hook, make 13ch and work first 2 rows as for back. 12 sts. Rep 2nd row 25[29] more times. 27 [31] rows.
Change to larger hook and work along top edge of cuff as for back inc one st in centre. 28[32] sts.
Next row (WS) 1ch, (1htr into next dc, 1ss into next dc) 4[5] times, 1dc into each of next 10dc, 1ss into next dc, (1htr into next dc, 1ss into next dc) 4[5] times. Turn.
Cont in patt as set, inc one st at each end of 7th and every following 6th row, working extras sts into edge patt, until there are 44[48] sts. Work straight until sleeve measures 46cm, ending with a WS row.
Shape top
Next row Ss over first 5 sts, 2ch, patt to last 4 sts. Turn.
Dec one st at each end of next and following 5[6] alternate rows, then at each end of next 8 rows. 8[10] sts. Fasten off.

Front band

Using smaller hook, make 7ch and work first 2 rows as for back. Rep 2nd row twice more. 6 sts.
5th row (buttonhole row) 1ch, 1dc, 2ch, miss 2dc, 1dc into last 2dc. Turn.
6th row 1ch, 1dc, 2dc into 2ch sp, 1dc into last 2dc. Turn.
Cont in patt, making 5 more buttonholes at intervals of approx 6cm, then cont until band is long enough to reach up front edge, round back neck and down other front. Fasten off.

To make up

Press or block, as appropriate.
Join shoulder seams.
Using smaller hook, work surface slip stitch (see page 19) over each panel of 10dc as shown in diagram.
Join side and sleeve seams. Set in sleeves. Sew on front band. Press seams.
Sew on buttons.

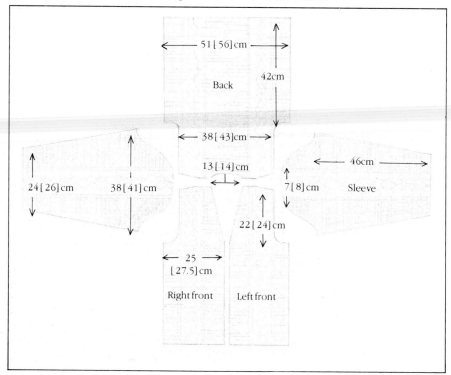

SHAWL-COLLARED JACKET

This stylish edge-to-edge jacket has turn-back cuffs and a shawl collar.

Sizes

To fit *81* [*86:91*]*cm bust*
Length *69* [*71:72*]*cm*
Sleeve seam *(with cuff turned back)43cm*

Note *Instructions for larger sizes are in square brackets [ ]; where there is only one set of figures it applies to all sizes.*

Materials

Approx 1280 [*1360:1440*]*g of a double knitting yarn*
Synthetic wadding for shoulder pads
20cm by 90cm lining fabric for pockets
6.00mm crochet hook
7.00mm crochet hook

Tension

15 sts and 15 rows to 10cm over patt using 7.00mm hook

To save time, take time to check tension.

Back pocket linings

Using smaller hook, make 19 [23:23] ch.
Base row 1dc into 2nd ch from hook, 1dc into each ch to end. Turn. 18 [22:22] sts.
Next row 1ch to count as first dc, miss first st, 1dc into each st to end. Turn.
Rep last row until work measures 12cm from beg. Fasten off and break yarn. Work a 2nd pocket lining in the same way. *Do not break yarn.*

Back

Using larger hook and new ball of yarn, make 73 [77:83] ch.
Base row (WS) 1dc into 2nd ch from hook, 1dc into each ch to end. Turn. 72 [76:82] sts.
Patt row Inserting hook from front to back work 1dc round stem of first 0 [2:2] sts – raised dc formed –, *1dc into each of next 3 sts, 1 raised dc into each of next 3 sts, rep from * to last 0 [2:2] sts, 1dc into each of last 0 [2:2] sts. Turn.
Rep patt row until work measures 20cm, ending with a WS row.
Fasten off and place a marker at the end of last row.
Join in back pocket linings
Next row Using larger hook and yarn left on 2nd pocket lining and beg at first st of 2nd pocket lining, work (1dc into each of first 3 sts, 1 raised dc into each of next 3 sts) 3 times, (1dc into each of next 3 sts, 1 raised dc into next st) 0 [1:1] time, patt across 72 [76:82] sts of back (with RS facing), (1 raised dc into first st of other pocket lining, 1dc into each of next 3 sts) 0 [1:1] time, (1dc into each of next 3 sts, 1 raised dc into each of next 3 sts) 3 times. Turn. 108 [120:126] sts.
Patt one row.
Shape pocket linings
Keeping patt correct, dec one st at each end of next and every following 5 [1:1] alternate row. 96 [116:122] sts.
Dec one st at each end of next 6 [14:14] rows, ending with a RS row. 84 [88:94] sts.
Next row Ss across first 7 sts, patt to last 6 sts. Turn. 72 [76:82] sts.
Place a marker at each end of last row.
Cont in patt until work measures 48cm from beg, ending with a WS row.

Shape armholes
Next row Keeping patt correct, ss across first 4 sts, patt to last 3 sts. Turn. 66 [70:76] sts.
Next row Ss across first 3 sts, patt to last 2 sts. Turn. 62 [66:72] sts.
Dec one st at each end of next 3 [4:5] rows. 56 [58:62] sts.
Work straight in patt until armhole measures 21 [23:24] cm, ending with a WS row.
Shape shoulders
Next 2 rows Ss across first 6 [6:7] sts, patt to last 5 [5:6] sts. Turn.
Next row Ss across first 6 [7:7] sts, patt to last 5 [6:6] sts. 26 sts. Fasten off.

Front pocket linings

Using back pocket linings as a guide and allowing 2cm for turning under on all edges, cut out 2 front pocket linings from lining fabric.

Left front

Using larger hook, make 37 [39:43]ch. Work base row as for back. 36 [38:42] sts.
1st row (RS) 1 raised dc into each of first 0 [2:2] sts, * 1dc into each of next 3 sts, 1 raised dc into each of next 3 sts, rep from * to last 0 [0:4] sts, (1dc into each of next 3 sts, 1 raised dc into last st) 0 [0:1] time. Turn.
2nd row (1dc into first st, 1 raised dc into each of next 3 sts) 0 [0:1] time, * 1dc into each of next 3 sts, 1 raised dc into each of next 3 sts, rep from * to last 0 [2:2] sts, 1dc into last 0 [2:2] sts. Turn.
Last 2 rows form left-front patt. Rep left-front patt until work matches back to first marker, ending with a WS row.
Make pocket extension
Next row 7ch, 1dc into 2nd ch from hook, 1dc into each of next 5ch, patt to end. 42 [44:48] sts.
Cont in left-front patt until work matches back to 2nd marker, ending with a RS row.
Next row Patt to last 6 sts. Turn. 36 [38:42] sts.
Cont in left-front patt until 10 rows less than on back have been worked to beg of armhole shaping, ending with a WS row.
Shape collar
Keeping patt correct, inc one st at front

edge on next and every following 4 alternate rows. 41 [43:47] sts.
Patt one row.

Shape armhole
Next row Ss across first 4 sts, patt to last st, inc 1 into last st. Turn.
Next row Patt to last 2 sts. Turn. 37 [39:43] sts.
Keeping patt correct, dec one st at armhole edge on next 3 [4:5] rows and *at the same time* cont to shape collar by inc one st at front edge on every following 4th row from last inc 4 [4:5] times. 38 [39:43] sts.
Patt 5 rows.
Inc one st at front edge on next and following 6th row. 40 [41:45] sts.
Work straight in left-front patt until work matches back to beg of shoulder shaping, ending with a WS row.

Shape shoulder
Next row Ss across first 6 [6:7] sts, patt to end. 35 [35:39] sts.
Next row Patt to last 5 [5:6] sts. Turn. 30 [29:33] sts.
Next row Ss across first 7 sts, patt to end. 24 [25:27] sts.

Collar extension
Work 14 rows more in left-front patt.
Fasten off.

Right front
Using larger hook, make 6ch for pocket extension.
Fasten off.
Using larger hook, make 37 [39:43] ch. Work base row as for back. 36 [38:42] sts.
1st row (RS) (1 raised dc into first st, 1dc into each of next 3 sts) 0 [0:1] time, * 1 raised dc into each of next 3 sts, 1dc into each of next 3 sts, rep from * to last 0 [2:2] sts, 1 raised dc into each of last 0 [2:2] sts. Turn.
2nd row 1dc into first 0 [2:2] sts, * 1 raised dc into each of next 3 sts, 1dc into each of next 3 sts, rep from * to last 0 [0:4] sts, (1 raised dc into each of next 3 sts, 1dc into last st) 0 [0:1] time. Turn.
Last 2 rows form right-front patt. Rep right-front patt until work matches back to first marker, ending with a WS row.

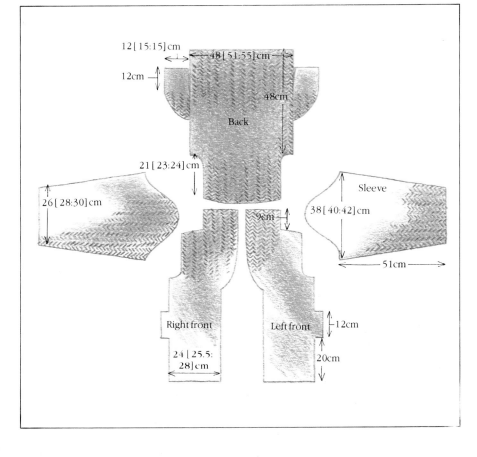

SPECIAL TECHNIQUE
Raised chevron pattern

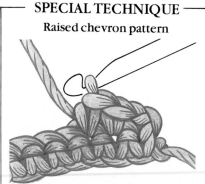

1 *The reversible pattern on the jacket shown here is formed by working round the stems of groups of double crochet. Begin with a base row of double crochet. If working the first size of the jacket, begin the next row with one double crochet worked into each of the first three stitches, beginning with one chain. (The number of stitches to be worked for larger sizes is specified in the pattern.)*

2 *Insert the hook from front to back and from right to left round the stem of the next stitch and work one double crochet. Repeat twice more to form a ridge of raised double crochet on the back of the work. On following rows work raised double crochet of the last row and vice versa.*

3 *When a row begins with raised double crochet, do not work a turning chain to count as the first stitch as usual; instead work a raised double crochet round the stem of the first stitch. When a row begins with double crochet, work one chain to count as the first stitch.*

Make pocket extension
Next row Patt to end, keeping patt correct work across 6ch formed at beg. Turn. 42 [44:48] sts.
Cont in patt and complete as for left front, reversing all shaping.

Sleeves (both alike)
Using larger hook, make 41 [43:47] ch and work base row (WS) as for back. 40 [42:46] sts.
Patt row 1 raised dc into first 2 [0:2] sts, * 1dc into each of next 3 sts, 1 raised dc into each of next 3 sts, rep from * to last 2 [0:2] sts, 1dc into each of last 2 [0:2] sts. Turn.
Rep patt row until work measures 14cm, ending with a WS row.
Shape sleeve
Keeping patt correct, inc one st at each end of next and every following 6th row until there are 58 [60:64] sts.
Work straight in patt until work measures 51cm from beg, ending with a WS row.
Shape top
Next row Ss across first 4 sts, patt to last 3 sts. Turn. 52 [54:58] sts.
Next row Ss across first 3 sts, patt to last 2 sts. Turn. 48 [50:54] sts.
Keeping patt correct, dec one st at each end of next and every following 7 [8:8] alternate rows. 32 [32:36] sts.
Keeping patt correct, dec one st at each end of next 6 [6:8] rows. 20 sts.
Next 2 rows Ss across first 4 sts, patt to last 3 sts. Turn.
Fasten off.

Shoulder pads (make 4)
Using smaller hook, make 31ch and work base row as for back pocket linings. 30 sts.
Work 3 rows in dc.
Shape top
Next row 1ch, miss first 2 sts, 1dc into each st to last 2 sts, miss next st, 1dc into last st. Turn. 28 sts.
Next row Work in dc.

Rep last 2 rows twice more. 24 sts.
Next row Ss across first 3 sts, work in dc to last 2 sts. Turn. 20 sts.
Next 3 rows As last row. 8 sts. Fasten off.

To finish
Do not press.
Using a zigzag machine st, or overcasting, finish edges of front pocket linings.
With WS facing, sew front pocket linings to front pocket extensions at side edges.
Join shoulder and sleeve seams.
Join side seams, leaving seams open between markers.
Join front and back pocket linings.
Set in sleeves.
Join collar extensions neatly at centre back and sew in place round neck.
Outer edging
With RS facing and using smaller hook, beg at beg of collar shaping on right front and work a row of dc and then a row of crab st (dc worked from left to right) round front and lower edges of jacket to beg of collar shaping on left front. Fasten off.
With WS facing (i.e. RS of collar), beg at start of collar shaping on right front and work a row each of dc and crab st along edge of collar to beg of shaping on left front. Fasten off.
Sleeve edging
With WS facing, work a row each of dc and crab st along lower edge of sleeves. Fasten off.
Press seams very lightly.
Shoulder pads (make 2)
Join 2 sections of shoulder pads, leaving one straight edge open. Insert wadding, grading thickness from a thin layer at the shaped edge to a thicker layer at flat edge.
Close open edge.
Sew shoulder pads in place.
Fold 8cm of sleeves to RS and catch loosely in place at sleeve seam.

AUTUMN STRIPES

Four shades of brown have been used for this warm jacket, perfect for a cool autumn day.

Sizes

To fit *81-86 [91-96] cm bust*
Length *74 [76] cm*
Sleeve seam *40 [42] cm*

Note *Instructions for the larger size are in square brackets [ ]; where there is only one set of figures it applies to both sizes.*

Materials

Approx 550 [650] g of a chunky yarn in main colour (A — cinnamon)
Approx 200 [250] g in contrasting colour (B — old gold)
Approx 150g in contrasting colour (C — pale gold)
Approx 150 [200] g in contrasting colour (D — cocoa brown)
5.50mm crochet hook
7.00mm crochet hook

Tension

18 sts and 16 rows to 15cm over moss st patt using 5.50mm hook

To save time, take time to check tension.

Back

Using smaller hook and A, make 55 [63] ch.
Base row (RS) Using A, 1dc into 2nd ch from hook, 1dc into each ch to end. Turn. 54 [62] sts.
1st row Using A, 1ch to count as first dc, miss first st, 1dc into each st to end.
2nd and 3rd rows Using A, as first row.
4th row Using B, 1ch to count as first dc, miss first st, 1dc into next st, insert hook into next st 2 rows below, yrh and draw through a long loop, insert hook into same st of working row, yrh and draw through first loop on hook, yrh and draw through rem 2 loops on hook – spike st formed –, * 1dc into each of next 3 sts, spike st into next st, rep from * to last 3 sts, 1dc into each of last 3 sts. Turn.
5th row Using D, 1ch to count as first dc, miss first st, 1dc into each of next 2 sts, (insert hook into next st, yrh and draw through a loop, yrh) 3 times, draw through first 5 loops on hook, yrh and draw through rem 2 loops on hook – bobble formed –, *1dc into each of next 3 sts, bobble into next st, rep from * to last 2 sts, 1dc into each of last 2 sts. Turn.
6th row Using B, 1ch to count as first dc, miss first st, * 1dc into each of next 3 sts, spike st into next st, rep from * to last st, 1dc into last st. Turn.
7th row Using D, 1ch to count as first dc, miss first st, * bobble into next st, 1dc into each of next 3 sts, rep from * to last st, 1dc into last st. Turn.
8th-10th rows Rep 4th-6th rows once more.
11th row Using A, ch 2, miss first st, * 1dc into next st, 1tr into next st, rep from * to last st, 1dc into last st. Turn. Last row forms moss st patt.
12th-16th rows Using A, work in moss st patt.
17th row Using C, work in moss st patt.
18th, 20th, 22nd, 24th rows Using A, work in moss st patt.
19th row Using B, work in moss st patt.
21st row Using D, work in moss st patt.
23rd row Using B, work in moss st patt.
25th row Using C, work in moss st patt.
26th-32nd rows Using A, work in moss st patt.
Rep 17th-32nd rows once more, then rep 17th-27th rows once more.

Shape armholes

60th row Using A, ss across first 5 [7] sts, 1ch to count as first st, miss ss at base of first ch, patt to last 4 [6] sts. Turn. 46 [50] sts.
61st-64th rows Using A, work in moss st patt.
65th-73rd rows Work as for 17th-25th rows.
74th row Using A, work in moss st patt.
2nd size only
Using A, work 2 rows in moss st patt.
All sizes
75th [77th] row Using A, 1ch to count as first dc, miss first st, 1dc into each st to end. Turn.
76th [78th] row Using B, 1ch to count as first dc, miss first st, 1dc into each st to end. Turn.
77th [79th] row Using D, 1ch to count as first dc, miss first st, * bobble into next st, 1dc into each of next 3 sts, rep from * to last st, 1dc into last st. Turn.
78th [80th] row Using B, 1ch to count as first dc, miss first st, 1dc into next st, * spike st into next st, 1dc into each of next 3 sts, rep from * to end. Turn and fasten off.

Shape shoulders

Miss first 14 [16] sts and rejoin D to next st.
Next row Using D, 1ch to count as first dc, miss first st, 1dc into each of next 0 [2] sts, bobble into next st, * 1dc into each of next 3 sts, bobble into next st, rep from * twice, 1dc into each of next 4 [2] sts. Turn.
Next row Using B, 1ch to count as first dc, miss first st, 1dc into each of next 1 [3] sts, * spike st into next st, 1dc into each of next 3 sts, rep from * twice, spike st into next st, 1dc into each of last 3 [1] sts. Fasten off.

Left front

Using smaller hook and A, make 27 [31] ch. Work base-11th rows as for back. 26 [30] sts.
Make pocket
12th row Using A, work 6 [8] sts in moss st patt, then, working into *back* loop only of each st, patt next 16 sts. Turn. 22 [24] sts.
Keeping stripe sequence correct, cont in moss st patt on these sts only until 30th row has been worked. Fasten off. Return to 12th row and rejoin A to

front loop of 7th [9th] st, working into *front* loop only of each st patt 16 sts, working into both loops of each st patt to end. Turn. 20 [22] sts.

Keeping stripe correct, cont in moss st patt on these sts only for 7 rows more.

20th row Ss across first 2 sts, 1ch to count as first dc, miss first st, work in moss st patt to end. Turn.

21st row Patt to last st, miss last st. Turn.

Keeping stripe sequence correct, cont in moss st patt, dec 1 st at pocket edge on each row until 10 [12] sts rem.

Keeping stripe sequence correct, work straight in moss st patt until 30th row has been worked.

31st row Patt first 4 [6] sts, bring up other part of pocket, patt next 6 sts through both parts of pocket, patt to end. 26 [30] sts.

32nd-59th rows Work as for back.

Shape armhole

60th row Using A, ss across first 5 [7] sts, 1ch to count as first dc, miss ss at

base of 1ch, patt to end. Turn. 22 [24] sts.

61st-72nd rows Work as for back.

Shape neck

73rd row Ss across first 4 sts, 2ch, miss ss at base of 2ch, patt to end.

74th row Patt to last 3 sts. Turn. 16 [18] sts.

75th row Ss across first 3 [3] sts, patt to end. Turn. 14 [16] sts.

Work straight for 3 [5] rows more as for back. Fasten off.

Right front

Work as for left front to pocket.

Make pocket

12th row Using A, patt 4 [6] sts, working into front loop only of each st, patt next 16 sts. Turn.

Keeping stripe sequence correct, cont in moss st patt on these sts only until 19th row has been worked.

20th row Patt to last st, miss last st. Turn.

21st row Ss across first 2 sts, 1ch to

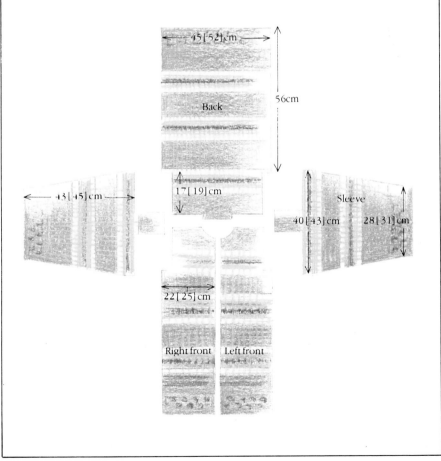
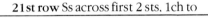

SPECIAL TECHNIQUE
Spiked stitches

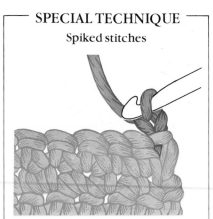

1 *Spiked stitches are used with bobbles to form the patterned bands at the lower edges and shoulders on the jacket. Work a few rows of double crochet. Change to a contrasting colour and work one chain to count as the first double crochet. Miss first stitch.*

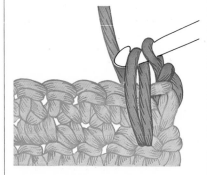

2 *Insert the hook into the next stitch two rows below. Wind the yarn round the hook and draw through a long loop, extending the yarn so that the previous rows do not curl and spoil the work.*

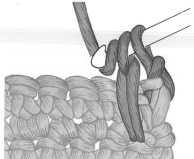

3 *Insert the hook into the same stitch of the current row, wind the yarn round the hook and draw through the first loop on the hook. Wind the yarn round the hook and draw through the remaining two loops to complete the spiked stitch.*

count as first dc, miss first st, work in moss st patt to end. Turn.

Keeping stripe sequence correct, cont in moss st patt, dec 1 st at pocket edge on each row until 10 [12] sts rem. Work straight in moss st patt until 30th row has been worked. Fasten off. Return to 12th row and rejoin A to back loop of 5th [7th] st, working into *back* loop only of each st, patt 16 sts, working into both loops of each st, patt to end. Turn.

Cont in moss st patt on these sts until 30th row has been worked.

31st row Patt first 16 [18] sts, bring up other piece of pocket, patt next 6 sts through both parts of pocket, patt to end.

Turn. 26 [30] sts.

Complete to match left front, reversing all shaping.

Sleeves (both alike)

Using smaller hook and A, make 35 [39] ch.

Base-5th rows Work as for back. 34 [38] sts.

6th row Work as for back, inc 1 st at each end of row. Turn.

Cont as for back, inc 1 st at each end of every following 5th [4th] row until there are 46 [54] sts.

Cont in moss st patt until 43 [45] rows have been worked from beg.

Next row Work as for 75th [77th] row of back.

Next row Work as for 76th [78th] row of back.

Next row Work as for 77th [79th] row of back.

Next row Work as for 78th [80th] row of back. Fasten off and turn.

Sleeve extension

Next row Miss first 19 [23] sts and rejoin D to next st, 1ch to count as first dc, miss first st, 1dc into each of next 3 sts, bobble into next st, 1dc into each of next 3 sts. Turn.

Next row Using B, 1ch to count as first dc, miss first st, spike st into next st, 1dc into each of next 3 sts, spike st into next st, 1dc into each of last 2 sts. Turn.

Next row Using D, 1ch to count as first dc, miss first st, 1dc into next st, bobble into each of next 3 sts, bobble into next st, 1dc into last st. Turn.

Next row Using B, 1ch to count as first dc, miss first st, 1dc into each of 2 sts, spike st into next st, 1dc into each of next 4 sts. Turn.

Work 18 [20] more rows in this way. Fasten off.

To make up

Block or press lightly, as appropriate for yarn used. Join side and sleeve seams, leaving 3cm open at top of sleeve to set into armhole.

Set in the sleeves, then join the shoulder seams.

Sew sides of pockets to fronts on WS.

Front band

Using larger hook and one strand each of A, B, C and D, make a length of ch to fit round neck and down both fronts. Work 2 rows of dc into ch. Fasten off. Sew band to front and neck edges.

Cuffs (both alike)

Using larger hook and one strand each of A, B, C and D, make a length of ch to fit round lower edge of sleeve. Work 1 row of dc into ch. Fasten off. Sew cuffs to lower edges of sleeves.

RED-EDGED BEACH CARDIGAN

This cool filet crochet cardigan is the perfect light cover-up over swimsuit or sun top.

Back

Using A, make 122 [130:138:146:154] ch.
Base row 1tr into 6th ch from hook * 1ch, miss 1ch, 1tr into next ch, rep from * to end. Turn. 119 [127:135:143:151] sts.
1st row 4ch to count as first tr and 1ch sp, 1tr into next tr, *1ch, 1tr into next tr, rep from * to end, working last tr into 4th of first 5ch. Turn.
2nd row As first row, working last tr into 3rd of first 4ch.
2nd row forms patt and is rep throughout.
Cont in patt until work measures 38cm. Mark each end of last row with contrasting thread to denote armholes.
Cont in patt until work measures 59 [60:62:64] cm. Fasten off.

Left front

Using A, make 62 [66:70:74:78] ch.
Work base row as for back. 59 [63:67:71:75] sts.
Cont in patt as for back until front measures 7 [7:8:8:8] cm less than back to shoulder, marking armhole as for back and ending at armhole edge.
Shape neck
Next row Patt to last 16 [18:18:20:22] sts. Turn.
Next row 3ch to count as first tr, miss first tr and 1ch sp, 1tr into next tr, * 1ch, 1tr into next tr, rep from * to end. Turn.
Next row Patt to last 3ch. Turn.
Rep last 2 rows 2 [2:3:3:3] more times. 37 [39:41:43:45] sts.
Work straight until front measures same as back to shoulder. Fasten off.

Right front

Work as for left front, noting that fabric is reversible.

Sleeves

Using A, make 114 [122:130:138:146] ch. Work base row as for back. 111 [119:127:135:143] sts. Cont in patt as for back until work measures 42 [43:43:45:45] cm.
Fasten off.

Neck band

Join shoulder seams. Using knitting needles, A and with RS facing, pick up and K 109 [117:125:137:145] sts round neck, picking up one st from each crochet st and 2 sts from each row end.
1st row (WS) P1, * K1, P1, rep from * to end.
2nd row K1, * P1, K1, rep from * to end.
Work 3 more rows of rib in A, then K 1 row in B, rib 1 row in B, K 1 row in A, then rib 5 rows in A. Alternatively, rib a total of 13 rows in A. Cast off in rib.

Lower edge

Join side seams as far as armhole markers. Using knitting needles, A and with RS facing, pick up and K 153 [167:183:197:213] sts along lower edge, picking up (one st from each of next 2 crochet sts, miss one st), ending with pick up one st from each of last 2 sts. Work in K1, P1 rib as for neckband.

Cuffs

Using knitting needles, A and with RS facing, pick up and K sts round cuff edge of sleeves, picking up every alternate crochet st. Work in K1, P1 rib as for neckband.
Then K 1 row in B, rib 1 row in B, K 1 row in A, rib 5 rows in A. Alternatively,

Sizes

To fit *81 [86:91:96] cm bust*
Length *61 [62:64:65:66] cm*
Sleeve seam *46 [47:47:49:49] cm*

Note: *Instructions for larger sizes are in square brackets [ ]; where there is only one set of figures it applies to all sizes.*

Materials

Approx 1500 [1650:1650:1850:2000] m of a No. 5 crochet cotton in main colour (A)
Small amount of contrasting colour (B)
2.00mm crochet hook
1 pair 2¾ knitting needles
61 [61:61:66:66] cm open-ended zip

Tension

28 sts and 13 rows to 10cm over patt worked on 2.00mm hook

To save time, take time to check tension.

rib a total of 21 rows in A. Cast off in rib.

Front bands
Using knitting needles, A and with RS of right front facing, beg at lower edge of ribbed welt and pick up and K sts up front edge to top of ribbed neckband, picking up one st from each ribbed row end and 3 sts from each crochet row end. Work 3 rows K1, P1 rib. Cast off firmly in rib.

Work along left front edge in same way, beg at top of ribbed neckband.

To make up
Press each piece lightly under a damp cloth with a warm iron, omitting rib. Join sleeve seams. Set in sleeves between markers, with underarm seam at side seam of jacket. Sew zip to front opening from lower edge of ribbed welt to top of neckband. Press seams.

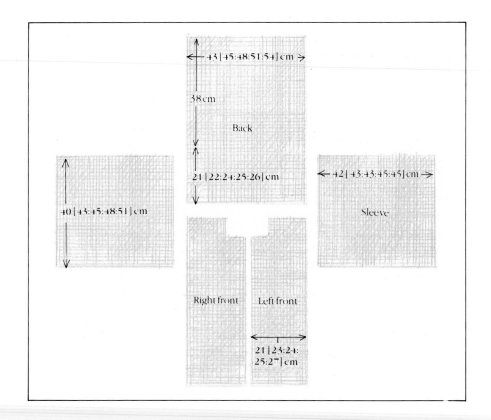

BABY'S JACKET

This simple jacket for a baby is worked all in one piece.

Sizes
To fit *46 [51] cm chest*
Length *22 [23] cm*
Sleeve seam *17 [18] cm*

Note *Instructions for larger size are in square brackets [ ]; where there is only one set of figures it applies to both sizes.*

Materials
Approx 100 [125] g of a 4 ply yarn in main colour (A)
Approx 25g in contrasting colour (B)
3.00mm crochet hook
1 button

Tension
24 tr to 10cm using 3.00mm hook

To save time, take time to check tension.

Back
Beg at lower edge. Using A, make 60 [66] ch.
Base row (RS) 1 tr into 4th ch from hook, 1 tr into each ch to end. Turn. 58 [64] sts.
1st patt row Ch 1, miss 1 tr, 1 sc into each tr to end, working last dc into top of turning ch. Turn.
2nd patt row 3ch, miss 1dc, 1 tr into each dc to end, working last tr into turning ch. Turn.
These 2 rows, with tr rows on RS, form patt. Rep until work measures 13 [14] cm, ending with a dc row. Turn.
Shape sleeves
Using a separate length of A, make 34 [36] ch, fasten off and leave aside until end of next row. Return to main piece.
Next row Work 36 [38] ch, 1 tr into 4th ch from hook, 1 tr into each of next 32 [34] ch, 1 tr into each dc of back, working last tr into turning ch; do not turn but work 1 tr into each of 34 [36] separate ch. 126 [136] sts.
Cont in patt on all sts until work

measures 22 [23] cm at centre, ending with a dc row. Mark both ends of this row (fold line) with a short piece of contrasting yarn.
Divide for fronts
Next row (RS) 3ch, miss 1dc, 1 tr into each of next 50 [54] dc. Turn and work on these sts only for right front and sleeve. 51 [55] sts.
Work 4 rows patt, ending at front edge. Turn.
Shape neck
Next row Ch 12 [13] ch, 1dc into 2nd ch from hook, 1dc into each of next 10 [11] ch, 1dc into each tr to end, working last dc into top of turning ch. Turn. 62 [67] sts.
Work straight in patt until front sleeve matches back sleeve, working same number of rows to marked row and ending with a tr row at front edge. Turn.
Shape sleeve
Next row 1ch, miss 1 tr, 1dc into each tr to last 34 [36] tr. Turn.
Cont in patt on rem 28 [31] sts until right front measures 22 [23] cm from

120

marked shoulder row, ending with tr row. Fasten off.

Return to front dividing row. Miss centre 24 [26] sts, join A to next st, 3ch, do not miss next st, but work 1tr into each dc to end. Turn and cont in patt on these 51 [55] sts for left front and sleeve.

Work 4 rows patt, thus ending at cuff edge. Turn.

Using a separate length of A, make 11 [12] ch. Fasten off and leave aside until end of next row. Return to main piece.

Next row Work in dc to end; do not turn but work 1dc into each of separate ch. Turn. Cont in patt until left sleeve matches right sleeve, ending at cuff edge. Fasten off.

Shape sleeve

With WS facing, miss first 34 [36] sts, join A to next st, 1dc into each st to end. Turn. Cont in patt on rem 28 [31] sts until left front matches right front. Fasten off.

To make up

Join side and sleeve seams. With RS facing, using A and beg at lower edge of right front, work 1 row dc evenly up front edge, round neck and down left front edge, working a multiple of 3 sts plus 1. With RS facing, join B to first st, 1ch, 1dc into each st to end. Turn.

Next row 1ch, (2ch, miss 2dc, 1dc into next dc) to end. Turn. 1ch, (3tr into 2ch sp, 1dc into next dc) to end. Fasten off.

Join A to first cuff st and work 1 row dc round cuff edge and join to first st with a ss, making this round a multiple of 3 sts. Fasten off A and join in B.

Next round 1ch, 1dc into each dc to end, join with a ss to first dc, 1dc, (2ch, miss 2 sts, 1dc into next st) to end, ending with a ss into first st.

Next round 1dc, (3tr into next 2ch sp, 1dc into next dc) to end, joining with a ss as before. Fasten off.

Press or block, as appropriate. Using 2 strands of B tog, work 46cm ch for each cuff. Fasten off. Insert tie through ch sps of cuff borders to tie. Sew button to neck edge; use top 2 ch sp as buttonhole.

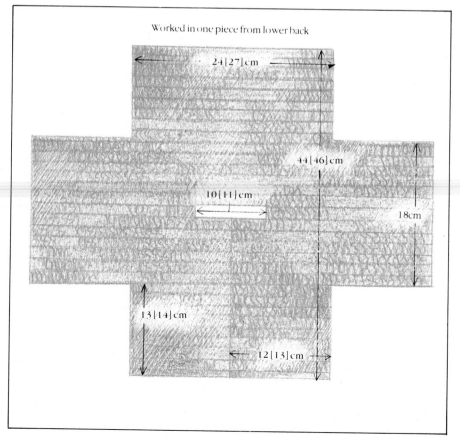

Worked in one piece from lower back

24 [27] cm

44 [46] cm

10 [11] cm

18cm

13 [14] cm

12 [13] cm

BABY'S SWEATER AND BLANKET

A sweater and matching rug, worked in bold navy and white checks, make a smart outfit for a baby.

Sizes

Blanket *76cm long by 65cm wide*
Sweater *To fit 6-9 months (43-45cm chest)*
Length *28cm*
Sleeve seam *20cm*

Materials

4 ply yarn:
Blanket *Approx 300g in main colour (A)*
Approx 300g in contrasting colour (B)
5.50mm crochet hook
Sweater *Approx 100g in main colour (A)*
50g in contrasting colour (B)
4.00mm crochet hook
4.50mm crochet hook
6 buttons

Tension

Blanket *16 sts and 20 rows to 11.5cm over patt using 5.50mm hook*
Sweater *16 sts and 20 rows to 9.5cm over patt using 4.50mm hook*

To save time, take time to check tension.

Note: *When changing colour complete last dc of every WS row with the new colour. Carry colour not in use loosely up side edge of work.*

Blanket

Using 5.50mm hook and A, make 90ch.
Base row (WS) 1dc into 2nd ch from hook, 1dc into each ch to end. Turn. 89dc.
1st row Using B, 1ch, 1dc into first dc, * (yrh, insert hook from front of work, from right to left round stem of next dc and work 1tr – 1tr front worked –, 1dc into next dc) 4 times, 1dc into each of next 8dc, rep from * to end, omitting 8dc at end of last rep. Turn.
2nd row Using B, 1ch, 1dc into first dc, 1dc into each tr and dc to end. Turn.
3rd row Using A, 1ch, 1dc into first dc, * (miss next dc of last row, 1tr front round stem of next tr of row before last, 1dc into next dc of last row) 4 times, 1dc into each of next 8dc, rep from * to end, omitting 8dc at end of last rep. Turn.
4th row Using A, as 2nd row.
5th row Using B, as 3rd row.
6th-10th rows Rep 2nd-5th rows once, then 2nd row again.
11th row Using A, ch 1, 1dc into first dc, 1dc into each of next 8dc, * (miss next dc to last row and work 1tr front round stem of corresponding dc of last A row, 1dc into next dc of last row) 4 times, 1dc into each of next 8dc, rep from * to end. Turn.
12th row Using A, as 2nd row.
13th row Using B, 1ch, 1dc into first dc, 1dc into each of next 8dc, * (miss next dc of last row and work 1tr front round stem of next tr of row before last, 1dc into next dc of last row) 4 times, 1dc into each of next 8dc, rep from * to end. Turn.
14th row As 2nd row.
15th row Using A, as 13th row.
16th-20th rows Rep 12th-15th rows once, then 12th row again.
21st row Using B, 1ch, 1dc into first dc, * (miss next dc of last row, 1tr front round stem of corresponding dc of last B row, 1dc into next dc of last row) 4 times, 1dc into each of next 8dc, rep from * to end, omitting 8dc at end of last rep. Turn.
Rep 2nd-21st rows 5 times, then 2nd-10th rows again. Fasten off.

Edging

1st round With RS facing, join A to corner of long side at end of base row, work dc evenly into row-ends to next corner, 1dc into each st to next corner, work dc evenly into row-ends to next corner.
2nd round Working into other side of foundation ch, work 2dc into first ch, 1dc into each ch to last ch, 2dc into last ch, (2dc into first dc of next side, 1dc into each dc to last dc before corner, 2dc into next dc) 3 times, sl st to first dc. Fasten off.

Sweater
Front

Using 4.00mm hook and A, make 43ch.
Base row 1tr into 4th ch from hook, 1tr into each ch to end. Turn. 41 sts.
1st row (RS) 2ch, miss first tr, (yrh, insert hook from front of work, from right to left round stem of next tr and work 1tr – 1tr front worked –, yrh, insert hook from back of work, from right to left round stem of next tr and work 1tr – 1tr back worked –) to end, working last tr round stem of turning ch. Turn.
2nd row 2ch, miss first tr, (1tr back round stem of next tr, 1tr front round stem of next tr) to end, working last tr round stem of turning ch. Turn.
Rep first and 2nd rows once more, then first row again. Change to 4.50mm hook.
Next row 1ch, 1dc into first st, 1dc into each st to end, working last dc into top of turning ch. Turn**.
Work first-21st rows of blanket, then 2nd-19th rows again. Cont with A only and change to 4.00mm hook.
Buttonhole row 1ch, 1dc into first dc, 1dc into each of next 2dc, (1ch, miss next dc, 1dc into each of next 4dc) twice, 1ch, miss next dc, 1dc into each of next 13dc, (1ch, miss next dc, 1dc into each of next 4dc) twice, 1ch, miss next dc, 1dc into each of last 3dc. Turn.
Next row 1ch, 1dc into first dc, 1dc into each st to end. Fasten off.

Back

Work as for front to **. Cont in patt.
1st row Using B, 1ch, 1dc into first dc, 1dc into each of next 8dc, (1tr front round stem of next dc, 1dc into next dc) 4 times, 1dc into each of next 8dc) twice. Turn.

2nd row As 2nd row of blanket.
3rd row As 15th row of blanket.
4th row As 4th row of blanket.
5th row As 13th row of blanket.
6th-10th rows Rep 2nd-5th rows once, then 2nd row again.
11th row Using A, 1ch, 1dc into first dc, * (miss next dc of last row, 1tr front round stem of corresponding dc of last A row, 1dc into next dc of last row) 4 times, 1dc into each of next 8dc, rep from * twice, omitting 8dc at end of last rep. Turn.
12th row As 4th row of blanket.
13th row As 5th row of blanket.
14th row As 2nd row of blanket.
15th row As 3rd row of blanket.
16th-20th rows Rep 12th-15th rows once, then 12th row again.
21st row Using B, ch 1, 1dc into first dc, 1dc into each of next 8dc, * (miss next dc of last row and work 1tr front round stem of corresponding dc of last B row, 1dc into next dc of last row) 4 times, 1dc into each of next 8dc, rep from * to end. Turn.
Rep 2nd-21st rows once, then 2nd-10th rows again.

Front extensions
Next row Patt across 13 sts. Turn.
Keeping patt correct, work 9 more rows on these 13 sts.
Change to 4.00mm hook and using A, work 2 rows of dc. Fasten off.
2nd side
Next row With RS facing and using 4.50mm hook, miss centre 15 sts for back neck and rejoin A to next st.
Keeping patt correct, work 10 rows on these 13 sts.
Change to 4.00mm hook and using A, work 2 rows of dc.
Fasten off.

Sleeves
Using 4.00mm hook and A, make 25ch. Work as for front to ** on 23 sts. Cont in dc in stripes of 2 rows B and 2 rows A, inc 1dc at each end of 4th row and every following 6th row until there are 31dc. Work straight until sleeve measures 20cm from beg, ending with a 2-row stripe. Fasten off.

Neck edging
1st row With RS of back facing, using 4.00mm hook and A, work 9dc evenly down row-ends of inner edge of first front extension, work 1dc into each dc across back neck and 9dc evenly up row-ends of second front extension. Turn.
2nd row 1ch, 1dc into first dc, 1dc into each of next 7dc, miss next 2dc, 1dc into each of next 13dc, miss next 2dc, 1dc into each of last 8dc. Fasten off.

To make up
With side edges even, lap last 2 rows of front over last 2 rows of front extensions on back. Catch-stitch row-ends neatly at side edges. Sew buttons to front extensions to correspond with buttonholes. With centre of sleeve top even with first row of front extensions, sew in sleeves. Join side and sleeve seams with invisible seams.

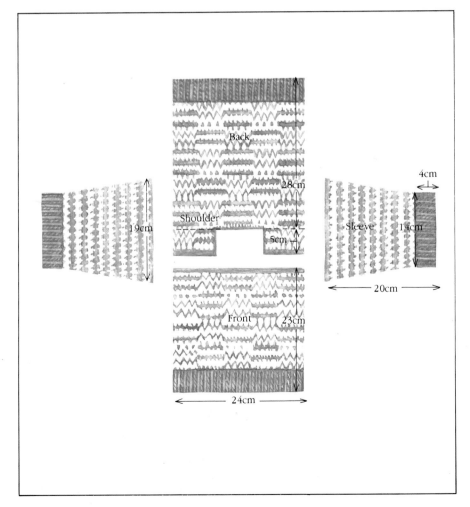

COAT OF MANY COLOURS

Make this brightly-striped, reversible quilted jacket in an assortment of soft or bright colours, using one of the colours for the towelling lining.

Size
To fit *9-12 months*
Length *27.5cm*
Sleeve seam *14.5cm*

Materials
Approx 50g of a double knitting yarn in main colour (A)
25g in each of seven contrasting colours: (B, C, D, E, F, G and H)
3.50mm crochet hook
1.75mm steel hook
1m of stretch towelling
75cm of medium weight washable wadding
Matching sewing thread

Tension
18dc and 22 rows to 10cm using 3.50mm

To save time, take time to check tension.
Note *Jacket is worked sideways in one piece, starting at left cuff.*

1st sleeve (started at cuff)
Using larger hook and A, make 51ch.
1st row 1dc into 2nd ch from hook, 1dc into each ch to end. Turn. 50dc.
Cont working in dc throughout. Work 7 more rows A, changing to B at end of last row. Cont in stripe patt, working 3 rows B, 4 rows C, 1 row D, 7 rows E, 1 row F, 8 rows A, 1 row G.

Shape sleeve
Next row Using G, 1ch, 2dc into first st, dc to last st, 3dc into last st. Turn. (2dc inc at each end of row.) 54dc.
Work 1 row G, changing to H at row end.
Next row Using H, 1ch, 2dc into first st, 1dc into each dc to last st, 3dc into last st. Turn. 58dc.
Fasten off.

Main body
Using D, make 20ch for back, with RS facing, work 1dc into each dc across sleeve, 21ch for left front. Turn.
Next row Using D, 1dc into 2nd ch from hook, 1dc into each of next 19ch, 1dc into each of next 58dc across sleeve, 1dc into each ch to end. Turn. 98dc.
Work 1 more row in D on these sts.
Cont in stripe patt on these sts working 2 rows E, 1 row F, 5 rows A, 8 rows B, 3 rows C, 1 row H and 3 rows C, changing to A at end of last row.
Next row Using A, 1ch, 1dc into each of next 44 sts. Turn and leave next 8sts for neck edge, placing marker at each end to mark neck opening, then leave rem 45 sts for front.

Back
Cont working in stripe patt on rem sts for back, working 5 more rows A, 6 rows D, 2 rows B, 4 rows H, 7 rows E, 1 row F and 2 rows G.

Right front and neck edge
Next row Using G, patt across 45 sts for back, make 54ch for neck edge and right front, placing markers at each end of first 8ch for neck opening. Turn.
Next row Using G, 1dc into 2nd ch from hook, 1dc into next 52ch, 1dc into each dc to end of back. Turn. 98dc.
Work 4 more rows G. Cont in stripe patt on all sts for right front and back, working 8 rows A, 5 rows C, 3 rows D, 1 row F, 3 rows B, 1 row E. Fasten off.

Second sleeve
With RS of body facing, miss first 20 sts, rejoin E to next dc.
Next row Using E, 1ch to count as first dc, 1dc into each of next 57dc. Turn and leave rem 20dc unworked. 58dc.

Shape sleeve
Next row Using E, 1ch, miss next 2sts, 1dc into each dc to last 2dc. Turn and leave rem sts unworked. 54dc.
Work 1 row E without shaping, then work 1 row E dec 2 sts at each end of row as before. 50dc. Cont in stripe patt on these sts working 5 rows G, 4 rows H, 8 rows D, 1 row C, 5 rows F and 8 rows A. Fasten off.

Left front
Using F and with WS facing, rejoin yarn at hem of left front. Work in patt across first 45dc, to neck edge. Turn.
Work one more row F on these sts.
Cont in stripe patt on these 45 sts for left front working 4 rows G, 4 rows E and 4 rows A. Fasten off.

Right front
With RS of front facing, rejoin A to hem of right front and work as for left front, working 3 rows A and 11 rows H.
Fasten off.

To make up

Lay crochet flat, WS down, on WS of towelling. Pin all round without stretching. Cut out towelling leaving 25cm seam allowance all round. Remove pins.

Place crochet on wadding and pin, then cut out wadding in same way again allowing 2.5cm margin.

Place three layers tog with WS of crochet and towelling facing inside and wadding in between them.

Quilting

With RS of crochet facing upwards, pin all three layers tog, working from centre outwards and placing pins parallel to work along edges of stripes. Turn work over and make sure that towelling has not become stretched. Smooth out any creases and pin again if necessary.

Work quilting by machine, using a medium length straight stitch, with thread matching towelling in the bobbin and appropriate colours in the needle. Stitch along stripes, starting and finishing 1cm in from edge each time and keeping work flat without pulling or stretching it. Alternatively, quilt by hand, using short running stitches.

Trim wadding to measure 1cm less than crochet all round. Turn towelling seam allowance inside between batting and crochet; trim off excess fabric to prevent bulk and facilitate working crochet edging. Pin in place.

Edging

Using smaller hook and A, and with towelling side of right front facing, work dc evenly down right front, working through towelling and crochet, 3dc into corner, dc up side and sleeve seam, 3dc into corner, dc round cuff, 3dc into corner, dc across hem, 3dc into corner, cont to work round other side of sleeve and side seam. Cont all round jacket in same way, making sure that dc are not worked too closely tog to prevent uneven, stretched edging. Starting at hem, join side and sleeve seam with 1 row dc. Work other side to match. Steam press lightly.

Ties

Using A and with RS of front facing, rejoin yarn at left front neck edge. Using smaller hook, make 50ch. Turn and work 1dc into 2nd ch from hook, 1dc into each ch to end, join with a ss to left front. Fasten off. Work 2 more ties in same way, spacing them evenly down left front. Work 3 ties to correspond on right front.

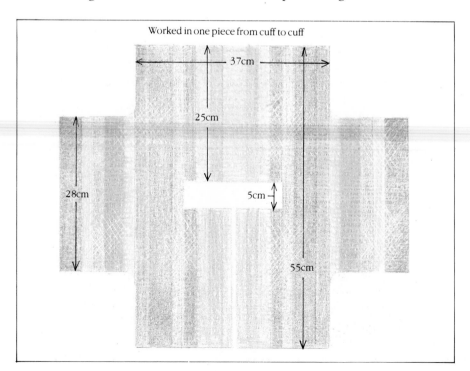

Worked in one piece from cuff to cuff

37cm
25cm
28cm
5cm
55cm

SPECIAL TECHNIQUE

Quilting a crocheted fabric

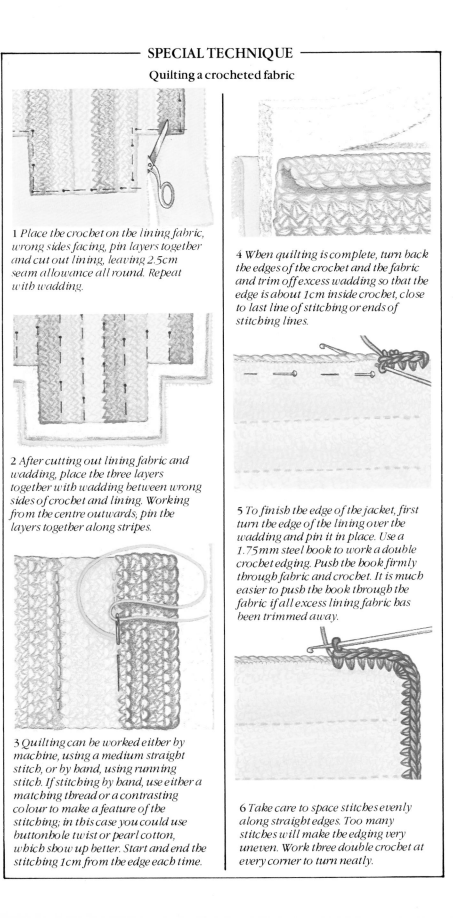

1 *Place the crochet on the lining fabric, wrong sides facing, pin layers together and cut out lining, leaving 2.5cm seam allowance all round. Repeat with wadding.*

2 *After cutting out lining fabric and wadding, place the three layers together with wadding between wrong sides of crochet and lining. Working from the centre outwards, pin the layers together along stripes.*

3 *Quilting can be worked either by machine, using a medium straight stitch, or by hand, using running stitch. If stitching by hand, use either a matching thread or a contrasting colour to make a feature of the stitching; in this case you could use buttonhole twist or pearl cotton, which show up better. Start and end the stitching 1cm from the edge each time.*

4 *When quilting is complete, turn back the edges of the crochet and the fabric and trim off excess wadding so that the edge is about 1cm inside crochet, close to last line of stitching or ends of stitching lines.*

5 *To finish the edge of the jacket, first turn the edge of the lining over the wadding and pin it in place. Use a 1.75mm steel hook to work a double crochet edging. Push the hook firmly through fabric and crochet. It is much easier to push the hook through the fabric if all excess lining fabric has been trimmed away.*

6 *Take care to space stitches evenly along straight edges. Too many stitches will make the edging very uneven. Work three double crochet at every corner to turn neatly.*

BUTTONED-NECK SWEATER

Crocheted buttons provide the finishing touch on this little sweater. They're comfortable for baby and washable, too.

Front

**Using larger hook and A, make 50ch.
Base row 1tr into 4th ch from hook, 1tr into each ch to end. Turn. 48 sts.
1st row 3ch, miss first tr, 1tr into each st to end. Turn.
Break off A. Join in B.
2nd row 3ch, miss first tr, * miss 1tr, 1tr into next tr, 1tr into tr just missed, rep from * to turning ch, 1tr into turning ch. Turn.
Break off B. Join in A.
3rd row As first row.
Break off A. Join in C.
4th row As 2nd row.
Break off C. Join in A.
5th row As first row.
Work 19 more rows in tr. Turn.
Next row 1ch, miss first tr, 1dc into each st to end. Turn.**

Shape neck
Next row 1ch, miss first dc, 1dc into next 14dc. Turn. 15 sts.
Work 2 more rows in dc on these 15 sts. Fasten off.
Miss next 18dc on neck edge and rejoin A to next dc, 1ch, miss first dc, 1dc into next 14 sts. Turn. 15 sts.
Work 2 more rows in dc on these 15 sts. Fasten off.

Back
Work as front from ** to **.

Shape neck
Next row 1ch, miss first dc, 1dc into next 14dc. Turn. 15 sts.
Buttonhole row 1ch, miss first dc, 1dc into next dc, (2ch, miss next 2dc, 1dc into each of next 3dc) twice, 2ch, miss next 2dc, 1dc into last st. Turn.
Next row 1ch, miss first dc, (1dc into each of next 2ch, 1dc into each of next 3dc) twice, 1dc into each of next 2ch, 1dc into each of next 2 sts. Fasten off.
Miss next 18dc on neck edge and rejoin A to next dc, 1ch, miss first dc, 1dc into next 14dc. Turn. 15 sts.
Buttonhole row 3ch, miss first 3dc, (1dc into each of next 3dc, 2ch, miss next 2dc) twice, 1dc into each of last 2 sts.
Next row 1ch, miss first dc, 1dc into next dc, (1dc into each of next 2ch, 1dc into each of next 3dc) twice, 1dc into each of last 3ch. Fasten off.

Sleeves (both alike)
With RS tog and with crossed treble rows corresponding, sew back to front at side seams, beg at lower edge and ending after 14th row. Pin dc rows at shoulder tog with buttonholes on top.
With RS facing, join A to underarm, 3ch, 16tr into row ends to dc rows at shoulder, 3tr into shoulders working through both thicknesses, 16tr into

Size
To fit 3-6 months (40-45cm chest)
Length *21cm*
Sleeve seam *11cm*

Materials
Approx 60g of a 4 ply yarn in main colour (A)
Approx 25g in each of two contrasting colours (B and C)
3.00mm crochet hook
1.50mm crochet hook
70cm of gathered eyelet lace edging

Tension
21tr and 12 rows to 10cm using 3.00mm hook

To save time, take time to check tension.

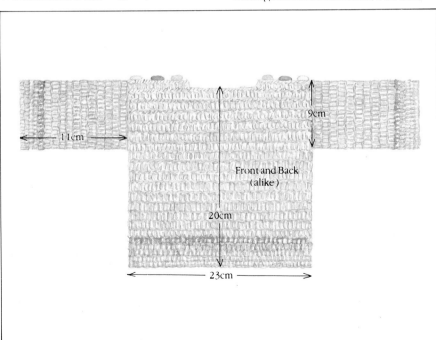

9cm

11cm

Front and Back
(alike)

20cm

23cm

Crossed treble

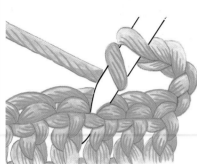

1 *Make three chain to count as the first treble and miss the first stitch. Then miss the next stitch. Take the yarn round the hook and insert the hook into the next stitch. Work the treble in the usual way.*

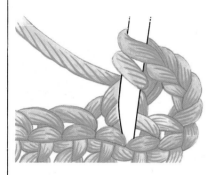

2 *Take the yarn round the hook and, working from the front, insert the hook into the last stitch just missed. Work the treble in the usual way. One pair of treble has now been crossed.*

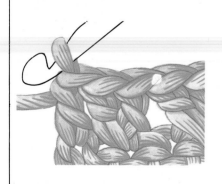

3 *Continue in this way to the turning chain, crossing treble by working into the stitch just missed. At the end of the row, work one treble in the usual way into the top of the turning chain.*

Working an invisible seam

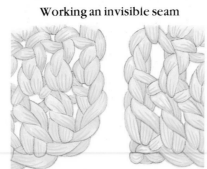

1 *This flat seam is used on the side and sleeve seams of the baby's sweater, since it enables patterns to be matched easily and does not produce a hard ridge. Place the pieces right side up, and edge to edge, matching patterns.*

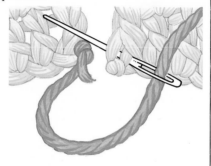

2 *Using a matching yarn (here a contrasting color is shown for clarity) and a tapestry needle, fasten the yarn to one lower edge. Take the needle over to the other side edge and pass it under one stitch.*

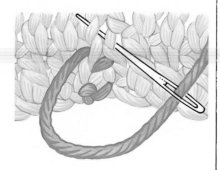

3 *Take the needle back to the first side edge and under the next stitch. Pull the yarn through firmly to make the stitch invisible, but not so tightly that the fabric puckers. Continue catching one stitch on each edge, until the seam is complete.*

row ends to underarm. Turn. 36 sts.
Next row 3ch, miss first tr, 1tr into each st to end. Turn.
Work 8 more rows in tr.
Break off A. Join in C.
Next row As 2nd row of front.
Break off C. Join in A.
Work 1 row in tr.
Break off A. Join in B.
Next row As 2nd row of front.
Break off B. Join in A.
Work 1 row in tr.
Fasten off.

Buttons
Make 2 in A, 2 in B and 2 in C as follows:
Using smaller hook, 3ch, ss to first ch to form a ring.
1st round 2ch, 7htr into ring, join with a ss to first ch.
2nd round Working *from left to right* and into front loops only, 1ch, miss first st, 1dc into each st to end, join with a ss to first ch.
3rd round Working from right to left and into back loops only of first round, ch 1, 1dc into each st to end, join with a sl st to first ch.
4th round 1ch, * dec 1dc over next 2 sts, rep from * to end, join with a ss to first ch. Fasten off.

To make up
Join sleeve seams.
Sew buttons to shoulders to correspond with buttonholes, placing buttons in A at neck edge, buttons in B at shoulder edge and buttons in C in between.
Cut lengths of eyelet lace to fit front and back neck edges and lower edges of sleeves, allowing 1cm extra on each piece. Turn under 5mm at each end of neck pieces and topstitch. Slipstitch lace to underside of neck edge. Join ends of sleeve lace, taking 5mm seam allowance. Slipstitch lace under edges of sleeves.

CLUSTER-STITCH WAISTCOAT

Clusters give a pleasing texture to this attractive little waistcoat. Make it in pretty pastel stripes or all in one colour.

Size
To fit *61cm chest*
Length *34cm*

Materials
Approx 40g of a double knitting yarn in each of five colours (A, B, C, D and E)
4.00mm crochet hook
1 pair 3¾ mm knitting needles
4 buttons

Tension
8 clusters to 10cm and 5 rows to 6cm using 4.00mm hook

To save time, take time to check tension.

Note Change colour while working the last st of each row.

Main part (worked in one piece to armholes)
Using crochet hook and A, make 103ch.
Base row (RS) Leaving last loop of each tr on hook, work 3tr into 3rd ch from hook, yrh and draw through all 4 loops – 1 cluster worked –, * 1ch, miss next ch, 1 cluster into next ch, rep from * to end. Turn. 51 clusters.
Working in stripes of 1 row each B, C, D, C, B, A, D and A, cont in patt.
1st row 2ch, * 1 cluster into next 1ch sp, 1ch, rep from * to end, ending 1htr into top of turning ch. Turn. 50 clusters.
2nd row 2ch, * 1 cluster into next 1ch sp, 1ch, rep from * to end, ending 1 cluster into sp formed by turning ch. Turn. 51 clusters.
Rep first and 2nd rows for patt. Cont in stripes and patt until a total of 12 rows has been worked from beg.
Shape front
Next row 2ch, miss first 1ch sp, * 1 cluster into next 1ch sp, 1ch, rep from * to last 1ch sp, 1 cluster into 1ch sp, 1ch, 1tr into top of turning ch. Turn. 49 clusters.
Rep last row once.
48 clusters.

Shape right front
1st row 2ch, miss first 1ch sp, (1 cluster into next 1ch sp, 1ch) 8 times, 1htr into next 1ch sp, turn. 8 clusters.
2nd row As first row of patt. 8 clusters.
3rd row 2ch, miss first 1ch sp, * 1 cluster into next 1ch sp, 1ch, rep from * to end, 1htr into top of turning ch. Turn. 7 clusters.
4th row As first row of patt. 7 clusters.
5th row As 3rd row. 6 clusters.
6th row As first row of patt. 6 clusters.
7th row As 3rd row. 5 clusters.
8th row As first row of patt. 5 clusters.
9th row As 3rd row. 4 clusters.
10th row As 2nd row of patt. 5 clusters.
11th row As first row of patt. 4 clusters.
12th row As 10th row. Fasten off.
Shape back
1st row With RS facing, miss next three 1ch sps after right front and join A to next 1ch sp, 2ch, (1 cluster into next 1ch sp, 1ch) 21 times, 1tr into next 1ch sp. 21 clusters. Work straight in patt until the same number of rows have been worked as on right front.
Fasten off.
Shape left front
1st row With RS facing, miss next three 1ch sps after back and join A to next 1ch sp, 2ch, (1 cluster into next 1ch sp,

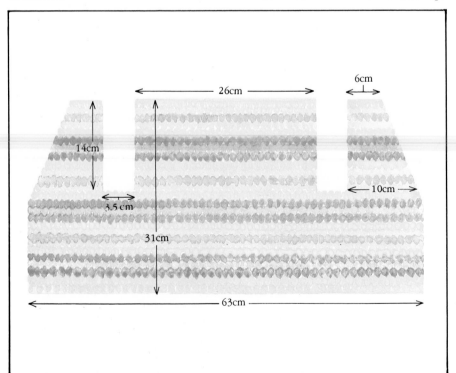

1ch) 8 times, 1htr into top of turning ch. Turn. 8 clusters.
Complete to match right front, reversing shapings.

Welt

With RS facing, using knitting needles and E, pick up and K 103 sts evenly along other side of foundation ch.
Work 3cm in K1, P1 rib, beg RS rows P1.
Cast off in rib.

Armbands

With RS facing, using knitting needles and E, pick up and K 81 sts evenly round armhole.
Rib 4 rows as for welt.
Cast off in rib.
Join shoulder and armband seams.

Front band

1st row With RS facing, using knitting needles and E, pick up and K 201 sts straightly up right front, across back neck and down left front.
2nd row P1, (K1, P1) to end.
3rd row K1, (P1, K1) to end.
4th row Rib 152sts, (cast off 2 sts, rib 12sts including st remaining on needle after cast-off) 3 times, cast off 2 sts, rib to end.
5th row Rib to end, casting on 2sts over those cast off on previous row.
Rib 2 rows.
Cast off in rib.
Sew on buttons.

SPECIAL TECHNIQUE
Cluster fabrics

1 *Clusters are simply formed by working a number of treble together. Make an straight number of chain. Yarn round hook, insert the hook into the fourth chain from the hook, yarn round hook and draw through the first two loops on the hook.*

2 *Working into the same chain, repeat step 1 until there are four loops on the hook, yarn round hook and draw through all four loops — one cluster worked. Work one chain, miss the next chain and work a cluster into the next chain. Continue in this way, working one cluster and one chain alternately.*

3 *Turn, work four turning chain and one cluster into the next one-chain space. Work one chain. Continue in this way to the end of the row, working one cluster into the space formed by the turning chain. To vary the size of the cluster simply work fewer or more treble together.*

PINEAPPLE-STITCH PULLOVER

Diamond-shaped motifs using pineapple stitch decorate the front and sleeves of this V-neck pullover.

Back

Using larger hook, make 57 [59:61:63] ch.

Base row 1dc into 2nd ch from hook, 1dc into each ch to end. Turn. 56 [58:60:62] dc.

Patt row 1ch to count as first dc, miss first st, 1dc into each st to end. Turn. Rep patt row until 44 [46:50:52] rows have been worked.

Shape armholes

Next row Ss across first 6 sts, 1ch to count as first dc, miss ss at base of first ch, patt to last 5 sts. Turn. 46 [48:50:52] sts.

Next row 1ch to count as first dc, miss first st, work next 2dc tog, patt to last 3 sts, work next 2dc tog, 1dc into last st. Turn. 44 [46:48:50] sts.

Next row Patt to end.
Rep last 2 rows 3 times more. 38 [40:42:44] sts.
Work straight in patt until 29 [31:33:35] rows have been worked from beg of armhole shaping.

Shape shoulders

Next row Ss across first 7 [7:7:8] sts, 1ch to count as first dc, miss ss at base of first ch, patt to last 6 [6:6:7] sts. Turn. 26 [28:30:30] sts.

Next row Ss across first 6 [7:8:8] sts, 1ch to count as first dc, miss ss at base of first ch, patt to last 5 [6:7:7] sts. 16 sts. Fasten off.

Front

Work as for back until 28 [30:34:36] rows have been worked.

Beg pineapple band

1st row (RS) Ss into each st to end. Turn.

2nd row 1ch to count as first dc, miss first st, inserting hook into front loop only of each st, work in dc to end. Turn.

3rd and 4th rows Rep last 2 rows once more.

5th row 1ch to count as first dc, miss first st, 1dc into each of next 4 [5:6:7] sts, * 1ch, draw up loop to approx 1cm in (yrh, insert hook into side of last dc, yrh, draw through loop to same height as first loop) 4 times, miss next st, insert hook into next st, yrh and draw through all 9 loops on hook, 1ch – pineapple st or ppst formed –, 1dc into each of next 7 sts, rep from * 5 times more, ending last rep with 4 [5:6:7] dc.

Turn.

6th row 1ch to count as first dc, miss first st, 1dc into each of next 3 [4:5:6] sts, *2dc into top loop of next ppst, 1dc into each of next 7dc, rep from * 5 times more, ending last rep with 5 [6:7:8] dc. Turn.

7th row 1ch to count as first dc, miss first st, 1dc into each of next 3 [4:5:6] sts, * 2ppsts, 1dc into each of next 5 sts, rep from * 5 times more, ending last rep with 3 [4:5:6] dc. Turn.

8th row 1ch to count as first dc, miss first st, 1dc into each of next 2 [3:4:5] sts, * (2dc into top loop of next ppst) twice, 1dc into each of next 5dc, rep from * 5 times more, ending last rep with 2 [3:4:5] dc. Turn.

9th row 1ch to count as first dc, miss first st, 1dc into each of next 2 [3:4:5] dc, * 3ppsts, 1dc into each of next 3 sts, rep from * 5 times more, ending last rep with 2 [3:4:5] dc. Turn.

10th row 1ch to count as first dc, miss first st, 1dc into each of next 1 [2:3:4] sts, * (2dc into top loop of ppst) 3 times, 1dc into each of next 3 sts, rep from * 5 times more, ending last rep with 3 [4:5:6] dc.

Turn.

11th row Work as for 7th row.

12th row Work as for 8th row.

13th row Work as for 5th row.

14th row Work as for 6th row.

15th row Work as for first row.

16th row Work as for 2nd row.

17th row Work as for first row.

18th row Work as for 2nd row.

Shape armhole and neck

Next row Ss across first 6 sts, 1ch to count as first dc, miss first st, patt 22 [23:24:25] sts. Turn. 23 [24:25:26] sts.

Next row 1ch to count as first dc, miss first st, work next 2dc tog, patt to last 3 sts, work next 2dc tog, 1dc into last st. Turn. 21 [22:23:24] sts.

Cont to dec at armhole edge as for back, then work straight while *at the same time* dec 1 st at neck edge on every following 3rd row until 11 [12:13:14] sts rem.

Work straight until 29 [31:33:35] rows have been worked from beg of armhole shaping.

Shape shoulder

Next row Ss across first 7 [7:7:8] sts,

Sizes

To fit [67:70:73] cm chest
Length 40 [42:45:47] cm
Sleeve seam 27 [29:31:36] cm

Note *Instructions for larger sizes are in square brackets [ ]; where there is only one set of figures it applies to all sizes.*

Materials

Approx 200 [200:250:250] g of a double knitting yarn
3.50mm crochet hook
4.00mm crochet hook

Tension

16dc and 20 rows to 10cm using 4.00mm hook

To save time, take time to check tension.

1ch to count as first dc, miss first st at base of ss; patt to end. Turn.
Next row Patt to end. Fasten off.

Sleeves (both alike)
Using larger hook, make 25 [27:29:29]ch.
Base row Work as for back. 24 [26:28:28] sts.
Patt 2 [2:3:3] rows as for back.
Shape sleeve
Next row 1ch to count as first dc, miss first st, 2dc into next st, patt to last 2 sts, 2dc into next st, 1dc into last st. Turn. 26 [28:30:30] sts.
Cont in patt, inc 1 st at each end of every following 4th [4th:5th:5th] row, until there are 40 [42:44:46] sts. Work straight in patt until 32 [36:42:50] rows have been worked.
Beg pineapple band
1st-4th rows Work as for first-4th rows of front pineapple band.
5th row 1ch to count as first dc, miss first st, 1dc into each of next 5 [6:7:8]

dc, * ppst, 1dc into each of next 7 sts, rep from * 3 times, ending last rep with 5 [6:7:8] dc. Turn.
6th row 1ch to count as first dc, miss first st, 1dc into each of next 4 [5:6:7] sts, * 2dc into top loop of next ppst, 1dc into each of next 7 sts, rep from * 3 times, ending last rep with 6 [7:8:9] dc. Turn.
7th row 1ch to count as first dc, miss first st, 1dc into each of next 4 [5:6:7] sts, * 2ppsts, 1dc into each of next 5 sts, rep from * 3 times, ending last rep with 4 [5:6:7] dc. Turn.
8th row 1ch to count as first dc, miss first st, 1dc into each of next 3 [4:5:6] sts, * (2dc into top loop of next ppst) twice, 1dc into each of next 5 sts, rep from * ending last rep with 5 [6:7:8] dc. Turn.
9th row 1ch to count as first dc, miss first st, 1dc into each of next 3 [4:5:6] sts, * 3ppsts, 1dc into each of next 3 sts, rep from * 3 times, ending last rep with 3 [4:5:6] dc. Turn.

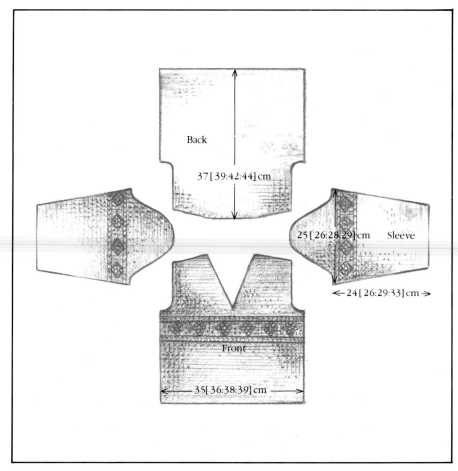

10th row 1ch to count as first dc, miss first st, 1dc into each of next 2 [3:4:5] sts, * (2dc into top loop of next ppst) 3 times, 1dc into each of next 3 sts, rep from * 3 times, ending last rep with 4 [5:6:7]dc. Turn.

11th row Work as for 7th row.

12th row Work as for 8th row.

13th row Work as for 5th row.

14th row Work as for 6th row.

15th–18th rows Work as for 15th–18th rows of front pineapple band.

Shape sleeve top

Next row Ss across first 6 sts, 1ch to count as first dc, miss first ss at base of first ch, patt to last 5 sts. Turn. 30 [32:34:36] sts.

Next row 1ch to count as first dc, miss first st, work next 2dc tog, patt to last 3 sts, work next 2dc tog, 1dc into last st. Turn. 28 [30:32:34] sts.

Next row Patt to end.

Rep last 2 rows until 10 sts rem.

Next row Ss across first 3 sts, 1ch to count as first dc, miss first st, patt to last 2 sts. Fasten off.

To make up

Do not press. If necessary, spray each piece lightly with water and pin out to correct shape to dry. Join shoulder, side and sleeve seams. Set in sleeves.

Neck edging

With RS facing and using smaller hook, join yarn to first row of neck at front,

1ch to count as first dc, miss first st, work in dc evenly round neck edge. Turn.

Next row 1ch to count as first dc, miss first 2 sts, 1dc into each st to last 2 sts, miss next st, 1dc into last st. Turn.

Next row Ss into each st to end. Fasten off. Join seam at V.

Cuffs

With RS facing and using smaller hook, join yarn to sleeve seam.

Next round 3ch to count as first tr, miss first st, work 1tr into each loop of foundation ch, ss to 3rd of first 3ch. 24 [26:28:28] sts.

Next round 3ch to count as first tr, miss first st, * inserting hook from front to back work 1tr round stem of next tr – 1tr front worked –, inserting hook from back to front work 1tr round stem of next tr – 1tr back worked –, rep from * to last st, 1tr front into last st, ss to 3rd of first 3ch.

Rep last round once more.

Fasten off.

Waistband

With RS facing and using larger hook, join yarn to lower edge at a side seam.

Next round 3ch to count as first tr, miss first st, work 1tr into each loop of foundation ch, ss to 3rd of first 3ch. 112 [116:120:124] sts.

Work 5 rounds of tr front and back as for cuff. Fasten off.

SPECIAL TECHNIQUE
Working pineapple stitch

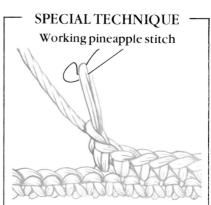

1 *Pineapples are formed from several loops worked together. Those on the pullover shown here are worked on a background of double crochet. Pattern to the position of the first pineapple. Make one chain. Draw the loop on the hook up to a height of approximately 1cm.*

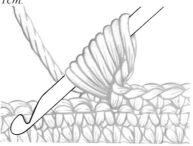

2 *Wind the yarn round the hook and insert the hook into the vertical loop at the side of the previous stitch. Wind the yarn round the hook and draw through a loop to the same height as the long loop in step 1. Repeat this step three times more, keeping the loops fairly high up the shaft and making sure that they are the same height.*

3 *Miss the next stitch and insert the hook into the next stitch. Wind the yarn round the hook and draw through all nine loops on the hook. Work one chain to complete the pineapple. On the following row work two double crochet into the top loop of the pineapple.*

CLASSIC CARDIGANS

Two classic cardigans for children. The girl's version has a crocheted lace collar.

Both cardigans
Back
Using 3.00mm hook, make 11ch.
Base row (RS) 1dc into 2nd ch from hook, 1dc into each ch to end. Turn. 10dc.
Rib row 1ch to count as first dc, miss first st, working into *back* loops only work 1dc into each st to end. Turn.
Rep rib row until there are 35[37:41] ridges on RS of work, ending with an RS row. Fasten off.
With RS facing and using 3.50mm hook, rejoin yarn to first row end on long edge of ribbed band.
Inc row (RS) 3ch, 1tr into base of 3ch, * 1tr into row end of next ridge, 2tr into row end of next ridge, rep from * to end. Turn. 53[56:62] sts.
Pattern row 3ch, miss first st, 1tr into each st to end. Turn.
Rep patt row until work measures 24 [26:28] cm from beg.
Shape armholes
Next row Ss over first 4 sts, 3ch, miss first st, 1tr into each of next 46[49:55] tr. Turn.
47[50:56] sts.
Dec 1 st at each end of next 3 rows. 41[44:50] sts.
Work straight in tr until work measures 37[40:43] cm from beg.
Shape shoulders
Next row Ss over first 3tr, 1dc into each of next 2tr, 1htr into each of next 2tr, 1tr into each of next 27[30:36]tr, 1htr into each of next 2tr, 1dc into each of next 2tr. Turn. 35[38:44] sts.
Next row Ss over first 2dc, 2htr and 2 [3:5]tr, 1dc into each of next 2tr, 1htr into each of next 2tr, 1tr into each of next 15[16:18]tr, 1htr into each of next 2tr, 1dc into each of next 2tr. Fasten off.

Sleeves (both alike)
Using 3.00mm hook, make 11ch and work in rib as for back until there are 14[15:17] ridges on RS of work, ending with RS row. Fasten off.
With RS facing and using 3.50mm hook, rejoin yarn to first row end on long edge of ribbed band.
Inc row 3ch, miss first row end, 2tr into each ridge to end. Turn. 29 [31:35] sts.
Work 3 rows in patt as for back. Inc 1 st at each end of next row. Cont to inc 1 st at each end of every 4th row in this way until there are 37[41:45] sts.
Work straight in tr until work measures 29[33:36] cm from beg.
Shape top
Next row Ss across first 4tr, 3ch, miss first st, 1tr into each of next 30 [34:38]tr. Turn. 31[35:39] sts.
Dec 1 st at each end of next and every following row until 19[23:27] sts rem.
Next row 1ch to count as first ss, miss first tr, 1dc into each of next 2tr, 1htr into each of next 2tr, 1tr into each of next 9[13:17]tr, 1htr into each of next 2tr, 1dc into each of next 2tr, ss into last st. Fasten off.

V-neck cardigan only
Right front
Using 3.00mm hook, make 11ch and work in ribbing as for back until there are 15[17:19] ridges on RS of work, ending with RS row. Fasten off. With RS facing and using 3.00mm hook, rejoin yarn to first row end on long edge of ribbed band.
Work inc row as for back. 23[26:29] sts.
Rep patt row as for back until work measures 24[26:28] cm from beg, ending at front edge.**
Shape armhole and neck
Next row 3ch, miss first st, work next 2tr tog, 1tr into each of next 17 [20:23] tr. Turn.
Dec 1tr at armhole edge on next 3 rows and *at the same time* dec 1tr at neck edge on every following alternate row until 13[14:16] sts rem.
Work straight until work measures same as back from beg. Fasten off.

Left front
Work as for right front, reversing all shaping.
Neckband
Join shoulder seams. Mark position of 4 buttonholes on left front, one at beg of neck shaping, one 2cm from lower edge and two spaced equally between.
With RS facing and using 3.00mm hook, rejoin yarn to first st on ribbed band of right front.
Work one row of dc up right front, across back neck and down left front, working 1dc into each st on ribbed

Sizes
To fit [60:65]cm chest
Length 37[40:43]cm
Sleeve seam 29[33:36]cm

Note *Instructions for larger sizes are in square brackets [ ]; where there is only one set of figures it applies to all sizes.*

Materials
V-neck cardigan *Approx 200 [250:350]g of a double knitting yarn*
4 buttons
Round-neck cardigan *Approx 200 [250:350]g of a double knitting yarn*
6 buttons
3.00mm crochet hook
3.50mm crochet hook
Collar *1 ball of a No. 5 crochet cotton*
1 small button
2.50mm crochet hook

Tension
Cardigans *17dc and 10 rows to 10cm using 3.50mm hook*
Collar *15cm at widest point*

To save time, take time to check tension.

141

bands, 2dc into each row end of fronts and 1dc into each st on back neck. Work 2 more rows in dc.
Buttonhole row (WS) 1ch to count as first dc, miss first st, (work in dc to position of buttonhole, 3ch, miss next 3dc) 4 times, 1dc into each st to end. Turn.
Next row 1ch to count as first dc, miss first st, (work in dc to next 3ch sp, 3dc into next 3ch sp) 4 times, 1dc into each st to end. Turn.
Work 2 more rows in dc. Fasten off.

Note *To make a girl's version of this V-neck cardigan, mark buttonholes on right front and work buttonholes on neckband to correspond.*

Round-neck cardigan only
Right front
Work as for V-neck cardigan to **.
Shape armhole
Next row 3ch, miss first st, 1tr into each of next 19 [22:25]tr. Turn. 20 [23:26] sts.
Dec 1tr at armhole edge on next 3 rows.
Work straight in tr until work measures 33 [36:39] cm from beg, ending at armhole edge.
Next row 3ch, miss first st, 1tr into each of next 14 [15:17]tr. Turn. 15 [16:18] sts.
Dec 1 st at neck edge on next 2 rows. 13 [14:16] sts.
Work straight until work measures same as back to shoulders, ending at neck edge.
Shape shoulder
Next row 3ch, miss first st, 1tr into each of next 5 [6:8]tr, 1htr into each of next 2tr, 1dc into each of next 2tr. Turn.
Next row Ss across first 2dc, 2htr and 2 [3:5]tr, 1htr into each of next 2tr, 1tr into each of last 2 sts. Fasten off.

Left front
Work as for right front, reversing all shaping.

Neckband
Join shoulder seams. With RS facing and using 3.00mm hook, rejoin yarn to first st on right front neck shaping. Work a row of dc up right neck, across back neck and down left neck, working 1dc into top of each tr and 2dc into each tr row end.
Work 4 more rows in dc. Fasten off.

Button band
With RS facing and using 3.00mm hook, rejoin yarn to first dc row end of neckband of left front.
Work a row of dc down left front, working 1dc into each dc row end of neckband, 2dc into each tr row end and 1dc into each st of ribbed band.
Work 6 more rows in dc. Fasten off.

Buttonhole band
Mark positions of 6 buttonholes on right front, one 2cm from top edge, one 2cm from lower edge and 4 equally spaced in between.
With RS facing and using 3.00mm hook, rejoin yarn to first st on ribbed band of right front. Work a row of dc up right front, working 1dc into each st of ribbed band, 2dc into each tr row end and 1dc into each dc row end of neckband. Work 2 more rows in dc.
Buttonhole row (WS) 1ch to count as first dc, miss first st (work in dc to position of buttonhole, 3ch, miss next 3dc) 6 times, 1dc into each st to end. Turn.
Next row 1ch to count as first dc, miss first st, (work in dc to next 3ch sp, 3dc into next 3ch sp) 6 times, 1dc into each st to end. Turn.
Work 2 more rows in dc. Fasten off.

Note *To make a boy's version of this round-neck cardigan, mark buttonholes on left front and reverse position of button and buttonhole bands.*

To make up (both cardigans)
Press or block, according to yarn used. Set in sleeves. Join side and sleeve seams. Sew on buttons to correspond with buttonholes.
Collar
Foundation braid Using 2.50mm hook, make 2ch. Holding ch between finger and thumb of LH work 1dc into 2nd ch from hook. Turn, inserting hook into back of loop work 1dc into foundation loop of 2nd ch, turn, * insert hook into 2 vertical loops on the LH side, yrh and

draw through 2 loops on hook, yrh and draw through rem 2 loops on hook, turn, rep from * until braid measures approx 28cm and has a multiple of 9 loops plus 7 extra on the LH long edge.

1st row (RS) Ss into first loop, 5ch, 1tr into same loop, *ch 4, miss next 2 loops, (1dtr, 4ch, 1dtr) into next loop, 4ch, miss next 2 loops, (1tr, 2ch, 1tr) into next loop, 1ch, miss next 2 loops, (1tr, 2ch, 1tr) into next loop, rep from * omitting 1ch, (1tr, 2ch, 1tr) at end of last rep. Turn.

2nd row 5ch, 1tr into base of 5ch, *5ch, (leaving last loop of each st on hook work 3dtr into next 4ch sp between 2dtr, yrh and draw through all 4 loops on hook – dtr cluster formed –, 3ch) 3 times into next 4ch sp between 2dtr, 1dtr cluster into same sp, 5ch, (1tr, 2ch, 1tr) into next 1ch sp,

rep from * to end. Turn.

3rd row 4ch, tr cluster into next 2ch sp, *miss next 5ch sp, (4ch, leaving last loop of each st on hook work 2dtr into 4th ch from hook, yrh and draw through all 3 loops on hook – small cluster formed –, dtr cluster into next 3ch sp) 3 times, 4ch, small cluster into 4th ch from hook, miss next 5ch sp, dtr cluster into next 2ch sp, rep from * to end. Fasten off.

Button loop With WS facing and using 2.50mm hook rejoin yarn to first loop on top RH loop of braid, 4ch, ss into top of last st on first row, turn, 6dc into 4ch loop, ss into same place as joining. Fasten off.

Pin out collar to correct size and spray lightly with water. Allow to dry naturally. Sew button to braid to correspond with button loop.

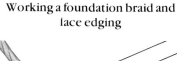

1 The lacy collar shown on the girl's cardigan is worked on a special braid. Detailed instructions for working the braid edging are given with the pattern. Shown here is the hook being inserted into two loops on the left-hand side, ready to draw a new loop through.

2 When calculating how much braid to work, treat it as a foundation chain — work for the length required so that the total number of loops on one edge is a multiple of the pattern repeat plus any loops required for edge stitches. Always begin the first row of the lace by slip stitching into the first loop on the left-hand long edge.

3 Then follow the instructions to work the first row into the loops of the braid. Insert the hook from front to back as usual. Work following rows into the first row. The braid forms a decorative edge which provides a firm base for heavy edgings such as collars.

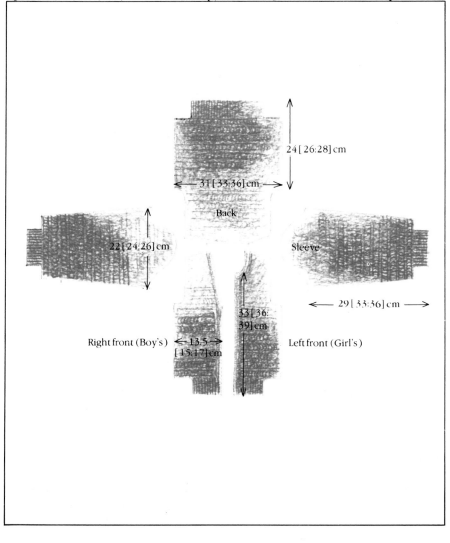

24[26:28]cm

31[33:36]cm

Back

22[24:26]cm

Sleeve

29[33:36]cm

33[36:39]cm

Right front (Boy's) 13.5 [15:17]cm Left front (Girl's)

143

DUFFLE COAT

Surface double crochet and puff stitches form the attractive design on this hooded duffle coat, which can be made for a boy or a girl.

Sizes
To fit 55 [60] cm chest
Length 42 [44] cm
Sleeve seam 22 [24] cm

Note *Instructions for the larger size are in square brackets [ ]; where there is only one set of figures it applies to all sizes.*

Materials
Approx 350 [400] g of a 4 ply yarn in main colour (A)
Approx 50g in contrasting colour (B)
3.00mm crochet hook
4 toggles

Tension
21 sts and 30 rows to 10cm over dc using 3.00mm hook

To save time, take time to check tension.

Back
Using A, make 71 [77] ch.
Base row (RS) 1dc into 2nd ch from hook, 1dc into each ch to end. Turn. 70 [76] sts.
1st row 1ch to count as first dc, miss first st, 1dc into each of next 20 [23] sts, (yrh, insert hook into next st and draw through a loop) 4 times, yrh and draw through first 8 loops on hook, yrh and draw through rem 2 loops on hook – puff st formed –, 1dc into each of next 5 sts, puff st, 1dc into each of next 14 sts, puff st, 1dc into each of next 5 sts, puff st, 1dc into each of next 21 [24] sts. Turn.
2nd row 1ch to count as first dc, miss first st, 1dc into each st to end. Turn.
3rd row 1ch to count as first dc, miss first st, 1dc into each of next 11 [14] sts, puff st, 1dc into each of next 11 sts, puff st, 1dc into each of next 20 sts, puff st, 1dc into each of next 11 sts, puff st, 1dc into each of next 12 [15] sts. Turn.
4th row As 2nd row.
5th row 1ch to count as first dc, miss first st, 1dc into each of next 9 [12] sts, puff st, 1dc into each of next 12 sts, puff st, 1dc into next st, puff st, 1dc into each of next 18 sts, puff st, 1dc into next st, puff st, 1dc into each of next 12 sts, puff st, 1dc into each of next 10 [13] sts. Turn.
6th row As 2nd row.
7th row As 3rd row.
8th row As 2nd row.
9th row As first row.
10th row As 2nd row.
11th row 1ch to count as first dc, miss first st, 1dc into each of next 7 [10] sts, puff st, 1dc into each of next 15 sts, puff st, 1dc into each of next 20dc, puff st, 1dc into each of next 15 sts, puff st, 1dc into each of next 8 [11] sts. Turn.
12th row As 2nd row.
13th row As 5th row.
14th row As 2nd row.
15th row As 11th row.

16th row As 2nd row.
First–16th rows form back patt. Cont in back patt until 115 [121] rows in all have been worked from beg, ending with a RS row.
Shape shoulders
Next row Ss across first 8 sts, 1ch to count as first dc, miss st at base of first ch, patt to last 7 sts. Turn. 56 [62] sts.
Rep last row twice more.
Fasten off.

Right front
Using A, make 43 [46] ch.
Base row (RS) 1dc into 2nd ch from hook, 1dc into each ch to end. Turn. 42 [45] sts.
1st row 1ch to count as first dc, miss first st, 1dc into each of next 20 sts, puff st, 1dc into each of next 5 sts, puff st, 1dc into each of next 14 [17] sts. Turn.
2nd row 1ch to count as first dc, miss first st, 1dc into each st to end. Turn.
3rd row 1ch to count as first dc, miss first st, 1dc into each of next 11 sts, puff st, 1dc into each of next 11 sts, puff st, 1dc into each of next 17 [20] sts. Turn.
4th row As 2nd row.
5th row 1ch to count as first dc, miss first st, 1dc into each of next 9 sts, puff st, 1dc into each of next 12 sts, puff st, 1dc into next st, puff st, 1dc into each of next 16 [19] sts. Turn.
6th row As 2nd row.
7th row As 3rd row.
8th row As 2nd row.
9th row As first row.
10th row As 2nd row.
11th row 1ch to count as first dc, miss first st, 1dc into each of next 7 sts, puff st, 1dc into each of next 15 sts, puff st, 1dc into each of next 17 [20] sts. Turn.
12th row As 2nd row.
13th row As 5th row.
14th row As 2nd row.
15th row As 11th row.
16th row As 2nd row.

First-16th rows form front patt. Cont in front patt until 100 [106] rows in all have been worked from beg, ending with a WS row.

Shape neck

Next row Ss across first 13 sts, 1ch to count as first dc, miss st at base of first ch, patt to end. Turn. 30 [33] sts.

Next row Patt to end. Turn.

Next row Ss across first 4 sts, 1ch to count as first dc, miss st at base of first ch, patt to end. Turn. 27 [30] sts.

Next row Patt to end. Turn.

Next row 1ch to count as first dc, miss first st, work next 2dc tog, patt to end. Turn. 26 [29] sts.

Rep last 2 rows until 115 [121] rows in all have been worked from beg.

Shape shoulder

Next row Ss across first 8 sts, 1ch to count as first dc, miss st at base of first ch, patt to end. Turn.

Next row Patt to last 6 sts, turn. Fasten off.

Left front

Work base row as for right front. Cont as for right front, reversing all shaping *and* reversing all front patt rows as follows:

1st row (WS) 1ch to count as first dc, miss first st, 1dc into each of next 13 [16] sts, puff st, 1dc into each of next 5 sts, puff st, 1dc into each of next 21 sts. Turn.

2nd row 1ch to count as first dc, miss first st, 1dc into each st to end. Turn.

3rd row 1ch to count as first dc, miss first st, 1dc into each of next 16 [19] sts, puff st, 1dc into each of next 11 sts, puff st, 1dc into each of next 12 sts. Turn.

Sleeves (both alike)

Using A, make 57 [61]ch.

Base row (RS) 1dc into 2nd ch from hook, 1dc into each ch to end. Turn. 56 [60] sts.

1st row 1ch to count as first dc, miss first st, 1dc into each of next 13 [15] sts, puff st, 1dc into each of next 5 sts, puff st, 1dc into each of next 14 sts, puff st, 1dc into each of next 5 sts, puff st, 1dc into each of next 14 [16] sts. Turn.

2nd row 1ch to count as first dc, miss first st, 1dc into each st to end. Turn.

3rd row 1ch to count as first dc, miss first st, 1dc into each of next 16 [18] sts, puff st, 1dc into each of next 20 sts, puff st, 1dc into each of 17 [19] sts. Turn.

4th row As 2nd row.

5th row 1ch to count as first dc, miss first st, 1dc into each of next 15 [17] sts, puff st, 1dc into next st, puff st, 1dc into each of next 18 sts, puff st, 1dc into next st, puff st, 1dc into each of next 16 [18] sts. Turn.

6th row As 2nd row.

7th row As 3rd row.

8th row As 2nd row.

First-8th rows form sleeve patt. Cont in sleeve patt until 62 [68] rows in all have been worked. Fasten off.

Hood

Using A, make 33 [37] ch.

Base row (RS) 1dc into 2nd ch from hook, 1dc into each ch to end. Turn. 32 [36] dc.

1st row 1ch to count as first dc, miss first st, 1dc into each of next 17 sts, puff st, 1dc into each of next 5 sts, puff st, 1dc into each of next 7 [11] sts. Turn.

2nd row 1ch to count as first dc, miss first st, 1dc into each st to end. Turn.

3rd row 1ch to count as first dc, miss first st, 1dc into each of next 20 sts, puff st, 1 dc into each of next 8 [12] sts, 2dc into next st, 1dc into last st. Turn. 33 [37] sts.

4th row As 2nd row.

5th row 1ch to count as first dc, miss first st, 1dc into each of next 19 sts, puff st, 1dc into next st, puff st, 1dc into each of next 8 [12] sts, 2dc into next st, 1dc into last st. Turn. 34 [38] sts.

6th row As 2nd row.

7th row As 3rd row. 35 [39] sts.

8th row As 2nd row.

First-8th rows form hood patt. Cont in hood patt, but omit incs (i.e. 2dc into one st at end of every alternate row) when there are 38 [42] sts.

Cont in hood patt without shaping until 66 rows in all have been worked, ending with a WS row.

Shape top

Next row 1ch to count as first dc, miss first st, work next 2dc tog, patt to end. Turn.

Next row 1ch to count as first dc, miss first st, patt to last 3 sts, work next 2dc tog, 1dc into last st. Turn. Rep last 2

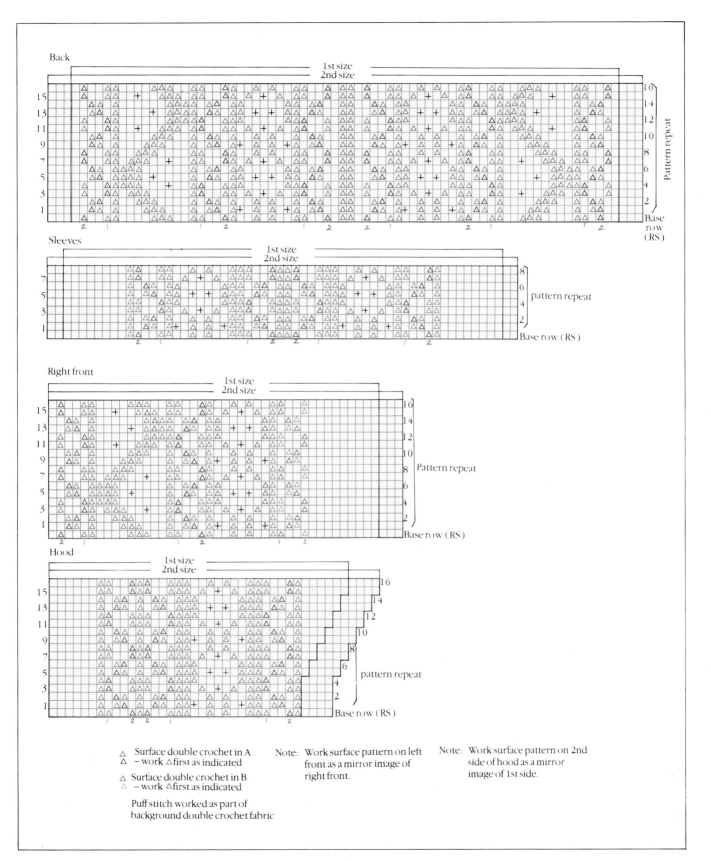

Back

Sleeves

Right front

Hood

△ Surface double crochet in A
△ – work △ first as indicated

△ Surface double crochet in B
△ – work △ first as indicated

Puff stitch worked as part of
background double crochet fabric

Note: Work surface pattern on left
front as a mirror image of
right front.

Note: Work surface pattern on 2nd
side of hood as a mirror
image of 1st side.

147

SPECIAL TECHNIQUES
Crochet frogging

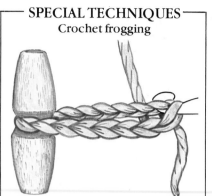

1 Make 16 chain. Fold the chain in half round the toggle so that the toggle lies at the fold. Holding the toggle in your left hand, work a slipstitch into the first chain to form a ring as shown.

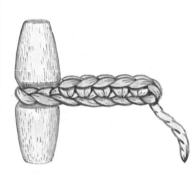

2 Work one chain to count as the first double crochet. Miss the first two chain joined in step 1. Work one double crochet into the next chain and into the next corresponding chain on the other side of the ring. Continue in this way until the toggle is held tightly. Fasten off.

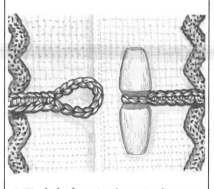

3 Work the frogging loops in the same way until the toggle slips easily through the loop. When all the toggle and loop frogging has been completed, sew them as required to the fronts of the coat.

rows once more. 34 [38] sts.

Next row Ss across first 4 sts, 1ch to count as first dc, miss st at base of first ch, patt to end. Turn. 31 [35] sts.

Next row 1ch to count as first dc, miss first st, patt to last 3 sts, turn. 28 [32] sts.

Rep last 2 rows once more. 22 [26] sts.

Next row Ss across first 4 sts, 1ch to count as first dc, miss st at base of first ch, patt to end. Turn. Fasten off. Work 2nd side of Hood to match first, reversing all shaping and reversing all hood patt rows as follows:

1st row (WS) 1ch to count as first dc, miss first st, 1dc into each of next 6 [10] sts, puff st, 1dc into each of next 5 sts, puff st, 1dc into each of next 18 sts.

2nd row 1ch to count as first dc, miss first st, 1dc into each st to end. Turn.

3rd row 1ch to count as first dc, miss first st, 2dc into next st, 1dc into each of next 8 [12] sts, puff st, 1dc into each of next 21 sts. Turn. 33 [37] sts.

To make up

Following charts on page 147 and using A or B as directed, work surface dc on back, fronts, sleeves and hood, beg at lower edge and rep patt to top edge of background fabric.

Join shoulder and sleeve seams.
Set in sleeves.
Join side seams.
Sew halves of hood tog and sew in place on neck edge.

Toggle frogging (make 4)
Using B, make 16 ch, fold in half round toggle, ss into first ch to form a ring.
Next row 1ch to count as first dc, miss first 2 joined ch, * 1dc into each of next corresponding 2ch on each side of toggle, rep from * to toggle so that it is firmly held.
Fasten off.

Frogging loops (make 4)
Work as for fastenings, leaving loop large enough to slip over toggle. Sew toggle frogging in place on left front (for girl) or right front (for a boy), the first 2cm from neck edge, the 4th 12 [13] cm from lower edge and the rem 2 evenly spaced in between.
Sew frogging loops to other front edge to correspond with toggles.

Edging
With RS facing, using A, work a row of dc round outer edge of coat, beg and ending at a side seam.
Work a row of dc round cuff edge in the same way.
Press seams very lightly.

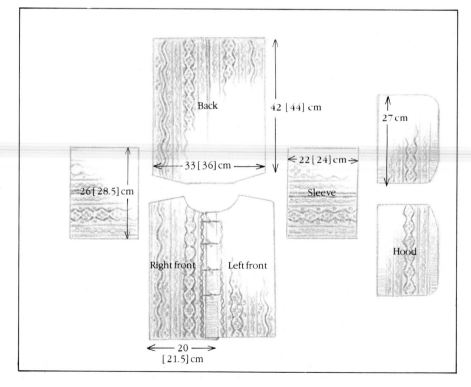

HOODED COAT

Patch pockets, frog fastenings and crab stitch edging give extra style to this comfortable coat.

Sizes

To fit 66 [71:76:81] cm chest
Length 63 [66:73:79] cm
Sleeve seam 25 [28:33:41] cm

Note *Instructions for larger sizes are in square brackets []; where there is only one set of figures it applies to all sizes.*

Materials

Approx 850 [900:100:1100] g of a double knitting yarn
4.50mm crochet hook
5.00mm crochet hook
6 toggles
3 press fasteners (optional)

Tension

16 dc and 16 rows to 10cm using 5.00mm hook

To save time, take time to check tension.

SPECIAL TECHNIQUE
Single chain braid

1 *The fastenings on the child's hooded coat are made of this simple braid. Begin with a length of chain. Turn and work a double crochet into each chain to make the braid. Make sure that you work each stitch into the lower loop of the base chain to make a firm edge. Fasten off yarn at the ends and sew them to the wrong side.*

2 *Sew the braid to the garment using a finer, matching thread if a thick yarn has been used for the braid. To make a toggle fastening, join in the ends of the single braid to form a ring. Bend the ring into the shape shown, then sew the edges together using sewing thread and slipstitch, from the wrong side.*

Back skirt

Using larger hook, make 84 [88:92:96] ch.
1st row 1dc into 2nd ch from hook, 1dc into each ch to end. Turn.
2nd row 1ch, 1dc into each dc to end. Turn. 83 [87:91:95] sts.
The 2nd row forms patt, rep until work measures 12 [14:20:25] cm.
Next row 1ch, 1dc into each of first 3dc, * (insert hook into next dc and draw through loop) twice, yrh and draw through all loops on hook – dec made – 1dc into each of next 6dc, dec over next 2dc*, 1dc into each st to last 13dc, rep from * to *, 1dc into each of last 3sts. Turn. 79 [83:87:91] dc.
Work straight for 7 rows.
Rep last 8 rows 5 times more. 59 [63:67:71] sts.
Work straight until back measures 48 [50:56:61] cm. Fasten off.

Left front skirt

Using larger hook, make 45 [47:49:51] ch. Work first and 2nd rows as for back. 44 [46:48:50] dc.
Work straight until work measures 12 [14:20:25] cm.
Next row 1ch, 1dc into each of first 3dc, work from * to * as for back, 1dc into each dc to end. Turn.
Work straight for 7 rows. Rep last 8 rows 5 times more 32 [34:36:38] sts.
Work straight until front measures same length as back. Fasten off.

Right front skirt

Work as for left front skirt, reversing all shapings by working dec row as follows: 1ch, 1dc into each st to last 13dc, work from * to * as on back, 1dc into each of the last 3dc. Turn.

Back yoke

Using larger hook, make 44 [48:50:54] ch. Work first and 2nd rows as for back skirt. 43 [47:49:53] dc. Work straight until armhole measures 15 [16:17:18] cm.
Shape shoulders
Ss over 6dc, work in dc to end. Turn. Rep last row once more.
3rd and 4th rows Ss over 6 [7:7:8] dc, work in dc to end of row. Fasten off. 19 [21:23:25] dc rem for back neck.

Left front yoke

Using larger hook, make 25 [27:29:31]

skirt. 24 [26:28:30] sts.
Work straight until yoke measures 11 [12:13:14] cm, ending at front edge.
Shape neck
Ss over 9 [10:11:12] dc, work in dc to end. Turn.
2nd row Work in dc to last 3 sts, dec over next 2dc, 1dc into last st. Turn.
3rd row 1ch, 1dc into first dc, dec over next 2dc, work in dc to end. Turn.
4th row As 2nd row.
3rd and 4th sizes only Rep 3rd row.
All sizes Work a few more rows until armhole measures same as back armhole, ending at side edge.
Shape shoulder
Ss over 6dc, work in dc to end of row. 6 [7:7:8] dc rem. Fasten off.

Right front yoke

Work as for left front yoke, reversing all shapings.

Sleeves

Using larger hook, make 49 [53:55:57] ch. Work first and 2nd rows as for back skirt. 48 [52:54:56] sts.
Work straight until sleeve measures 25 [28:33:41] cm. Mark both ends of last row, work another 5cm. Fasten off.

Hood

Using larger hook and beg at side edge, make 32 [34:36:38] ch, work first and 2nd rows as for back skirt. 31 [33:35:37] sts.
Work straight until work measures 23 [25:26:27] cm.
Next row Beg at front edge, work in dc to last 3 sts, dec over next 2dc, 1dc into last dc. Turn. Work 1 row straight.
Rep last 2 rows 3 times more. This marks the end of first half of hood. Work the 2nd half to match first, working incs at end of next and following 3 alternate rows as follows: work in dc to last 2dc, work 2dc into next st, 1dc into last dc. Turn.
Work straight in dc until work measures same length as first half of hood. Fasten off.

Pockets

Using larger hook, make 19ch. Work first and 2nd rows as for back skirt. 18 sts. Work straight for 11cm. Fasten off.

Braids (make 3)

Using smaller hook, make 16ch. Ss to first ch, make another 28ch, 1dc into 16th ch from hook, 1dc into each of next 12ch.

To make up

Join shoulder seams. Using smaller hook, and with RS facing, work 1 row of dc down left front yoke edge, along lower edge, left armhole edge, back lower edge, right armhole edge, right lower edge, and up right front edge, working 3dc into corners. Do not turn. Work 1 row of crab (dc worked from left to right) along previous row of dc. Fasten off.

Sew upper edge of sleeve to armhole, overlapping crab st edging to RS. Join back and front skirt to yoke, placing yoke at centre and sewing skirt extensions to rows above sleeve markers. Join side and sleeve seams.

With RS facing, using smaller hook and beg at top front edge of left skirt, work 1 row of dc down left front edge, along lower edge of skirt and up right front to yoke, working 3dc into corner. Do not turn. Work 1 row of crab st into row of dc. Fasten off.

Join back seam of hood. Sew hood to neck edge, beg and ending 5 sts from front edge. With RS facing, using smaller hook, work 1 row of dc round front edge of hood. Without turning, work 1 row of crab st into previous row of dc. Fasten off.

With RS facing, using smaller hook, work 1 row of dc all round pocket edges, working 3dc into corners. Without turning, work 1 row of crab st into previous row of dc. Fasten off. Sew on pockets in positions shown.

Shape and stitch fastenings as shown opposite. Sew in place on coat fronts. Sew on toggles.

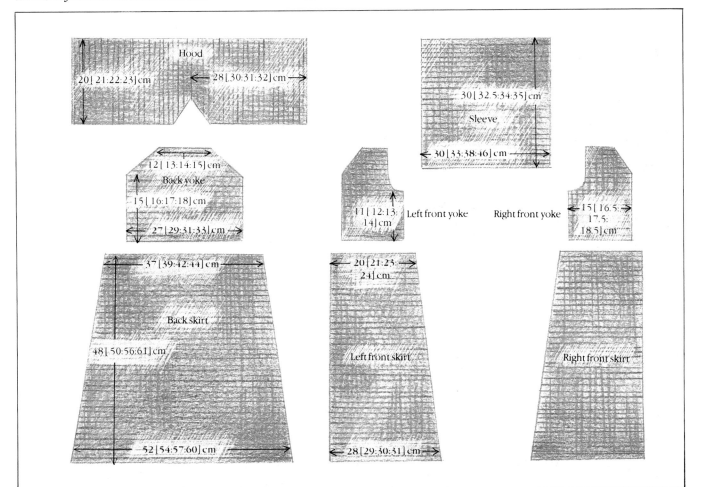

V-NECK SWEATER

Two shades of a Shetland yarn are used for this V-neck sweater.

Back

Note *Strand yarn not in use loosely up side of work.*

Using crochet hook and A, make 84 [88:92] ch.
Base row 1 tr into 4th ch from hook, * miss next ch, 1dc into next ch, miss next ch, 3tr into next ch, rep from * to end, ending last rep with 2tr into last ch. Turn. 81 [85:89] sts.
Beg patt as follows:
1st row 1ch, 1dc into first tr, *3tr into next dc, 1dc into 2nd of next 3tr, rep from * to end, working last dc into top of turning ch. Turn.
2nd row 3ch, 1tr into first dc, *1dc into 2nd of next 3tr, 3tr into next dc, rep from * to end, ending last rep with 2tr into last dc.
First and 2nd rows form back patt.
Cont in back patt until work measures 31cm from beg, ending with a 2nd row.
Shape armholes
Next row Ss across first 5 sts, 1ch, 1dc into ss at base of 1ch, patt to last 4 sts. Turn. 73 [77:81] sts.
Next row Ss across first 5 sts, 3ch, 1tr into ss at base of 3ch, patt to last 4 sts. Turn. 65 [69:73] sts.
Beg with a first row, work straight in patt until work measures 54cm. Fasten off.

Front

Using A, make 104 [108:112] ch.
Base row (RS) Using A, 1tr into 4th ch from hook, *miss next 3ch, 3tr into next ch, rep from * to end, ending last rep with 2tr into last ch. Do not turn, but return to beg of row.
Next row (RS) Join B with a ss to top of first 3ch, * 3tr into centre ch of next 3ch missed on base row, rep from * to end, ss into last tr of base row. Turn.
Beg patt as follows:
1st row Using A, 3ch, 1tr into first ss, * 3tr into centre tr of next 3tr worked on previous row in A, rep from * to last ss, 2tr into last ss. Do not turn, but return to beg of row.
2nd row Using B, ss into top of first 3ch, * 3tr into centre tr of next 3tr worked on previous row in B, rep from * to last tr, ss into last tr.
First and 2nd rows form front patt.

Cont in front patt until work measures 31cm from beg, ending with a 2nd row.
Shape armholes
Next row Ss across first patt rep, patt to last patt rep. Turn.
Rep last row twice more. 19 [20:21] patt reps.
Divide for neck
Next row Work 9 [10:10] patt reps. Turn.
Shape left neck
Cont on these sts only, work straight in patt for 3 rows.
Next row Patt to last patt rep. Turn.
Rep last 4 rows 3 times more. 5 [6:6] patt reps.
Work straight in patt until work measures 54cm from beg. Fasten off.
1st and 3rd sizes only
Return to beg of neck shaping, miss centre patt rep and keeping patt correct, rejoin yarn to next patt rep.
2nd size only
Return to beg of neck shaping and keeping patt correct, rejoin yarn to next patt rep.
All sizes
Next row Work to end. Turn. 9 [10:10] patt reps.
Shape right neck
Cont on these sts only, patt 3 rows without shaping.
Next row Work to last patt rep. Turn.
Rep last 4 rows 3 times more. 5 [6:6] patt reps.
Work straight in patt until work matches left side of neck. Fasten on.

Back welt
With RS facing, using knitting needles and A, pick up and K 104 [110:114] sts straightly along lower edge.
Work 7cm in K1, P1 rib.
Cast off loosely in rib.

Front welt
With RS facing, using knitting needles and A, pick up and K 102 [106:110] sts evenly along lower edge.
Work 7cm in K1, P1 rib.
Cast off loosely in rib.

Front neckband
Fold corners of front decs to WS and sew in place using slipstitch.
With RS facing, using knitting needles

Sizes
To fit 96 [101:106] cm chest
Length 61cm

Note: *Instructions for larger sizes are in square brackets [ ]; where there is only one set of figures it applies to all sizes.*

Materials
Approx 30 [300:350] g of a double knitting yarn in main colour (A)
Approx 100 [150:150] g in contrasting colour (B)
4.00mm crochet hook
1 pair 3¼ knitting needles

Tension
4 patt reps and 12 rows to 10cm over back patt using 4.00mm hook
5 patt reps and 14 rows to 10cm over front patt using 4.00mm hook

To save time, take time to check tension.

SPECIAL TECHNIQUE
One-row stripes

1 *When changing colour at the end of each row in a two-colour pattern, you can avoid breaking yarn (and having to darn in dozens of ends later) by turning only after every alternate row as in the pattern. Work the base row. Remove the hook from the loop and leave the first colour at the side of the work. The loop can be held with a safety pin.*

2 *Do not turn, but return to the beginning of the row. Join the second colour to the top of the first stitch with a slipstitch. Pattern to the loop left in step 1. Insert the hook first into the top of the last stitch and then into the loop. Remove the safety pin, wind the second colour round the hook and draw through all loops on the hook. Turn.*

3 *Drop the second colour and draw the first through the loop on the hook. Pull both ends of yarn firmly but not so tightly that the fabric puckers. Pattern to the end, leaving a loop as in step 1. Return to the beginning of the row, rejoin the first colour as in step 2 and pattern to the end, working into the last stitch and loop as before.*

and A, pick up and K 68 sts down left front neck, one st from centre V and 68 sts up right front neck.

1st row (P1, K1) to within 2 sts of centre st, K2 tog, P1, K2 tog, (K1, P1) to end.

2nd row K1, (P1, K1) to within 2 sts of centre st, P2 tog, K1, P2 tog, (P1, K1) to end.

Rep last 2 rows twice more.

Cast off loosely in rib, at the same time dec one st at each side of centre st as before.

Back neckband

Place a contrasting marker on last row of back 5 [6:6] patt reps from each armhole edge.

With RS facing, using knitting needles and A, pick up and K 45 sts between markers.

Work 6 rows in K1, P1 rib. Cast off loosely in rib.

Armbands (both alike)

Join shoulder seams.

With RS facing, using knitting needles and A, pick up and K 130 sts evenly along armhole edge.

Work 6 rows in K1, P1 rib.

Cast off loosely in rib.

To make up

Press or block as appropriate.
Join side and armband seams.
Press seams lightly.

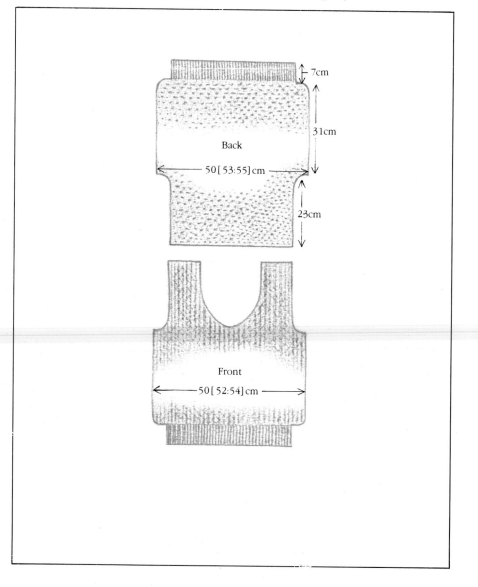

DIAGONAL-STITCH PULLOVER

This comfortable V-neck pullover has a diagonal stripe pattern worked in surface crochet.

Sizes
To fit *91-96 [102-107] cm*
Length *69 cm*
Sleeve seam *48 [49] cm*

Note *Instructions for larger size are in square brackets [ ]; where there is only one set of figures it applies to both sizes.*

Materials
Approx 950 [1000] g of a double knitting yarn
4.50mm crochet hook
5.50mm crochet hook
1 pair 3¼mm knitting needles

Tension
16dc and 20 rows to 10cm using 4.50mm hook

To save time, take time to check tension.

Back
Using smaller hook, make 81 [89] ch.
Base row (RS) 1dc into 2nd ch from hook, 1dc into each ch to end. Turn. 80 [88] dc.
Next row 1ch, miss first dc, 1dc into each st to end. Turn.
Work straight in dc on these 80 [88] sts until work measures 61cm from beg, ending with a WS row.
Shape shoulders
Next row 1ch, miss first dc, 1dc into each dc to last 7 [8] sts. Turn.
Rep last row 7 times more. 24 sts. Fasten off.

Front
Work as for back until work measures 38cm from beg, ending with a WS row.
Divide for neck
Next row 1ch, miss first dc, 1dc into next 34 [38] dc. Turn.
Working on first set of sts only, dec 1dc at neck edge on next and every following 3rd row 7 times in all. 28 [32] dc. Work straight in dc until work measures 61cm from beg, ending with a RS row.
Shape shoulder
Next row 1ch, miss first dc, 1dc into each dc to last 7 [8] sts. Turn.

Next row 1ch, miss first dc, 1dc into each dc to end. Turn.
Rep last 2 rows twice more.
Fasten off.
Return to rem sts. With RS facing, miss next 10dc and rejoin yarn to next st, 1ch, miss first dc, 1dc into each of next 34 [38] sts. Turn.
Complete to match first side, reversing shaping. Fasten off.

Sleeves (both alike)
Using smaller hook, make 41ch and work base row as for back. 40dc.
Cont in dc as for back on these 40 sts, inc 1dc at each end of next and every following 4th row until there are 72dc.
Work straight until work measures 40 [41] cm. Fasten off.

Surface diagonals
Back
With RS facing and using larger hook, follow chart to work surface slip stitch (see page 19) over first 78 rows of back and front to form diagonals, each 4 sts wide.

Front
Work as for back.

Welts (back and front alike)
Using knitting needles, pick up and K 104 [114] sts evenly along lower edge.
Work in K1, P1 rib for 8cm.
Cast off loosely in rib.

Cuffs
Using knitting needles, pick up and K 56 sts evenly along lower edge.
Complete as for welts.

Neckband
Using knitting needles, cast on 140 sts and work in K1, P1 rib for 5cm.
Cast off loosely in rib.

To make up
Press or block, as appropriate.
Join shoulder seams. Set in sleeves, placing centre of top of sleeve at shoulder seam. Join side and sleeve seams, matching surface crochet diagonals on front and back.
Sew neckband in place, overlapping left over right at centre front as shown.

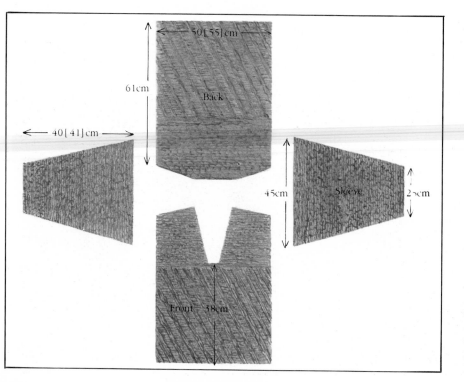

TRIANGLE PATCHWORK SWEATER

This rugged sweater, worked in a yarn with an interesting tweedy fleck, is great for the outdoor life.

Size
To fit 96-102cm chest
Length 68cm
Sleeve seam 48cm

Materials
Approx 650g of a tweed double knitting yarn in main colour A (dark brown)
Approx 500g in contrasting colour B (medium brown)
Approx 500g in contrasting color C (beige)
5.50mm crochet hook
1 pair 3¾mm knitting needles

Tension
14 sts and 10 rows to 10cm over patt using 5.50mm hook

To save time, take time to check tension.

Large triangles
Make 2 in C.
Make 97ch.
Base row 1tr into 4th ch from hook, 1tr into each ch to end. Turn. 95 sts.
1st row (RS) 2ch, miss first 2 sts, inserting hook from right to left and from front to back work 1tr round stem of next tr – 1tr front worked –, * inserting hook from right to left and from back to front work 1tr round stem of next tr – 1tr back worked –, 1tr front, rep from * to last 2 sts, miss next st, 1tr into top of turning ch. Turn. 93 sts.
2nd row 2ch, miss first 2 sts, 1tr front, * 1tr back, 1tr front, rep from * to last 2 sts, 1tr into next st. Turn. 91 sts.
3rd row As 2nd row. 89 sts.
4th row 2ch, miss first 2 sts, work next 2tr tog, 1tr front, * 1tr back, 1tr front, rep from * to last 4 sts, work next 2tr tog, 1tr into next st. Turn. 85 sts.
5th row 2ch, miss first 2 sts, 1tr back, * 1tr front, 1tr back, rep from * to last 2 sts, 1tr into next st. Turn. 83 sts.
6th-8th rows As 5th row. 77 sts.
9th row 2ch, miss first 2 sts, work next 2tr tog, 1tr back, * 1tr front, 1tr back, rep from * to last 4 sts, work next 2tr tog, 1tr into next st. Turn. 73 sts.
10th-13th rows As 2nd row. 65 sts.
Rep 4th-13th rows once more, then rep 4th-12th rows once more. 19 sts.
33rd row As 4th row. 15 sts.
34th-36th rows As 5th row. 9 sts.
37th row 2ch, miss first 2 sts, work next 2tr tog, 1tr back, work next 2tr tog, 1tr into next st. Turn. 5 sts.
38th row 2ch, miss first 2 sts, 1tr front leaving last loop on hook, 1tr into next st leaving last loop on hook, yrh and draw through all 3 loops on hook. Fasten off.

Medium triangles
Make 4 in B. Make 53ch.
Work base row as for large triangle. 51 sts.
Work first-17th rows as for large triangle. 11 sts.
18th row As 9th row of large triangle. 7 sts.
19th row As first row of large triangle. 5 sts.
20th row As 38th row of large triangle. Fasten off.

Small triangles
Make 6 in A, 4 in B and 6 in C.
Make 39ch. Work base row as for large triangle. 37 sts.
Work first-12th rows as for large triangle. 9 sts.
13th row 2ch, miss first 2 sts, work next 2tr tog, 1tr front, work next 2tr tog, 1tr into next st. Turn. 5 sts.
14th row As 38th row of large triangle, work 1tr back instead of 1tr front. Fasten off.

Sleeves (both alike)
Using A, make 47ch.
Base row 1tr into 4th ch from hook, 1tr into each ch to end. Turn. 45 sts.
Beg patt as follows:
1st row (RS) 2ch, miss first st, 1tr front, * 1tr back, 1tr front, rep from * to last st, 1tr into top of turning ch. Turn.
2nd row 2ch, miss first st, 1tr back, * 1tr front, 1tr back, rep from * to last st, 1tr into top of turning ch. Turn.
First and 2nd rows form patt.
Shape sleeve
Keeping patt correct, inc one st at each end of next and every following 5th row until there are 59 sts.
Work straight in patt until work measures 34cm from beg, ending with a WS row.
Divide for top
Next row Pat first 29 sts. Turn.
Next row 2ch, miss first 2 sts, patt to end. 28 sts.
Next row Pat to last 2 sts, 1tr into next st. Turn. 27 sts.
Rep last 2 rows 3 more times. 21 sts.
Fasten off.
With RS facing, return to sts missed at beg of top, miss next st and rejoin A to next st.
Next row 2ch, miss st at base of joining, patt to end. 29 sts.
Complete to correspond with first side of sleeve top, reversing all shaping.

To make up
Block if necessary.
Cuffs (both alike)
With RS facing, using knitting needles and A, pick up and K 44 sts along lower edge of sleeve.
Work 6cm of K2, P2 rib. Cast off in rib.
Place a contrasting marker 20cm from

each end of longest side of large triangles.

Join triangles as shown in diagram on page 159 to form back and front. Join long edges of large triangles between corners and markers, leaving edges between markers open for neck.

Back welt
With RS facing, using knitting needles and A, pick up and K 92 sts along lower edge of back.
Work 6cm of K2, P2 rib as for cuffs.
Cast off in rib.

Front welt
Work as for back welt.
Set in sleeves.
Join side and sleeve seams.
Press seams very lightly.

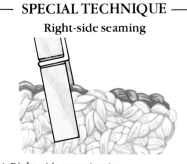

SPECIAL TECHNIQUE
Right-side seaming

1 *Right-side seaming is an easy method of achieving an exact match on seams when joining a complex garment like the sweater shown here. Hold the edges of the two triangles together with wrong sides facing — clothes pegs are better than dressmaker's pins on thick crochet. Use a blunt-ended yarn needle and two strands of spliced yarn matching one of the triangles.*

2 *Join the yarn to the wrong side of the corner of the triangle nearer to you. Insert the needle from back to front into the edge of the further triangle, catching one strand only of the edge stitch. Then insert the needle from front to back slightly further along the edge of the same triangle. Draw up the yarn tightly.*

3 *Insert the needle from front to back into the edge of the nearer triangle. Insert the needle from back to front slightly further along the same edge. Draw up the yarn tightly. Continue in the same way to the end. This method produces a flat, invisible seam which is very strong.*

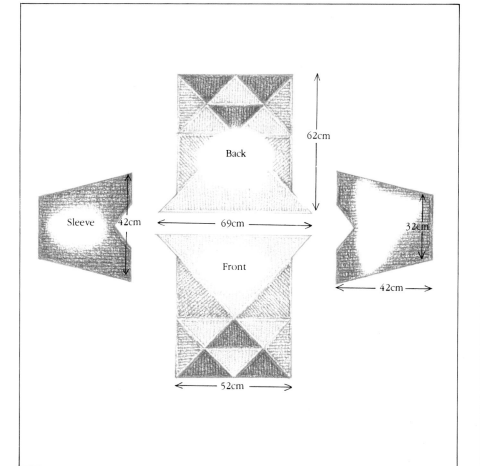

Back

62cm

Sleeve   42cm

69cm

32cm

Front

42cm

52cm

SPECIAL TECHNIQUES
Tunisian crochet

Also known as Afghan stitch, Tunisian crochet is worked with a long hook of uniform thickness with a knob at the end to retain the stitches. The firm fabric produced by this technique has in the past been used mainly for articles that receive hard wear such as rugs, jackets and coats. At one time Tunisian crochet was called "shepherd's knitting" and was used to make peasant garments.

The Victorians used Tunisian crochet to make rugs and blankets with very long so-called "blanket hooks". These were made from three detachable pieces which could be screwed together to make a hook approximately 75cm long.

With modern yarns such as mohair and bouclé, however, it is now possible to use the same traditional techniques to create unusual and exciting fashion garments. Some of the close, firm stitches found in Tunisian crochet look very much like knitting, but they produce a much firmer fabric, which in some cases can even be cut up to make tailored coats and jackets using dressmaking patterns.

The fluffy texture of mohair and other similar yarns appears on the wrong side of the work, and often this can be so attractive that, with care, you can make a completely reversible garment – one which is fluffy on one side and much smoother on the other.

Different stitches can be combined, as can different textures of yarn, although it is important that the yarns be of the same thickness. The end result can be an extremely wearable high fashion garment in an exciting mixture of colours and textures.

Hooks The special hooks used for Tunisian crochet are extra long to hold a large number of stitches and are available in sizes ranging from 2.50mm to 10.00mm and in various lengths.
Yarns and wools Any yarn or wool suitable for knitting and crochet can be used for Tunisian crochet. It is advisable, however, to begin with a small sample using smooth thread such as crochet cotton, worked with a 3.50mm hook, until the basic techniques have been mastered.

The basic technique
Tunisian crochet is quite easy to learn, especially if you have already learned normal crochet techniques. It is worked from one side only: one row is worked from right to left in a crochet stitch (for example, double or treble crochet), but with one loop per stitch left on the hook; then the next row is always a return row worked from left to right. For this row, the yarn is wound round the hook and pulled through the first loop on the hook. The yarn is then wound round the hook a second time and pulled through two loops. Keep winding the yarn round the hook and pulling it through two loops on the hook until the row has been completed and one loop remains on the hook. The next row can then be started in crochet stitch. These two rows form the basic Tunisian crochet stitch repeat, (see basic Tunisian stitch opposite).
Casting off A firm edge can be produced by working a row of double crochet or slip stitches into the last return row.

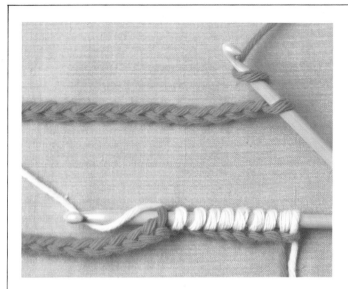

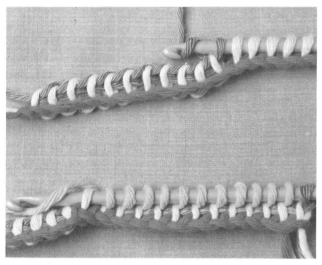

Basic Tunisian stitch (Tst)

This is also called knit stitch. It resembles a woven fabric and can be used as a background for cross stitch embroidery. Begin with a length of chain as for ordinary crochet (the pattern will specify the number, which will include 1 extra for turning).

1st row Work from right to left: miss 1 ch, * insert hook into next rch, yrh and draw through a loop, leave loop on hook, rep from * to end.

2nd row (return row) Yrh, draw through 1 loop, * yrh, draw through 2 loops, rep from * to end of row. 1 loop on hook.

3rd row 1ch, * insert hook from right to left under next vertical st, yrh and draw through a loop, leave loop on hook, rep from * to end.

Rep 2nd and 3rd rows throughout.

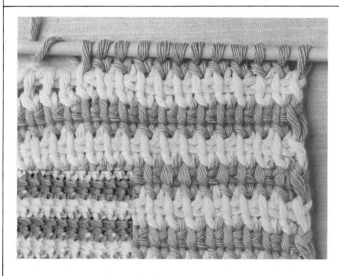

Tunisian double crochet (Tdc)

Work any number of ch plus 1.

1st and 2nd rows As first and 2nd rows of basic Tunisian st.

3rd row 1ch, miss first vertical thread, * insert hook from right to left under next vertical thread of previous row, yrh and draw through 1 loop, yrh and through 1 loop, leave loop on hook, rep from * to end of row.

4th row As row 2 of basic Tunisian st. Rep 3rd and 4th rows throughout.

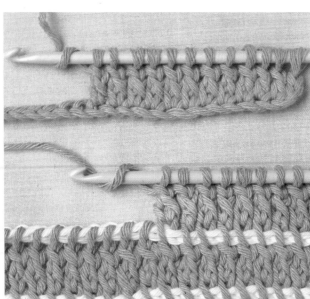

Tunisian treble (Ttr)

Work any number of ch plus 2.
1st row Yrh, insert hook into 4th ch from hook, yrh and draw through 1 loop, yrh and draw through 2 loops, yrh and draw through 1 loop, * yrh, insert hook into next ch, yrh and draw through 1 loop, yrh and draw through 2 loops, yrh and draw through 1 loop, rep from * to end.
2nd row As 2nd row of basic Tunisian st.
3rd row 1ch, * yrh, insert hook into 2nd vertical loop, yrh and draw through 1 loop, yrh and draw through 2 loops, yrh and draw through 1 loop, rep from * to end. Rep rows 2 and 3 throughout.

Tunisian purl stitch (Tp)

Work any number of ch plus 1.
1st and 2nd rows As first and 2nd rows of basic Tunisian st.
3rd row 1ch, miss first vertical thread, * with yarn to front insert hook from right to left under next vertical thread, pass yarn under, then over hook and draw through loop, rep from * to end.
4th row As row 2 of basic Tunisian st. Rep 3rd and 4th rows throughout.

Casting off

The edge that is produced by the return row of Tunisian crochet can be left as it is and joined in a seam in the usual way; however, this is not always satisfactory, since holes tend to appear along the seam line. A neater and much firmer edge can be obtained by working a row of slip stitch, as shown here, or double crochet, using either an ordinary or a Tunisian hook.
The seam can then be joined by sewing or crochet as appropriate.

Bobble stitch (Tb)

The bobbles are worked on a background of Tunisian dc.
Work a multiple of 6 ch plus 4.

1st and 2nd rows As first and 2nd rows of basic Tunisian st.

3rd row 1 Tdc, * yrh, insert hook from front to back into next st, yrh and draw through 1 loop, ** yrh, insert hook into same st, yrh and draw through 1 loop**, rep from ** to ** once, yrh and draw through 6 loops, yrh and draw through 1 loop (1 bobble made), 5 Tdc *; rep from * to *, working 1 bobble into next-to-last st, 1 Tdc.

4th-8th rows Work Tdc.

9th row 4 Tdc, * 1 bobble into next st, 5 Tdc *, rep from *, 1 Tdc into last st.

10th-14th rows Work Tdst. Rep rows 3-14 throughout.

Tunisian triple treble (Ttrtr)

This is a decorative stitch worked over a background of basic Tunisian stitch or Tunisian treble. Here it is worked over a background of basic Tunisian stitch in colour A, using a contrasting colour, B, to produce a pattern called "brick stitch."

1st and 2nd rows Using A, as first and 2nd rows of basic Tunisian st.

3rd row Using B, as 3rd row of basic Tunisian st.

4th row Using B, return (2nd) row of Tst.

5th row Using A, as 3rd row of Tst.

6th row Using A, return row.

7th and 8th rows As 5th and 6th rows.

9th row Using B, 1ch, * 2Tst, yrh 3 times, insert hook into vertical loop 5 rows down, yrh and draw through a loop, (yrh and draw through 2 loops on hook) 3 times – called Tunisian triple treble or Ttrtr; rep from * to within last 4 sts, 4Tst.

10th row Using B, return row.
Rows 5-10 form the patt.

Hairpin crochet

The origins of hairpin lace crochet are obscure. The special prong or staple which is used resembles a hairpin – hence the name. In the nineteenth century women often used their large bone hairpins for the work. Recently the adjustable hairpin staple has appeared on the scene, eliminating the necessity of buying an assortment of staples to produce strips of different widths.

The technique consists of looping yarn round the staple and joining the loops in the centre, using an ordinary crochet hook. The lace strips thus produced are then joined edge to edge, using one of several methods, to make the fabric. Individual strips can also be used as edgings or trimmings.

Any kind of yarn can be used for hairpin lace. Experiment with yarns of different textures and colours to see for yourself the variety of effects you can create.

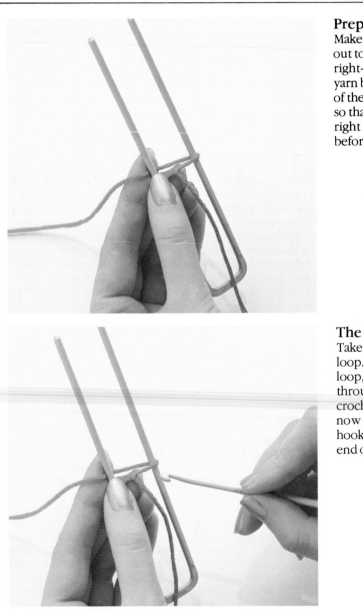

Preparing to crochet
Make a slip loop as for the start of a chain stitch and 〔 〕ll it out to half the width of the staple, then put it over the right-hand prong, with the knot in the centre. Hold the yarn behind the left prong with the thumb and forefinger of the left hand, then turn the prong over from right to left so that the yarn is passed round what has now become the right prong. Hold the yarn behind the (left) prong as before.

The first stitch
Take the crochet hook and insert it through the left-hand loop. Put the yarn round the hook and draw it through the loop, then put the yarn round the hook again and draw it through the loop on the hook to complete the first crochet stitch at the centre of the work. (There should now be a loop round each prong and one on the crochet hook.) Keeping the loop on the hook, take the other, free end of the hook over the right prong to lie behind it.

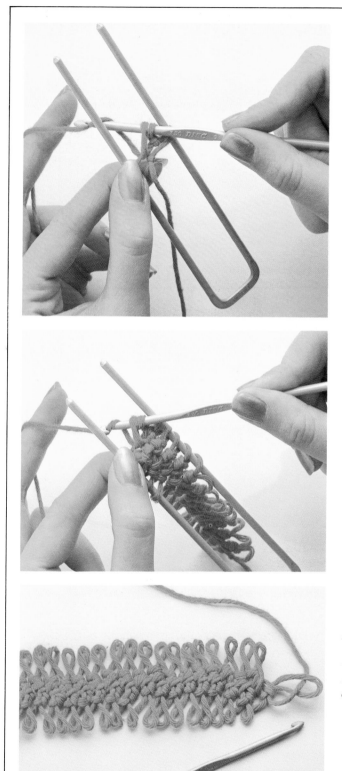

A double crochet
Turn the prong from right to left so that the yarn passes round the prong and insert the crochet hook from below through the front of the loop on the left prong. Take the yarn round the hook and draw a loop through so that there are two loops on the hook. Put the yarn round the hook and draw it through both loops, completing a double crochet into the loop. Lift the end of the crochet hook over the right prong and turn the prong from right to left.

Continuing
Continue turning the hook and working the double crochet as described to form a braid of loops with a centre ridge of double crochet. When the staple is filled with loops, slip the work carefully off the staple and gently replace the last four or five pairs of loops worked back on their respective prongs, while leaving the rest of the braid to hang free.

Finishing a strip
When you have worked the number of loops required (check that you have an equal number on each side of the strip), simply cut off the yarn and draw the end through the loop on the hook. Do not pull a strip round too much while working, for the loops are easily unravelled at this stage and the work does not become firm until the loops of the separate strips have been joined (see next page).

Joining strips

The simplest method of joining is to pull the loops through each other. Place two strips side by side on a flat surface, making sure that each strip has the beginning knot at the bottom and the last loop end at the top. Working up from the bottom, insert the hook into the first loop of one strip. Insert it through the first loop of the other strip (two loops on hook) and then pull the second loop through the first.

Joining – continued

Insert the hook into the next loop on the second strip and draw it through the loop already on the hook. Proceed in this way, alternating sides and checking continually on the wrong side of the work to make sure that you have not missed any loops. Pass the ends of the yarn through the last loop to finish off. The appearance of the work may be varied by linking loops two, or even three, at a time.

Abbreviations used in this book

approx	approximately	qtr	quadruple treble
beg	begin(ning)	rem	remain(ing)
ch	chain(s)	rep	repeat
cm	centimetre(s)	RH	right hand
cont	continu(e)(ing)	RS	right side
dc	double crochet	sp(s)	space(s)
dec	decreas(e)(ing)	ss	slip stitch(es)
dtr	double treble crochet	st(s)	stitch(es)
g	gramme(s)	tog	together
gr(s)	group(s)	tr	treble crochet
htr	half treble crochet	trtr	triple treble crochet
inc	increas(e)(ing)	WS	wrong side
K	knit	yrh	yarn round hook
LH	left hand		
m	metre(s)	Additional abbreviations are explained within the pattern in which they are used.	
P	purl		
patt	pattern		

INDEX